COLOR ME FLO
My Hard Life and Good Times
by **Flo Kennedy**

Prentice-Hall, Inc., Englewood Cliffs, N.J.

**Color Me Flo: My Hard Life and Good Times,
by Flo Kennedy**

Copyright © 1976 by Florynce R. Kennedy

Printed in the United States of America

Prentice-Hall International, Inc., London
Prentice-Hall of Australia, Pty. Ltd., Sydney
Prentice-Hall of Canada, Ltd., Toronto
Prentice-Hall of India Private Ltd., New Delhi
Prentice-Hall of Japan, Inc., Tokyo

10 9 8 7 6 5 4 3 2 1

Design and Art Direction by Hal Siegel

Library of Congress Cataloging in Publication Data

Kennedy, Florynce
    Color me Flo.

    1. Kennedy, Florynce
2. Lawyers—United States—Correspondence, re-
miniscences, etc.
I. Title.
KF373.K45A3   340′.092′4 [B]   76-17893
ISBN 0-13-152471-6
ISBN 0-13-152363-5 pbk.

CONTENTS

With Judge Bruce Wright at Joann Little demonstration, Union Square, 1975

Acknowledgements

If this project is not to yield a book which
is a more exploitative ripoff than any complained of herein, this cannot be a routine
brush-off acknowledgement.

Robert Stewart, Special Projects Editor
at Prentice-Hall, seriously offered to do
this biographical project. This was in
November of 1975. After a false start or
two and a few weeks' delay, he produced a
miracle editor called Carol Saltus. We
typed, collected, selected. Stewart and Saltus queried, phoned, tracked down docu-
ments, films, poems, word portraits, clips,
photos, and letters.

I balked, whined, blustered, tantrum-
med. There was so much available, but we
had the usual limitation of time and space,
so what we've produced is a sketch.

Sixty years is a lot to boil down, but with
the help of the implacable Irene Davall
and the unflappable Lena Meyers to fill
out the editorial team, it now appears that
in very little more time that it takes to have
a baby, we have a book.

My family were really important. They
dug into their memories and photograph
albums and helped reconstruct bits of the
Kansas City days. They cooperated; so did
my friends, photographers, news reporters, associates, film-makers and everybody
who was asked.

But lots of what anybody is about is re-
flected in glimpses of what's been said and
glimpses of what's been done, so there are
lots of fragments of reflections to augment
the words my friends and relatives and I
said about me. It's not much, but it's more
than likely enough. Most everything is too
much, anyway.

JUST A MIDDLE-AGED COLORED LADY

Rummaging through a lifetime—60 years' accumulation of papers, news clips, letters, pictures, to write this book, I came across this paper I wrote for a creative writing class at Columbia University in 1946, when I was just half the age I am now:

"To whom it concerns:
"I am one of those thousands of people whose head is swimming with unwritten books: novels, short stories, articles, and non-fictional outbursts of every imaginable sort. Naturally, I'm goose-pimply to write the inevitable autobiography.

"I'm thirty, and what with working eight hours a day as a dreary (even if rebellious) clerical in the U.S. Treasury Department and taking eleven units of extension work as a pre-law student at Columbia, my chances seem sickeningly slim. From where I sit, it looks as if I'll be older and much grayer before I have either the time to write, or enough money saved to quit work and—you know the story.

"I've done publicity for organizations in Kansas City—articles and accounts written in this connection have appeared in the *Kansas City Call*, a weekly. I am completing a course in professional writing at school, where I have a lot of fun, but have rather made a fool of myself.

"I think the folks in my writing class all love me, but they (especially my friends) can't help laughing at my long, tumbling, "wordy" sentences (see above and below), my crazy ideas. (I don't believe in marriage, horizontal romance or religion, church, and/or the Bible; I love the hiccups, words, and fighting; I do not smoke, except other people's, and I don't drink because I don't like the flavor of alcohol.)

"I'm very poor, very proud, and a Negro—but I don't think very much about it, and I run like everything to keep out of organizations.

"I can't say anything about quality, as regards my writing, but I suffer from an acute case of word diarrhea, and there has never been a time when I couldn't write on and on about almost anything. The only thing is that no one ever agrees with what I write, although it makes perfectly good sense to me."

Now, thirty years later, I'm still rebellious, still making a fool of myself, and most people still don't agree with what I have to say. The big difference is that now they pay me to say it anyway. So I'm saying to you, "Be patient. It may take thirty years, but sooner or later they'll listen to you, and in the meantime, keep kicking ass."

I'm just as opinionated today as I was then. I'm saying a lot of things now I never said before, but I'm also saying things I've been talking about all my life. Back in 1946 I wrote a monograph called "The Case Against Marriage," the idea being that marriage is a crock, and I still think it is. Why should you lock yourself in the bathroom just because you have to go three times a day? The church, the Establishment, the family, media, business are all into persuading people that marriage is the appropriate thing to do at a given time. I wasn't out of my teens before I began to see that the attitude toward marriage made as little sense as if people at a certain stage of your life were to tell you you had to move to Pittsburgh. People in Pittsburgh may not be unhappy, and Pittsburgh may not be a hideous place, but why anybody with taste and brains would want to uproot themselves and move to Pittsburgh at a given time was beyond me. And then I began to question, as I started to look around me and saw that married people didn't seem particularly happy, or else they'd been married and split, or been abandoned, and I could see nothing that persuaded me there was a great haven

Singing with NOW members in Atlantic City, 1974 ▶

called marriage that was worth looking for, let alone going out of your way to crawl into.

But you soon learned that there is supposedly a connection between marriage and lovemaking or, as I put it, fucking. And you discover that this is supposed to be a great experience, so then the question I asked, assuming sex was this incredibly gorgeous rose (no thorns, obviously), was, how much shit would you walk across to get this rose?

I believe that some women have what I call the Permanent Post-Partum Psychosis; they are so horrified by the actuality of marriage and children, the three o'clock screaming in the middle of the night. There you are, sleeping away, and all of a sudden you hear these shrill shrieks, and you wake up and think, "What in the hell is going on?"—if you forget momentarily who this strange creature screaming in the night is. Even with all the orange blossoms, the pink and white layettes, the blue enameled brushes, and the silver rattles, I still don't understand why women are so inclined to have children.

Lesbians don't impress me as being ecstatically happy, and unfortunately many of them are mothers—I guess motherhood accounts for as much

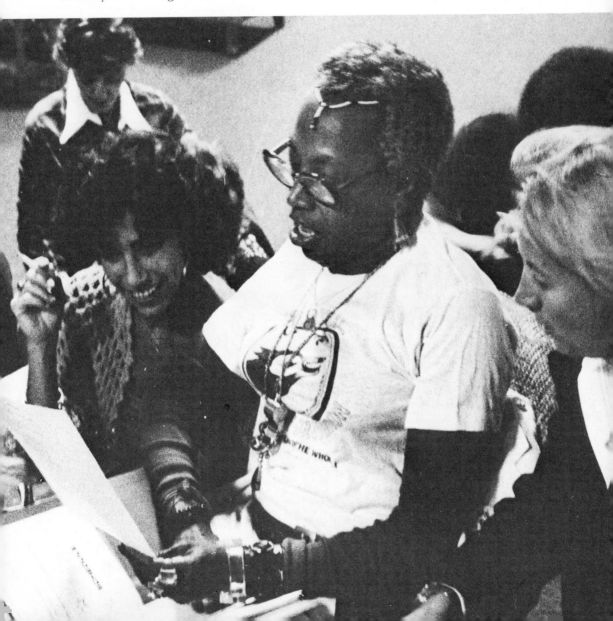

lesbianism as anything else—but the church discourages lesbianism, and at the same time talks about the right to life. They tell you, "You must not kill this child, you must have this unwanted baby," and then they say the horror of the Equal Rights Amendment is that it might lead to homosexual marriages. I tell these right-to-life people, partly with tongue in cheek but partly very seriously, that it seems to me that there is one program, at least, that they would be very vocal about: encouraging homosexual love affairs, because that would be one way of cutting down on the number of unwilling parents. The National Organization of Nonparents, which is a group I belong to, doesn't impress me as superbrave, but if it had the courage it should have to use up as much printing and postage as it does, I would think they'd come out openly and declare in favor of homosexual romance, marriage arrangements, tax deductions, or whatever. It seems to me that Planned Parenthood and all the other communities that are concerned about the population explosion should be pushing homosexuality—what better way to get your jollies, since our society has overrated sex to the point where it's imperative for people to have some sort of sexual recreation.

There ought to be a sort of smorgasbord, and I think society has a nerve to say that the church has a monopoly on the license to fuck, that you must lie one on top of the other (which is fairly boring in two senses of the word), and that you must not suck. I don't know why anyone would want to give anybody else a blow job, but in my opinion it's not for me or the church or anybody else, to tell people which of these rather unesthetic activities they ought to be involved in.

SUNWORLD / SUNWORLD / SUNWORLD / SUNWORLD / SUNWORL

'Foul-mouth' Flo, the fighting feminist

FLORYNCE Kennedy is a branded woman.

By Mary Murranka

Branded in the sense that she's been called anything and everything at one time or another.

At 59, she's now America's most well-known Black woman and a member of the National Black Feminist Organisation.

She's also a lecturer, lawyer and writer.

Her two most recent books are "Abortion Rap" and "The Pathology of Oppression."

I had the chance to talk with her at length during her brief stay at Suva's Club Hotel when she stopped off here for two days on her way home to the United States after attending the Women in Politics Conference in Canberra.

She came here at the invitation of Claire Slatter of the Y.W.C.A. and last night delivered a stirring speech at the Y.W.C.A. gymnasium, and is to speak again at the U.S.P. today at 1pm.

While in Australia she came under constant attack for her foul language.

"I don't use foul language." she said, "I use White House language...what's good enough for Nixon is good enough for me."

SUPER SUN

Yet beneath it all there is a staggering amount of warmth and love which irradiates any room she's in, whether it's a hotel lobby or a massive lecture hall.

Flo attended a meeting in Queensland with some Australian Aborigines and Torres Strait Islanders.

"They have a bunch of dumb politicians in Queensland," she said •

"And, boy, the State Senate Premier Bjelke-Petersen... he's a real prize.

"I don't give a damn what people say or think. I say what the hell's on my mind and that's that."

A handsome woman with an electrifying personality, she commands respect instantaneously.

Flo maintains two residences in the U.S., one in San Francisco, the other in New York.

But she spends more time in the air than on the ground and her schedule reads like a politician's diary of appointments.

She has vast self-confidence and shows no signs of tiring.

Jet lag is a permanent condition with her and there are a few signs of fatigue around her eyes.

But she keeps on going... and going...and going.

"Relaxation?" she said.

"I have little or no time for that."

But when she isn't on the warpath about something or other she likes to curl up and read, watch T.V. or play Scrabble.

Back in the U.S., she's been labelled the Black Queen of women's movements.

She engages all over the country constantly overseeing the diverse doings of dozens of feminist groups.

She's a radical in every sense.

She stops at nothing when it comes to protesting.

Last year she organised a 'pee-in' to protest the lack of toilet facilities for women at Harvard University.

Flo Kennedy was born and raised in Kansas City, Missouri, the second of five daughters.

She moved to New York at 26 and enrolled at Columbia University to study law, working in libraries and museums during the day to pay tuition fees.

She's faced discrimination on two scores, by being Black and being a woman.

And she's overcome both 'handicaps' by using the tactics for which she's most famous.

Protesting is something that's part of her life.

"I like to fight for anything and everything which I feel needs backing," she said.

And in the U.S. there's no lack of causes.

She's organised so many affairs she can't remember them all.

Talking with her, I got the feeling that she tired quickly of recitals of past events, preferring to keep ahead of what's happening.

With Margo St. James, Lydia, and Alma at COYOTE demonstration, San Francisco

Nobody Ever Died From a Blow Job

Talking about sexual recreation reminds me that a very average prostitute in almost any part of this country can get $100 a night minimum, or if she is fairly well-known she might make as much as $500. A run-of-the-mill file clerk nets about $100 a week, and a run-of-the-mill housewife will get zero a week for filing, fucking, ironing, having the baby, nursing the baby, baby-sitting, and the whole megillah. In my opinion, a government that cannot provide full employment for women who don't have degrees, and even those who do, has a pretty big nerve making the most lucrative occupation a crime. Recently, when I was lecturing in the Midwest, I talked to a young woman who was in law

school and also worked in a massage parlor. She told me she was somewhat conflicted as to whether to bother finishing law school, because she was earning more in a massage parlor than she would after five years of law school. And she was serious. I have the feeling that if she continued at law school, it would be because society disapproves of people who work in massage parlors, and that if she continued to work there she might very soon need a lawyer herself to prevent her going to jail. I think that neither the feminists nor the church nor the government nor anybody else has the right to say to women that they cannot choose whichever endeavor, for whatever reason, is best suited to their lives.

Prostitutes are accused even by feminists of selling their bodies; but prostitutes don't sell their bodies, they rent their bodies. Housewives sell their bodies when they get married—they cannot take them back—and most courts do not regard the taking of a woman's body by her husband against her will as rape. And I am inclined to think that the right to get up and go home afterwards might almost be worth sleeping with strangers for money, instead of going out to work in a laundry, or carrying around some stranger's shit floating in a shallow pan of piss, as nurses do. Yet you rarely hear the church come down on nurses—in fact, it sponsors nurses. I'm sure there is no nurse who has been working in a hospital for more than a year who hasn't washed some strange man's ass, and I think that a whore might find fucking a stranger not too much less pleasant than that, or, even worse, getting crotch-grabbed by a patient.

Now, even when I was young I wasn't good-looking, so I was never confronted with the possibility of becoming a prostitute, and I am not suggesting that I want my child or my sister or even my feminist friends all to become prostitutes. But I just don't see that women have such fascinating jobs, for the most part, that a job that pays ten times as much as most others should be outlawed.

Society's concern to eliminate prostitution from the scene is very political, in my opinion. In Boston during the World Series there was a kind of sweep of the "Combat Zone," the area where the prostitutes are. And in New York before a major convention like the 1976 Democratic Convention, you always have our brilliant municipal officials running around talking about "cleaning up" this or that erogenous zone—in this case, Times Square. And the mayor, the corrupt police, and the "good people" form an almost solid phalanx between the whores and those of us who think the city has better things to do than chase whores. Instead of worrying about the massage parlors, why doesn't the government

think about cleaning up Times Square by getting rid of tobacco and alcohol? There's a billboard, which dominates the whole area, of a man blowing smoke out over Times Square to encourage people to smoke, but tobacco kills 52,000 people a year from lung cancer, and there's no telling how many lives have been ruined through drinking. But to my knowledge, no one has ever died of a blow job, except, Margo St. James tells me, a whore who choked to death recently on the West Coast, and a few men who have died of heart attacks—but what better way to go, if that's how you get your jollies?

The Package and the Product

Like the cleanup of prostitution, I think that clothes are also very political, both dressing up and not dressing up. Everything in our culture is political, and when people say someone is "apolitical," they mean Establishmentarian, because there is no such thing as not being political. If you do what the Establishment wants and says, you do it in the name of peace and approval by the Establishment. If you do the opposite, then you are not being political, particularly—you are just not sucking.

I have a mink jacket I was given by Jeannie Bach, who is the producer of the Arlene Francis show and one of the prime movers in the Fortune Society, and I decided I would take this mink jacket to Australia when I went there for the Women in Politics Conference in Canberra City. The first night the Prime Minister gave a reception for us at Parliament House, but earlier in the day I had learned that the Black and aboriginal women—as they usually put it, the "aboriginal and island women"—were going to hold a demonstration with some other, more radical feminists. Now, I had to let my hosts and the TV people know I was going to join that demonstration. I didn't know whether I would be sent back home, ostracized, or thrown out of my hotel; but all they said was, "Good on you, but please come in and meet the Prime Minister (the "PM," as they call him), before you split from the reception." So I put on an incredibly expensive sheer chiffon dress that Diane Schulder gave me after I persuaded her to buy it, and I wore this very dressy, filmy print with the mink jacket. And later on, after I had held up my fist as I walked up the steps to Parliament House, I talked to the demonstrators and agreed to meet them the next day and discuss their grievances.

A couple of days later I was doing a radio program with a woman who is one of the better feminists down there, and she said, "Oh, one thing struck me, when you went to the aboriginals and island women, you had on this luxurious mink and this elaborate dress—the contrast was so great." "What the hell are you talking about?" I said. I am very conscious of the fact that some people think that when you talk to poor people they like you better if you dress the way they do. And it's my position that if I happen to have on jeans, that's cool, but I don't understand how anyone can be so stupid as not to realize that poor people are set forward by meeting people who look as if they can afford to live well, and are still interested in them.

To me it's a part of the phoney baloney to wear ragged clothes to go talk to poor people. I should imagine they'd think—it was certainly true when I was poor—"Who would wear raggedy clothes if they don't have to?" I know that some poor people have a sort of inverse snobbery, and they might very well like to see people who are able to afford $120 boots in $7 jeans from the Army-Navy

With aboriginal and island women at Canberra City, Australia, "Women in Politics" Conference, 1975

store. And that's fine if you want to, but I think it's very important for poor people to see people taking their position and arguing in favor of them, who look as if they don't have to side with them. It's just a superior attitude some people have, that poor people would be uncomfortable with anyone who wasn't dressed shabbily.

Clothes are like packages— sometimes they are indicative of the contents: for example, in a rape situation, a jury can be made to believe a woman almost invites rape when she's wearing tight pants or jeans, whereas a man in an expensive coat doesn't suggest he should be mugged, and wearing a diamond doesn't mean you are inviting robbery. And women supposedly invite rape by wearing miniskirts. I am sure that nobody in our society is absolutely free of that feeling, but it would not occur to anyone seriously to suggest that a bank invites robbery by having all that money there.

When women began wearing pants there was a tremendous backlash. I can remember—I was still practicing law at that time—going to court in pants and the judge's remarking that I wasn't properly dressed, that the next time I came to court I should be dressed like a lawyer. He's sitting there in a long black dress gathered at the yoke, and I said, "Judge, if you won't talk about what I'm wearing, I won't talk about what you're wearing," because it occurred to me that a judge in a skirt telling me not to wear pants was just a little bit ludicrous. It's interesting to speculate how it developed that in two of the most anti-feminist institutions, the church and the law court, the men are wearing the dresses.

I've never heard women complaining about men in dresses, but since the day we started wearing pants there was all this talk about women's asses and big hips. We all know that you don't have to go to Barney's to see men with asses as wide as a doorway in pants, but suddenly when women start wearing

pants the big ass becomes so prominent. When men comment about the size of a woman's ass in pants, what they are really saying is women have no right to wear them, although men's pants and jeans are very kind to the figure, and if somebody does have an extraordinarily big or fat ass, it probably looks as well in pants as in anything else. One of the reasons women look better in men's clothes is that the standard of beauty for men is not as high, and therefore when a woman wears a tailored shirt or a man's hat or cap, she looks less homely, if she happens to be a homely type. I wear funny hats all the time, mostly designed for men, and I think it's a gas. It's important for us to understand that one reason men's clothes are off limits is that they carry a message: "If you only want a woman who wears lace and ruffles, I am not the one for you." And anything a woman does that suggests she may not be the person for some man, is regarded as impudent.

But that mink jacket upset a lot of anti-Establishment or liberal people. It was amazing how uncomfortable it made some of the women, especially from America, in the trade-union movement. "Do you have to keep your jacket on?" they kept saying, and "Shouldn't you take off your jacket now?" when the TV people came around. For some reason they seemed to think it inappropriate for this Black woman to wear a mink jacket, but I would just say, "No, why should I take it off? I'm not hot."

It got to be a kind of acid test, even when I got back to the States. I relate to certain things as acid tests; for instance, during the deballing of Adam Clayton Powell I judged people's hidden or subconscious racism by the way they responded to the mention of his name. Some people would say, "Oh, he isn't good for the Black people; he doesn't show up in Congress often enough and he has an awful absentee record." Now that's what I call the "Nothing But the

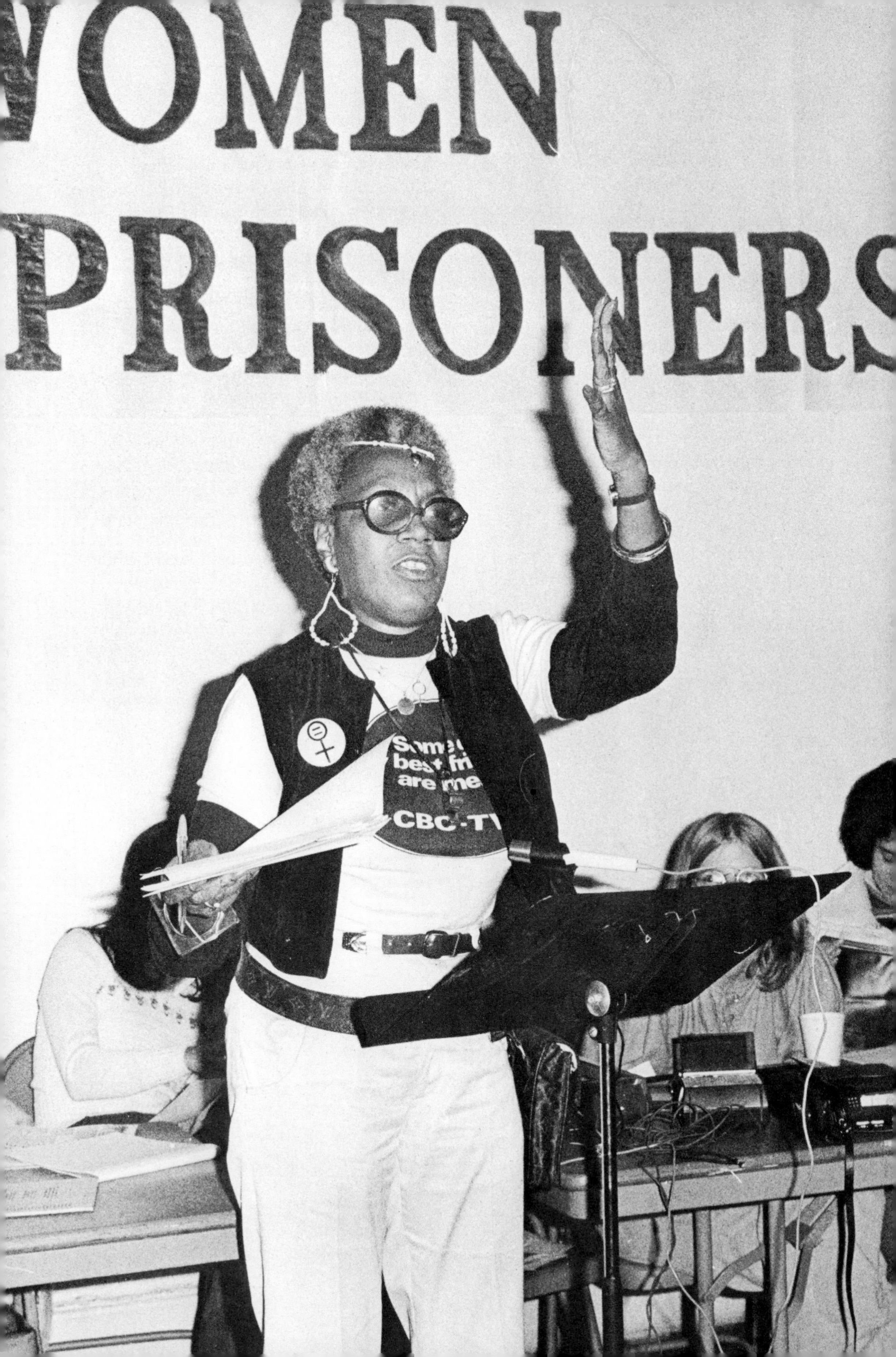
WOMEN
PRISONERS
CBC-TV

Best for the Oppressed" syndrome, and the people who have it want you to think they are so concerned for oppressed people that nothing is good enough for them. You see it in criticism of movies for Black people, and there even got to be a label for them—"Black exploitation." And it doesn't only apply to white people; Black people also joined in the attack.

I don't mean that Black films or Adam Clayton Powell should be beyond criticism, but it's ironic that these people never comment on the bad housing, the lack of jobs, the absence of day care centers, white teachers taking away Black teachers' jobs, the terrible education Black people get, and the fact that in the Black communities the schools, the houses, the restaurants, the department stores are infested with rats and roaches, and even in the streets of Harlem you see rats and roaches. But they worry that their Congressman, who had the brains to upset their society enough to get hundreds of thousands of dollars into Harlem, and who was their only effective representative in Congress, had a bad

absentee record, or was married twice, or was screwing his secretary. So they pretend that they want only the best for the oppressed, but of course the best is not available, and therefore the oppressed have nothing. But these critics don't seem the slightest disconcerted at this absurdity.

I come under a fair amount of criticism myself, and I have to say that I don't take kindly to it. Somehow I've got the reputation of being a very nice person, and some people are shocked when they find out what I'm like. For instance, I refuse to work under conditions that I regard as oppressive, and any time someone hisses me or talks while I'm trying to talk, I say to the people who organized the rally, "Just shut them up or I am going to leave, and I don't care what you paid, and I don't care about any contracts. I am not going to work if I am being insulted and harassed. I don't like it, and you just shut them up or I am leaving."

A lot of people have romantic ideas—I don't know where these ideas

"Give 'Em the Fist," Oneonta, New York

come from, but occasionally they try to scold you if you don't live up to them. Years ago, before I was speaking in public a lot, a woman in Washington started asking about my rings and my lipstick, and I said, "Let me tell you something. I didn't ask you why you had on blue jeans and a green sweater. I don't call anyone up in the morning and ask them what I should wear. I wear anything I want. I'm wearing an Afro and false eyelashes, and that's the way it's supposed to be. And I don't really give a shit what you've got on, and I don't know what what I've got on has to do with you."

a boulder alternative since 1892

Colorado Daily

Vol. 24, No. 75   Thursday, February 19, 1976   Boulder, Colorado

daily photo by john puerner

daily photo by john puerner

Feminist-activist Flo Kennedy (left) and former Assistant Watergate Prosecutor Jill Volner both spoke to the same group on campus Wednesday night. In widely differing styles, both addressed the subject of oppression.

From stereotypes to pigocracy

Two lawyers address oppression

By LYNNE DOMASH

The crowd in the UMC Ballroom was treated to a study in contrasts Wednesday night, as former assistant Watergate prosecutor Jill Volner and political activist Flo Kennedy each took center stage to air her views about oppression and how to deal with it.

Volner appeared the model career woman, in her orange dress and carefully applied make-up. Kennedy, with her boots, rakishly tilted hat and bracelets, was obviously the trouble-maker in the crowd.

The differences in dress were echoed by the differences in style and politics. Volner, speaking slowly, not always surely, described the problems women lawyers face because of their sex, and how she personally has dealt with some of them.

Kennedy, in a whiz-bang speaking style that sometimes left the listener far behind, described how she would deal with what she called the "pigocracy," and both her language and her tactics differed from Volner's.

Kennedy deals with the pigocrats by using the "testicular approach." That was described as the "nice colored lady," the kind who wears housedresses — "not Kimberly knits" — going to the dentist, and, when he proceeds to

carelessly hurt her with the drill, grabbing him by the testicles "just short of enough to make him go down on the floor and die," and saying "We are not going to hurt each other, are we?"

Or, to put it another way, "Somebody has got to go for broke in this country if we're going to make any changes."

One place to start, Kennedy suggested, would be with the University's law school faculty. Law school students have charged that the school is not making a good-faith effort to find minorities and women to fill several slots in the law school faculty. The faculty is now almost 100 per cent white male.

Students have written letters to the dean of the law school and the faculty, trying to solve the problem, but that's like "committing suicide," Kennedy said. Those "noble niggers" are still asking the pigocrats what to do about pigocracy."

However, "I am gonna take care of it for you," Kennedy promised. "I am going to go to every campus, and make this school very, very famous." Kennedy has friends in Washington, in the Office of Education, and "these people had better get this shit together. There ain't nothing old black Flo can't do to make them understand that they cannot diddle anybody after all those years."

She doesn't have anything to lose, Kennedy said, since "When I get through with this campus, I don't expect to be asked back." And besides, at 60, "my blood pressure is so high, I'm so near crazy and near dead" that there's not much they can do to her.

The University "is such a perfect prototype of all the ills," Kennedy said, that it is a perfect place to start. "If you want to give the whole academic community an enema, where better to start than the University of Colorado at Boulder?"

But, while both minorities and women have the right to demand preferential hiring until the problems are corrected, Kennedy reminded women that blacks have "more service time on the line," and deserve the chance to go first. "Racism is to sexism what cancer is to a very bad toothache," she said.

To charges of reverse sexism and reverse racism, Kennedy answers that that cannot exist "until we have lynched as many whites as they lynched blacks, until as many women have raped as many men, until they've put as many fists in as many mouths as men have to them."

"We have got to stop thinking about what humanitarians we are and fight this thing like it's got to be fought."

Meanwhile, back in the courts, Volner, who was on hand to speak to pros-

pective law students for Women's Law Day, described the discrimination she has faced in the courtroom. Often upon entering to try a case, she is asked, "Whose secretary are you?" Volner said. The papers report what she wears, not what she says.

But there are advantages to the stereotyped role women play, Volner said. "Women can get more information from a witness." She advised women to be themselves, rather than try to play the same role as men. "Do it your own way."

As an example, Volner said, when she cross-examined Rose Mary Woods, former President Nixon's secretary, about the 18-and-a-half minute gap in the tapes, "I did not yell at her as a man might have done. The press would have been sympathetic to her," and that would have hurt the government's case, Volner said.

"Do your job and do it well, and you'll be accepted," she said.

Not that she is above using her "special abilities" as a woman to gain the advantage, Volner said. When an opposing lawyer insisted on calling her "young lady," she could have asked him to stop. But she saw that the jury was as irritated as she was by his practice, so she let him go on, and she won the case.

continued on page 3

11

The Tyranny of the Weak

If you are part of a movement and some people perceive you as a leader or representative, they sometimes get so goddamn possessive, as if they're entitled to tell you whatever is wrong, and that's when I really go crazy. It's amazing, but a lot of people in the movement feel that they have to answer to other people about what they do. I remember when Kate Millett first wrote her book, people said to her, "You can't put your name on this book because this belongs to the movement and we are all part of it." Of course, nobody ever said that to me, because they know I am so crazy I would go to pukesville with them. But it's part of what I call the tyranny of the weak. They call it ego-tripping, and they don't want stars. Seemingly, the idea is that we are all the same in the women's movement, and maybe even in the Black movement —there are no celebrities, no stars. And, of course, what I say is, "If I'm not a star, what the hell are you doing on my phone at 3:00 o'clock in the morning, telling me about somebody getting busted for pot? Go tell your roommate about it, if we are all the same, don't call me. If we're all the same, why do you want me to come down and make a speech? I'm tired and I want to go to bed." When they want to use you, you're a star, but if you do anything it looks like you're going to get any credit for, then they try to bulldoze you.

I have definite ideas about what the Establishment does when they finally decide to recognize a member of an oppressed group and put him in power: I call it the "Pig's Prerogative." It's a concept I made up when Nixon made his trip to China and, after opposing the recognition of Communist China for 25 years, all of a sudden became asshole buddies with Mao Tse-Tung and Chou En-Lai. The chances are that John Kennedy or Ted Kennedy or McGovern could never do that, because if a liberal had done it, there would have been a great hue and cry from the pigs. But if the pigs decide for whatever reason to sell all our wheat to Russia so that the price of bread triples, or if they decide to deal with Mao and Chou, then it's not Communist China anymore, and Barbara Walters and the newscasters start calling it "The People's Republic of China," whereas they would have lost their jobs if they had said that five years before.

When Nixon went to China, the pigs were silent in their disapproval, except for an occasional super-pigocrat like Arizona's Junior Senator, Barry Goldwater, who rather astutely suggested Nixon get a one-way ticket. I would only add that Barry Goldwater should have joined him on the same basis.

Of course, it's occasionally suggested on campuses and television talk shows that I do the same. Cupcakes, anti-ERA Sellout Sals, and Female Fetus Fetishists accuse feminists and Black protesters of being pro-Communists, but Master-baiter Media people played wise monkey when Smiling Whitey Ford made charitable wheat deals with the U.S.S.R.

Wrinkles Reagan was up in arms over a Chicago welfare mother who managed to cop three or four welfare checks when she was entitled to only one, but he was tomb-silent about multimillion-dollar Lockheed payoffs and $41,000 C.I.A. liquor bill ripoffs.

The use of a woman's body is another example of the stylistics of the Pig's Prerogative. The mother is a madonna unless she has a so-called "illegitimate" child (I don't know what that is, unless it's a child made out of plastic that isn't real), but then, of course, all of a sudden the madonna language no longer applies. It's like the way the attitude changes toward a mother who has given her child up for adoption and then tries to get it back—suddenly the legitimate mother is the villain and the adoptive parents are the victims who get all the sympathy.

I think I'd better take advantage right here of the fact that our Bicentennial year coincides with my sixtieth birthday. What a crock this decade is going to be! I see the Bicentennial year as a launching pad, as it were, to look backward and forward in assessing the entire system of pathological oppression: what I call the Establishment CON Game (Control-of-Niggers) that we're into, but good. And of course, the great symbol of the 1960's was Martin Luther King, whose birthday so many people now ignore. He was not really a revolutionary, although in order to turn this country one degree you might as well get ready to die, as indeed he had to. But because he was in favor of serious social change, the Establishment took the attitude—usually through the media, but of course in other ways as well—that he was a dangerous rebel who had contacts with the enemy, that he was going to sell out the country to the enemy, that he was a Communist, in effect—or else that he wasn't getting anything done, that he was trying to get himself killed, that he was just a troublemaker looking for trouble.

All he was really trying to do, as it got down to the procedures of his program, was to make relatively minor social changes which seemed major because this country is so opposed to even the smallest change in the direction of less racism or sexism (of course, in those days sexism was not a major issue). But anyone who tries to make even the least social change is confronted with the kind of antagonism and resistance he would meet trying to stop an alcoholic from drinking. Although an alcoholic probably realizes

Dee Dee Wright on the left, convenor of the International Conference on Black Women, Atlanta, 1975   **13**

that alcohol is not good for him, that it will cut down his life expectancy and destroy relations with his family, his career, his boss, whoever he has to deal with, he will not stop drinking. And the addiction to racism in our country is such that people get very angry if you suggest that racism and sexism are poisoning our lives. It's the same with a person who is 70 pounds overweight who really digs very greasy, fatty, weight-increasing foods. You find that they resist, with great hostility and tension, any effort to reduce their food intake by even twenty calories a day, as they take their twelfth piece of salami or whatever. If you say, "Wouldn't eleven be enough?" they really feel put upon.

The pathology of this country has a similar pattern. All Martin Luther King was trying to do was reject the oppression that came down on Rosa Parks, the woman who sat in the wrong part of the bus in Montgomery, Alabama. She wasn't trying to make any major social change, but she was tired, she was not in the mood for shit, and she simply sat down and said, "I ain't moving." So Martin Luther King, a minister in the area, decided they had no right to arrest that woman, and he organized the Montgomery boycott. It took months, but they finally changed the segregationist attitude of that bus company, and in the meantime, coverage of that particular boycott proved to be the nucleus of what later became the civil rights movement of the 1960's. Now with a minimum of intelligent leadership this country could very easily have headed off all that, but in the same pathological way that you almost have to wreck a person to make him break a bad habit, you almost had to wreck the area, and of course kill Dr. King, before you could get people to kick their habit of racism in the smallest degree. Ten years later we had the phenomenon of Jimmy Carter, the former governor of Georgia, presidential hopeful in 1976, our Bicentennial year,

and people like Terry Sanford, the former governor of North Carolina, appealing to the northerners not to freak out over busing. They're like reformed alcoholics who go out and try to save the other pathological communities from freaking out—"Look, it's not that bad, we did it. We started the busing, we desegregrated the schools, and poor white kids don't die when Black kids come and sit in the same room with them, and they don't catch anything." In fact, it's much more likely that Black kids will catch head lice from the white kids.

The Baby Blanket

I think we should all be kicking ass fairly regularly, and one of my favorite targets is the media. I don't think we should continue to permit the Establishment to feed us only what they think we should have. Marshmallows are not dangerous food—I dig marshmallows myself—but a strictly marshmallow diet for diabetics is what we get from the media. Rhythm and blues for Black community radio, "I Love Lucy" for women, jockocracy for men, heroin for the junkies: Nielsen says they like it.

In September 1971 the *New York Times* came out with an article, probably based on a handout from Albany, that the guards at Attica had their throats slit by the inmates, and that one of them had been castrated. Later it turned out that this was just not true, and the *Times* had to back away from this horrendous tale for the simple reason that it never happened. And this sort of thing goes on often enough for people to start being a little skeptical of the *Times*, and not only those people who challenge the mass media version of events. There must be recognition of media's role in the Control-of-Niggers Game.

This is one absolute necessity for anyone who is prepared to leave his "Four-I" status: ignorance, innocence, impotence, and incompetence. Ignorance is, "I didn't know. I'm a good German, I never heard of Dachau, way over in Munich, ten miles away. Isn't this terrible, who would have guessed?" Innocence is, "I'm not to blame, I never kicked a nigger." (They'd better not, or they'd come back with a bloody ankle stump.) Then impotence: "I am just little me, what can I do?" And, incompetence: "The government knows better than I what to do about this terrible situation. What can I do about the fact that the President of the United States was killed in Dallas?" They tell you first that it was a lone assassin, then under pressure they admit he had worked for the government, and then after further checking, they admit that Ruby did know Oswald, and the net effect is that it was only the people's pressure that forced them to admit as much as they have.

So I think it is imperative, even for people who are not anti-Establishmentarian, to turn to alternate media.

Every woman should read at least one feminist paper without expecting too much; while it probably won't be too much worse than the *New York Times*, there's no reason to expect it to be better. The point is that it will be different. People say that papers like the *Militant*, the *Guardian*, and *Worker's World* are so slanted. My answer to that is, "What isn't slanted? You mean to tell me the *New York Times* isn't slanted?" You can find out what happened in Lebanon easier than you can find out what happened at 125th Street in New York City. But of course the *Times* has a bureau in Lebanon that will keep you abreast of who slept at the Holiday Inn there, while you may not be able to learn about an ongoing struggle in Harlem, and if you hear about it at all, it will be in the most biased form imaginable. To read about the death of Paul Robeson or the MPLA in Angola or

At the MORE Convention, Hotel Commodore, New York, 1975

prison conditions, in the media and then in *Worker's World*, is almost to read about entirely different events.

And I think it is important that people read what the assassinologists, the Weisbergs, the Mae Brussells, Mark Lanes, Sherman Skolnicks, and Dick Gregories have to say. We should demand that the media make these people available to us, but as it is, many of the better articles on the assassination come from discredited journals like the *National Tatler* and the *National Enquirer*, and from books that the writer has to publish himself. It seems to me that assassinologists don't have to be right to have their ideas circulated; they have as much right to theorize as William E. "Simple" Simon or Casper "Milquetoast" Weinberger. Some of these big minds in the government are almost totally crazy, and yet when someone writes a serious book analyzing an alternative theory to the official bullshit version of a political assassination, why is it that publishers who can find editors and paper and print to put out a book on the Long-Haired Dachshund Society, refuse, flatly and consistently, to publish it?

Whenever the Zapruder film has been shown on late night network TV talk shows, the impact has been unforgettable. Its frame-by-frame inspection of the Kennedy assassination is devastating to the defenders of the Warren Commission Report and the psyche of the average American. But the result of the tremendous interest shown by people who saw it on ABC was that the media gave you the CBS "Comedy Hour" on the Kennedy assassination, which claimed to lay to rest all our questions about it, as the Warren Commission promised to do, but only succeeded in making a baby blanket.

I see the Warren Commission as a large body trying to cover itself with a baby blanket, so if you cover your legs, your arms are out; if you cover your ass, your head is out; you cover your shoulders, and your ass and legs are out. The truth is too big for the Warren Report or the CBS "Comedy Hour" to cover up, but they try to cheer you up and convince you that all these people who are saying that Kennedy was killed by someone other than Oswald are all wet, and they promise, "We will show you that we have the truth to cover this problem." And they take this baby blanket and try to put it crosswise and tell you, "Look, now we've covered the shoulders," while you are supposed to be courteous enough to look away and not see that the ass is sticking out. So they just keep pulling the baby blanket from one end of the truth to the other, while you are supposed to be so dumb that you politely agree they have covered the situation, when of course they have not.

From the day the Warren Commission Report was published, as I remember, there was virtually no criticism of it; any critical analysis took the form of the media nodding its head at the blind rape. For instance, they've never explained to my satisfaction that magic bullet—the one that leaped from Kennedy's body, having first gone through his neck, made a slight right turn, went into Connolly, went through Connolly's body, through his wrist, into his thigh, and ended up practically pristine. If you shoot a bullet even just through cotton, you get all kinds of distortions, and a bullet that could make turns, go down, up, and across without showing any signs of wear must have magical properties.

And when Frank Burkholtzer interviewed William and Emily Harris in a California jail for the "Today" show, one wonders why he didn't probe the question of whether either of them was a narc in Indiana, and why George Hirsch's *New Times* magazine and Mae Brussell scooped NBC on this question.

So I think it's important that people read the alternate press and be more open to their version, be less suspicious

of what they are saying. After reading the underground material, we should then go back to the Establishment media and say to them, "We have Mae Brussell or Mark Lane or Harold Weisberg over here, and if you want to tell us they are wild-eyed, you can, but we have this other version and we want you to tell us, not with the "Comedy Hour" but with some believable facts, what in fact you have to say about their work. We also want you to explain to us why you didn't see it before they did, and why you have to be driven to the wall before you get around to answering it, and then answer it with a bunch of bullshit."

We should have a much more hostile attitude toward the Establishment press. We accept too much from them, we question them too little, and worst of all, we turn the hostility that should be directed at the Establishment upon the people who are trying to wake us up.

Social Change Is Where It's At

The ultimate challenge is social change, and to me, nobody who isn't slightly into social change has a sense of complete fulfillment. I don't care how many orgasms you have, I don't care how many diamonds, how many martinis, how many rock and roll records—there is no satisfaction, in my view, that dares to compete with the ability to make social change. What establishes power better? Money helps, but it doesn't establish it: in a whorehouse society, obviously, the two dollars or two thousand dollars or two million dollars on the dresser makes a hell of a difference, but the ultimate realization is social change, and anybody who isn't into that, and who is trying to be something, is falling short.

And for that reason I feel that unless people who make the money somewhere else take some of that money and get about the business of social change,

they are not just apolitical, they're collaborators. If I see a three-year-old getting raped and I don't say anything until the rapist has gone and then I get out my Vaseline jar and give her some Vaseline for her raped ass—that's what I call the Vaseline dispenser, the grass-roots organizer.

The grass-roots organizer is, in effect, a kind of collaborator. Now this is a tough position to take, but grass-roots organizing is like climbing into bed with a malaria patient to show how much you love him or her, and then catching malaria yourself. That's what people do who go to the ghetto to establish their sincerity and credentials of anti-Establishmentarianism. I say, go to the ghetto, listen to the people there—but don't stay too long, and for Christ's sake, don't get into bed with the malaria patient. If you want to kill poverty, go to Wall Street and kick ass or disrupt. There's a difference between Vaselining the rapee and catching the rapist, and the witness to the rape who doesn't do anything is what I mean by the "good people-collaborators."

The Big Screw

The spending of our tax dollars by the Pentagon represents the greatest social disease of our country; I call it Pentagonorrhea. We're paying $15 billion for the Trident missile submarine (and don't forget that a billion is a thousand million dollars, and that's a lot of money), while college students are forced into a trick-or-treat "financial aid" situation where they were promised total subsidies and then switched over to loans, where they become sharecroppers, or else have to scuffle up the money as best they can or drop out of school. My suggestion, when I talk to people who are commiserating with each other about libraries and hospitals being closed down or any of the rest of it, is that we should have telethons for the Pentagon, and people could write checks if they want to go to war as they do for sickle cell anemia or cystic fibrosis of heart disease or multiple sclerosis or cerebral palsy, and the other people who don't want war could have their taxes used for health, education, welfare and wages for housewives. And that way, the disease of Pentagonorrhea would be treated the way we treat any other disease, and our taxes could be used to improve our society instead of destroying it.

Vote Power vs. Zombie-ism

It is very important that people begin to get interested in the electoral process. It seems to me there is something lemming-like about people who trust the media and the "good people" in this country to give them a president. Those who are still relying on government and business delinquents to bring them a good president or a good society have got to be the most dense, the most stupid, the most illiterate people in the world. I call them zombies. And when people criticize those of us who are interested in electoral politics, I have to wonder how far up their asshole they have their head, because the alternative is to let the pigs of the society, of which there are plenty, be in charge of all the taxes, of all the advertising dollars, of the gross national product.

So I don't think we should sit elections out—I think we should all get involved in some campaigns. The only 1976 candidate I personally thought worth working for was Fred Harris—or Birch Bayh, a long way behind Harris. There are a lot of reasons why I dug Fred Harris, not the least of which is here is this poor boy from Oklahoma who had the brains and the good taste to marry a Comanche Indian.

If LaDonna Harris's husband Fred had made it, she would have been our first Comanche First Lady. Harlem, 1976

Some people say they don't see the difference between Democrats and Republicans. Well, if they can't, then there's a reason to ignore the electoral politics, if they're doing anything else more important. But it's my experience that these people who say the electoral process doesn't matter aren't doing anything else either, so I just wonder why, if one candidate is no better than the other, they don't try to see what difference the pressure of their numbers might make.

In this Bicentennial year, we don't have to worry about going to jail, we don't have to worry about getting arrested or getting shot—and yet, when you think about it, why were we ever worried about it? Five hundred people can die over a Labor Day weekend, and we still drive our cars at 60 miles an hour on our highways. And it's not even that easy to get arrested—we didn't get arrested when we sang "Tired of Fuckers Fucking Over Me" on the steps of St. Patrick's Cathedral to protest the abortion laws. The point is that when anybody does get arrested, it's more or less deliberate, even in a demonstration. There's not that much danger, it's a pathology, it's inside us. The problem with us is our sense of worthlessness, our horizontal hostility, our piranhaism, a whole lot of things that are working, and we have got to undo them.

Fortunately, we now have the chance to use all three of our major powers; because we do have three powers, however limited we are. We've got body power: that's what you kick with, what you have babies with, what you kiss with, dance with, demonstrate with. They call me an activist; everybody's an activist. You're an activist when you put your pants on instead of coming out with your tail hanging out, or when you stir a pot of beans or put mustard on your sandwich: everything you do is action. If you're trying to improve a sick society, that makes you an "activist"?

So what I am saying to you now is, use your powers: your body power, your dollar power, your vote power. We've got business to take care of. Zombie-ism is for worms.

Flo Kennedy
New York City,
1976

Rally protesting transfer of Judge Bruce Wright, 1975; Attorney Conrad Lynn, wearing glasses ▶

We Demand Constitutional Bail, Reinstate Wright

MY HARD LIFE AND GOOD TIMES

Kansas City: Twelfth Street Rag

I started out in Kansas City, Missouri, in a little house in Walrond Avenue. It was an all-white neighborhood for about ten blocks around, but there were tiny little enclaves of Black families in this two-block area between Howard Avenue and 25th Street. At first it was Lynn, Grayce, and I, and our mother Zella and our father Wiley. Joy and Faye, our two other sisters, came almost 25 years later. White people lived across the street from one end of the block to the other except for Mrs. Banks's house. Of course they were poor white trash, but even so they considered that we were infiltrating.

We were very little when we first learned about white people, because early in the game, when we'd been on Walrond Avenue for only a couple of years, the Klan came over to our house. They stood on the sidewalk, at the bottom of the wooden stairs going up to the porch—they never touched our porch—and said they wanted to see our daddy. When Daddy came out, they told him, "You have to get out of here by tomorrow." "Just a minute," he said, and went into the house. He brought his gun back out with him and said, "Now the first foot that hits that step belongs to the man I shoot. And then after that you can decide who is going to shoot *me*." They went away and they never came back.

At first Daddy was a Pullman porter on the trains. By the time I was born, porters belonged to the most exclusive class—they were the "pooristocrats" of the Black community—when we were little kids Daddy was working as a waiter at the Blue Goose, and later on he had a taxi business.

My grandmother was very snobbish about color, and hated my daddy because he was black, though she had married a dark man herself and therefore Zella was fairly dark. My uncle Pruitt Simpson, a maintenance engineer and the aristocrat of the family, looked like an Italian; he wouldn't even have been taken for Puerto Rican. He had a long, narrow face like George Washington's, and his white hair was probably not even as wavy. Nowadays, of course, Black people are unhappy if they can't make a "natural," if their hair is relaxed and limp like white people's, but at that time the whole idea was to have some Indian blood in you and have straight or "good" hair.

In those days—the early 1920's—Black people always described a person by their color and their hair. The first thing you noticed—before shape or legs or anything—was dark brown skin or yellow skin—"real light," you might say—with bad hair or good hair, "good" meaning that you didn't have to

Daddy

Daddy in the middle, Zella on the end of the second row, on a picnic when they were young

straighten it. Bad hair was of course like Black people's hair.

My grandmother had pretty good hair—she didn't have to straighten it—but because she had married a dark man, Zella had "bad" hair and had to straighten hers all the time. And when we were so little we couldn't even sit by ourselves, Zella would secure us in the high chair and straighten our hair—it was a family joke, that she was straightening our hair even before we could sit in a chair.

Her hair was longer and thicker and "better" than ours, and she had a long, straight nose and lighter skin, so that meant she was prettier than we were. We thought she was beautiful. She was awfully smart, too; she had gone to normal school at a time when very few Black people did. She and Daddy hardly ever quarreled at all, but they did have one major quarrel when she wanted to go out and work and Daddy wouldn't let her. He cried about that, and we always felt that Joy and Faye missed out on the really good part of our lives, because Zella stayed home and took care of us.

Later on she had to go out and work, but that wasn't till the Depression.

She was not into housekeeping, though; she liked to lie in bed and read Street and Smith love stories, and later on she read *The Delineator* and *Cosmopolitan*. She was always getting different recipes and dress patterns from the magazines, and making us cute little dresses. She was a total failure when it came to cooking, but she loved the idea of having special food and she never really accepted that she was an awful cook.

Our house was a very tacky little frame house with a narrow yard on one side, and a porch with little snaggle-toothed wooden bannisters and a wooden swing suspended from chains. Off the porch there was a tiny little room, which was my grandmother's. The living room, where the piano and Victrola were, looked out onto the front porch, with a window you could crawl in and out of. Behind that was the room where the stove was, a black stove with a pipe that went up and an elbow that turned and went into the wall. The three of us, Grayce, Lynn, and I, slept in that room, all in the same bed. When we got older we had a davenport that let out into a bed. Daddy and Zella slept in the next room. It had no door, just a wooden rod and a plush curtain that hung right beside the stove. The john and the kitchen were downstairs, and when it was too cold to go down there we had a bucket on the steps which was emptied every morning.

By the side of the house there was a cistern, but we never really got water out of it, not that I recall. The real economic tragedy of our life came during the Depression, when our pipes froze in the winter and we needed an inordinate amount of money to have them fixed, a tremendous amount, maybe as much as $140. Anyway, we didn't have it, so we didn't have water for six or eight months, and we had to borrow water from Mrs. Turner next door. That was the worst humiliation in the world, to have to go out our back door and into her back yard and get water. We just felt sort of pitiful.

Most of the time we didn't feel really poor. When we were growing up my daddy had a taxi business. He always wanted to work for himself, and he started with one car and then later he had two. He worked at night—he never ate dinner with us. Once in a while he would get a drunk at three or four in the morning who just wanted to ride and ride, and he made a lot of money if he stayed with the drunk. Sometimes it was a white drunk who would just have him take him here and there and stay with him, and that's when he really made money. But usually he was gone by the middle of the afternoon and would come in at three o'clock in the morning, and he loved to bring us something. He would have what we called a "fit," and for days on end he'd have, say, a bakery fit and bring milk, doughnuts, and cinnamon rolls in a big bag. And then he'd have a "barbecue fit" and bring us nothing but barbecue sandwiches and hot chili, and

my mother would say, "You stop bringing this junk home, Wiley Kennedy, you are going to ruin those children's stomachs." One night she had a tantrum; she got so mad that she snatched a cherry pie away from him and threw it against the wall behind the stove. We were stunned; she almost never had any temper displays, but we started to laugh, and we were screaming and laughing so hard we didn't realize that this cherry pie syrup had spread itself in a pattern, and with the heat from the stove had stuck like plastic on the wall. It must have stayed there on that wall for a year or more.

Neither Daddy nor Zella was very strict with us, but, of the two, he was crankier. One time I remember he didn't come home until late. We'd been jumping on the bed until the springs broke—it was a brass bed with a metal bar from head to foot, and the three of us were jumping up and down on it like on a trampoline. Just as he came in the door, the metal bar broke and the springs and mattress hit the floor with a crash. As we leaped off the bed he gave each of us a swat, not more than one, but we were so horrified—we were maybe eight, six, and four years old at the time—that we took all his belongings and threw his leggings in the hollow next door. He used to wear leather leggings, like boots, the kind policemen sometimes wear, separate from the shoes, and we threw them into the hollow in the vacant lot next door, full of tin cans and junk, where they mildewed. We just devastated all his belongings. But we weren't completely crazy, because we gave his bankbook to Zella, and she cooperated and didn't tell us not to throw his leggings in the hollow. So that taught him, of course, that he wasn't to hit us any more. We only learned later that they had a policy of not hitting us. We never were hit, even though I always assumed that we might be.

They never allowed anyone else to

hit us, either, and in fact we were taught from very early on never to take any shit from anyone. I remember one time when some white kids were chasing us. They had been chasing us on a regular basis, quite a few of them, and we would walk very slowly because we were so scared, and they would call us "niggers." So one day we got evil and we said, "Let's go get 'em," and Grayce, Lynn, and I turned around and started running after them and calling them "pecker-wood." They were so scared they just ran as fast as they could, and after that we had no more trouble, because whenever they started anything we would turn on them like we were going to get them, and they would just fly. And that established very early that although they were the enemy they were scared of us, and anybody calling us "nigger" had to be a rare thing, and we'd just start after them, throwing rocks, and not taking any shit at all off of anybody. And as soon as we started doing that, it got to be fun to go home from school.

One time Lynn came in the house crying because Gladys Hyromus, who was about her age but much smaller, had hit her. Lynn was about six then and I must have been four, and Zella made her go out and hit Gladys back. I don't know

Daddy in New York after Zella died

why, but that was very important to me. Now, of course, I would have been the one to go out and smear her, but when we were little I was pretty scared of people, and Lynn was always getting hit because she was very meek and mild. There were a couple of big guys, older than she, who hit her at school, and I was very scared. It never occurred to me to hit them back, but I was always more inclined than Lynn was to turn around and go after people who were trying to bother us.

When I was about ten I hit Cornelius Lucas in the head and made it bleed. He was about thirteen then and I think he was adopted. Anyway, he was sort of pitiful, and some neighborhood kids must have told the principal. So the principal was keeping me after school. He was going to give me a whipping with the strap, and my father—the same kids must have told him I was going to get a whipping—came to school with his gun and told the principal, "You don't ever hit my girls, or I will kill you." So at that point it was established that nobody in school was to hit us.

I suspect that that's why I don't have the right attitude toward authority today, because we were taught very early in the game that we didn't have to respect the teachers, and if they threatened to hit us we could just act as if they weren't anybody we had to pay any attention to. We had a standing order that if any principal or teacher tried to hit us, we were to leave school and come home, and then Daddy or Zella or Grandmother would take care of it. Other folks would tell their kids, "You get a licking at school, you come home and you'll get another one." They didn't care whether the teacher was right or wrong, but our parents' assumption was, "Whatever you did, we don't hit you and they are not to hit you. If they can't discipline you without hitting you, you come home and we will take care of it." So that made us feel kind of precious; everything that was done in a crisis tended to make us feel more, rather than less, precious. And of course Daddy was ready to shoot somebody and kill him to keep our house.

Most Black people don't have these things, so that's a plus, but when you come to Zella's hair-straightening scene and that kind of stuff, that's on the minus side. It's important to establish that for all the plusses I had in my life, I had plenty of minuses, because I don't want anybody to take comfort in the idea, "Oh, you never had to be afraid, you can do anything, and that's why you're political." The main thing to me is the theory that you never have troubles bigger than you can handle, as long as you don't panic. People tend to feel that the enemy is so much bigger than they are, and uncrushable, but I think everyone can handle their pro rata share of everything. And that's the reason I'm surprised when people ask me, "Aren't you discouraged? How can you go on?" I can go on because I have no sense that I can change the world, or that I should be able to, and I think I must do only as much as I am able to do in order to satisfy myself. When people say, "What good is what you are doing?" then I say, "What good is *not* doing what I am doing?"

The main thing was that all of us had such a sense of security because we were almost never criticized. It was as if our shit abolutely did not stink. Zella always treated us like precious people, but everyone at school sort of made fun of us and admired us at the same time, because we were quite smart, and we were always nice to each other.

Zella lived somewhat in a state of unreality—she didn't think of us as Black people. She was determined that we should have a better life than Black people are supposed to, and when we were little kids, and fairly prosperous, she would buy us crepe de chine dresses and we would have white high-topped shoes and black patent leather shoes with three straps. From the time we were about seven until we were in high school Grayce and I were dressed alike. We were, of course, exhibitionists and flaunted everything. We just loved being noticed, and we loved it when people thought we were twins, although sometimes Lynn wanted to sink into the woodwork. She was embarrassed because she thought her

Back row: Aunt Lottie, Zella, and Grandma; second row: Grayce and me; sitting: Lynn and Cousin Lil

ankles were too thick. She worried all the time about her ankles or pimples, or whatever. But she was the one who could draw and play the piano by ear.

Zella would sew for us, and once we had little pink and white gingham dresses. She probably got the pattern out of a magazine, I now realize, and she made them with flared skirts and long waists and sleeves and little bands at the cuffs that tied. When Zella told us how she was going to make the dress she would say, "and it will have a little yoke," and we would always laugh at Zella and her little yoke. When we went to California we all had the same dresses, black sateen, each one with a different color binding. Lynn's was lavender and Grayce's was apricot and mine was rose, and they had slits on the side and pants that matched the dress, and they were appliquéd in different colors. We were very fashionable, and we thought we were very cute. Of course we knew we were Black, and in those days you couldn't be Black and be very cute, but nevertheless we felt really sharp.

Zella never accepted poverty, and yet she didn't resent it either, and we laughed a lot when we were really desperately poor. She always made an effort to maintain some kind of esthetic surroundings. Every year she would go down to the Jones Company and get five rose bushes for a dollar. She was determined to have rose bushes, although our yard had too much shade—there was a maple tree right in front, and the house shaded it too, and nothing would ever grow there. But every year Zella decided she was going to have grass and roses. She would plant them and get all excited when one leaf came out, but they never lived through the season. We never had a single rose from any of those bushes, yet she persisted in going out and buying them. It was Zella who epitomized hope for us—she never gave up.

During Prohibition she was set on making home brew, and that was another disaster. Usually it would mold in the crock, but once we got as far as the bottles and they all exploded, and we were screaming and laughing at all these popping bottles. It was the same when she tried to make light rolls. She would do everything meticulously, but they just never would come out right—they'd either be gummy and soft in the middle or hard as a rock, but never fit to eat. I think she tried to cook because she wanted to be a good person, but she didn't take housekeeping seriously; she never thought it was a particularly good idea.

She never was very rugged about the housework, although each of us had a few little chores. Most of the time she didn't want to do anything, but once in a while she would get fired up about cleaning the house. She'd put the rugs out in back and beat them with a rug beater, and we would clean out the closets. She was so much like me: if she decided to clean the closets she'd put everything out on chairs and it would lie around out there for weeks. (I can't dye a sweater, or do anything with my hands, and my house is always a mess.)

I never liked dolls much, although I did have a cat named Walker that I liked better than Grayce or Lynn or anybody else in the family, but that was more because it was mine than because I loved it so much. We had a few dolls around the house, but I was never overwhelmed by the doll scene. I did have wagons and skates and the other things that kids have, but I fell on skates twice and that was the end of skates. I fell off a bike twice and that was the end of the bike. I never learned to skate or ride a bike; the idea of hurting yourself learning to ride a bike seemed like a crock of shit, and that's still very much my thing. I can see suffering on a picket line and maybe getting your head smashed, but to get smashed up just to be able to ride a bike—who the hell needs to ride a bike? That was one of the ways in which I was always different. Joy could ride a bike, as I remember, and Grayce and Lynn skated more than I did, but none of us was really into the athletic scene.

The things I remember about our childhood happened mainly in the summer. I don't remember much about winter, except that we didn't like to wear long underwear, and when we would get out of sight of the house we would roll up our underwear so we didn't have all that thickness under our stockings. There was a drugstore on Indiana Avenue and 25th Street, and sometimes we would go and get ice cream there in the summertime. We had a tiny little rocking chair that we used to sit in and watch the fireflies—we called them lightning bugs, and we would catch them and smell the phosphorus on their tails. Once we had a grasshopper, and of course there were caterpillars. We had mice downstairs, but we were scared of them.

When there was going to be a storm we would sit in the swing and watch the lightning, and the leaves turning inside out, but mainly in the summer Daddy would take us for rides. That was when we were little, like nine, seven, and five, and we would ask him to take us for a ride around the block. If he said okay, we would scamper into the back of the car, like mice, thinking if we were very quiet and very small he would take us further, which he often did.

When we were about eight, six, and four, Zella took us to California. She thought it would be warmer there; Kansas City was cold and terrible. This was before the Depression, and Daddy didn't want to go. He was always more conservative than she was, and he wouldn't move. We stayed there for two or three years, in a house in Los Angeles. There was a fig tree in the back yard and we grew fresh tomatoes, neither of which

I liked. But we loved California. We wore "King Tut" sweaters and switched our asses a lot. We loved the beach and the grass and trees and flowers in our yard, and we ate a lot of steak. I don't remember missing Daddy very much. Zella worked while we were in school. The whole education scene was different there; we went to an integrated school, for one thing, and the educational standard was much higher, but what I remember best about it was learning to play on the acting bars.

When Zella got ptomaine poisoning, Daddy came to California. He took us out to the ocean, and when we got there he said, "Well, we won't try to walk across it because it looks like it is very far across." He was extremely ignorant and never said very much, but what he did say was kind of profound, somehow. He went back to Kansas City, and later we all went back. We found that he'd been just working and plugging away and sending us money and writing us letters with small "*i*"s, but he didn't do a thing in the house while we were gone. In two years he hadn't even changed the sheets— they were coal black.

At that time Daddy had his taxi stand on Twelfth Street and Vine, as in "Twelfth Street Rag." All of the jazz people used to hang around there, but then business moved further south, toward Eighteenth Street. There were three theaters in the immediate vincinity, and a little hotel, the Booker T, where the jazz musicians stayed. George E. Lee was from Kansas City, and Jimmie Rushing and Benny Moten; Count Basie had been the pianist in Benny Moten's orchestra. As the town began to move toward Eighteenth Street, Zella wanted Daddy to move his business down there, which he could easily have done, but he wouldn't budge from Twelfth Street, and that was one of the reasons we felt the Depression so bad.

Zella was always very adventurous,

and it was easy for us to feel smart. We never felt like losers; we were the exact opposite of the Marilyn Monroe syndrome, the beautiful golden goddess who because of her bad childhood and sense of worthlessness was never able to feel like a goddess. We were little Black pickaninnies, but because of the way we were treated by our family, we felt very favored. I remember how at Christmas time Zella would call all the creditors and tell them she wouldn't be able to pay them because she had to buy something for her kids. She always made it clear to us and to everybody else that we were something special and to be indulged. Some families have the wherewithal, but they act as if it were some kind of betrayal of parental responsibility to indulge their kids. Her feeling was, "I want these children to know we care about them, that we give them the best we have," and yet there was no great sense of sacrifice, at least none that we knew of. I can remember her crying because she couldn't pay the bills—she was very conscientious about that—but bad as we had it during the Depression, she was determined not to go on welfare.

Neither Zella nor Daddy would ever take any shit from people, although they weren't really political—there wasn't much way for Blacks to be political in those days—but Daddy would hit anybody in the mouth if he had to. Once he got the worst of it and broke his hip, and that was when the Depression really hit us hard. Then Zella absolutely had to work.

At first she tried to get a loan from the Welfare Department because she liked the idea of being able to pay it back, but they said, "No, we can't make loans, you can't pay us back." So she went to work for a lady who apparently wasn't the most reasonable person in the world, yet Zella always got along with those people. She treated them like invalids when really they were just unhappy housewives. And

so naturally they were quite preoccupied with dirt and constantly running their fingers over things to see if they were dusty, but this lady went beyond the pale one day and accused Zella of stealing. Zella had a fit and started ranting and raving. Her manner was always so gentle that when she had a burst of temper it was frightening. She wound up taking off every stitch of clothes, and on that day she happened to have the "curse," so she tore off her sanitary napkin too and shook it in the lady's face and said, "There, you see, I don't have to steal from you," and stormed out of the house. This became a legend in our household, we were so proud of her, and the outrageousness of Zella slapping her unmentionable at that lady was something that we've cherished all our lives.

Unless you are political or intellectual, events like the Depression are seen as personal events. We thought of the Depression as something that made the pipes freeze; we thought it hit us because Daddy didn't move his taxi stand and because he broke his hip. It was only later I found out it was a national phenomenon. You think of it as an incident, a condition within your own family. I suppose we must have heard about the Depression, but we weren't very down in the mouth about it, although I remember once when we didn't get any Easter outfits, we hid in the house and turned off all the lights and pretended we weren't at home.

About this time the fellows started chasing us after school, and we would run away. That was the beginning of sex. They never caught us, but it was all very thrilling and exciting, and when we were about twelve or thirteen we would go to the show almost every Sunday and pet with the guys up in the balcony. I think we were regarded as pretty fast—we would get in a car with almost anybody. We didn't have much money, but we had

Daddy's car and we would go down to Eighteenth Street and park. Teenage girls having their own car in those days was almost like having your own plane would be now; it was almost unheard of. Of course it was a taxi, but you couldn't tell, it didn't have a meter or anything; it was a big new Dodge sedan, and we would pick up all these guys. We thought we were terribly hot shit.

In the depths of the Depression we would give parties. You could buy gallon jugs of syrup with carbonated water added, and Daddy would bring home five or six gallons of this twenty-cent soda pop. We were so poor that we had a leather sofa with bricks under it where the leg was broken, and we were embarrassed, but we gave parties anyway. Once we even got a girl from the orphan's home and paid her $1.50 for the entire night to serve us all. There wasn't room to sit down; we may have had as many as 60 people. We always entertained a lot, and Daddy was cooperative about that—he was grouchy, but very cooperative.

And we used to go to the public dances at Fifteenth and Paseo, where they had the "battles of the bands," a band at each end of the hall, like Jimmy Lunceford and Andy Kirk and his Twelve Clouds of Joy or George E. Lee and Benny Moten. Julia Lee sang with George E. Lee, and Mary Lou Williams was a big-name pianist even then. Lots of times we didn't have the money to go in, so we would stand on the outside looking in, watching the dancers and ducking around trying to see them without anybody we knew seeing us. When I got out of grade school, Uldine Johnson and I were the shortest ones in the class, but then at some point I shot up and got tall, so another peril was to be sitting down when someone came over to ask you to dance—you might rise up and tower over him. You didn't particularly like to refuse anyone, because your chances of getting

another dance were better out on the floor, and yet we didn't want anybody to see us dancing with someone shorter than we were. We were terribly snobbish about that.

Next door to us was a Black lady named Mrs. Turner who had three sons, Herbert, Louie, and Alfonso, whom we called Palmy. He was big, African-faced and very black. He played football and went to college, and we all had a crush on him. He thought we were just a joke; he was the hope of the family and I think ultimately went to Arkansas and became a school principal. When I was a teenager none of us drank, but once I went to a speakeasy, and I just drank and drank and drank. They served the liquor in a sort of creamer, a cheap little glass pitcher, and it held half a pint of whiskey. Lots of the kids went there, although it was a little beyond our crowd. That night we must have gone without our own friends, and I got totally drunk and sick and passed out, but Palmy, who by then was probably in college, was there and he brought me home.

Now it was typical of Zella that when I woke up in the morning she was laughing at me. She said, "Palmy brought you home with your head and your arms and legs hanging down, and you looked just like a dishrag." Instead of going into a big excitement and upset—"You came home drunk, what were you drinking, where were you and who were you with?"—she just said, "Well, I have never seen a funnier sight in my life than Palmy carrying you in here flopping like a dishrag." She must have been pretty scared, but she was cool. And of course that was the end of it, and I don't drink at all now.

I remember coming home once and telling her that Ernest and Virgin Woods, two brothers who were in show business, had given a party where people could go down in the basement and smoke, and she said, "Don't you ever sneak a smoke.

You smoke right here. I don't like the idea of you going places especially to smoke. This is your house, and anything you do you can do right here."

Nothing really bad ever happened to me because of anything I did, right or wrong. Some kids get punished if they do something wrong and admit it, and after that they're afraid to admit it. Other times they get punished if they don't admit it, and then they're in a terrible quandary. But punishment is one thing I almost never received, so since neither doing something wrong nor admitting it ever brought punishment, it was not difficult for me to tend to try (a) not to do something wrong, and (b) not to deny it if I did. Even now, I tend to admit to myself what it is I did wrong, and I think that if you admit anything to yourself, the most important person in the world knows it, and then other people are not so important. I'd like other people to have a good impression of me and like me, but my first feeling is that the only person who stays for the entire show is me. Therefore, since everybody else is just passing through, they can't possibly be as important as I am. If I can satisfy myself, earn my own respect and keep from being totally embarrassed by myself, that is really the essence. And I think I came to that realization quite early, because Dad always admitted everything, and Zella was so big on urging us to be honest with her.

All of us were very smart in school, although we just learned the usual shit. Zella used to read aloud to us from continued stories in the magazines, and then later of course we would read them for ourselves. I remember reading A.E.W. Mason and Kathleen Norris, and we used to get books out of the library. I must have been almost ready for high school when I decided to become a lawyer. My theory has always been that whatever the people who have all the

money don't want you to do, that's what you ought to do, but I must have been pretty old when I came to that realization. And Grandmother would say, "When you grow up you are going to be somebody, you are going to be something." She was a terrific snob, although Zella was ambitious too, and that ambitious attitude was part of our background. But Zella was not one to lecture or make any rules. If anyone did that, it would have been Grandmother.

I graduated from Lincoln High School at the top of my class, but I didn't have the slightest thought of college, at least not then. In the first place there was little chance in the Black communities —there was only K.U., which at that time was almost completely white. I thought I might somehow get to college eventually, but it was really kind of unheard-of. Zella had a feeling that if there was something we really wanted to do, we would ultimately do it, but at the time college was certainly totally out of the question.

Me in my neck brace, in Kansas City ▶

We thought very little about it, anyway—what we mainly had on our minds were parties and boys and things that had very little to do with the future. I was quite clear that I didn't want to marry and settle down, but I remember thinking more about fellows and kiss lists and fun and how we were going to get the car and whether we could go to the dance. We were not profound in any sense of the word; we did well in school, but I don't remember being any great shakes intellectually. I was probably a little more outspoken, a little crazier than the rest of the kids, but I was more into acting crazy with fellows than being crazy-political.

Then my life was interrupted by several months spent flat on my back. When I was about thirteen I had fallen and hurt my back when the swing on our porch broke. They didn't automatically do X-rays back then the way they do now, and by the time I was out of high school I was in a lot of pain. Then, several years later, Grayce and I went to Chicago. On the way, somewhere in Illinois, they refused to serve us at the bus stop coffee shop and dragged me off a stool, and my back really got hurt badly. I was having such trouble I had to go into a cast. They had rented a hospital bed for me but we were poor by then and I decided to help save money, so I had to lie immobilized in a cast that ran from underneath my arms down to my tail, with my head twisted. Later on, after I got to New York, I sued the luncheonette and the bus company with the help of Adam Clayton Powell. His staff recommended a lawyer, Harrison Jackson, whom I went to see. All I got out of it was a few thousand dollars, and a fused spine.

After that episode, the main thing we wanted was to make some money. In high school I had had various jobs: I once had a job doing housework that paid $3 a week—the people I worked for were almost as poor as we were—and once I took care of two dogs, a Pekinese and a Pomeranian. And then I had a job with Eva Lucas. She worked in a really rich area out past Swope's Park for a woman who had just had a baby, and she explained to me that the idea was that you were supposed to take work away from her. She didn't ask you to do something, but when you saw her starting to do it you were supposed to take it away from her and say, "Oh, I'll do that." She was Jewish, and we had the feeling that Jewish people were harder to work for because they wanted their houses so clean. They were very meticulous. But we thought the men treated the women horribly—there was one house where the man screamed and yelled at his wife, and another where the kids were mean to the mother and talked awfully to her. In the four or five families I worked for—all of them Jewish—the women were all treated very badly, they were just pitiful—but some of the houses were beautiful.

In order to get away from the housework scene after we graduated from high school, we opened a hat shop, "Kay's Hat Shop," on Eighteenth and Vine. We'd get hats from the millinery district, and when Grayce went to New York she sent some back to us. We'd decorate the windows with little orange and peach blossoms, make the place as cute as we could, and sell little straw hats for $3 or $5. The shop made money only at Easter and Christmas, but we were able to pay the rent and it was a lot of fun. The jazz musicians would pass by, people like Ellis Fletcher, who wrote "Prisoner of Love," which was stolen from him. We heard he never got a cent for it, and that was a big scandal.

The other thing we did was sing on the radio. We had our own radio program every Saturday night, when we were too poor to have a radio at home. Lynn could play the piano by ear, and she, Grayce and I were a trio. Our theme song was, "Fit as a fiddle and ready to sing, we might sound like any old thing, fit as a fiddle and ready to sing. Haven't a worry, haven't a care, feel like a feather just floating on air, fit as a fiddle and ready to sing." And we'd sing "Mississippi Mud" and "Honeysuckle Rose." But Grayce and Lynn got embarrassed because we didn't have a change of clothes every week to go to the station. I didn't care—it was only radio—but they were too embarrassed to continue, so that was the end of our fling at show business.

Besides running the hat shop, we worked on the two elevators in the office building where our Uncle Pruitt was maintenance engineer. Zella worked there too, the elevator was a family affair; there were four or five people on it, and we all worked there at one time or another, all of us except Lynn. She was too shy, so she stayed home and helped with the house, and after Zella had her operation for cancer—in 1938 she had a breast removed—Lynn took care of her. Later on she had to nurse Daddy too. I learned from that that sometimes the least brave person in the family has the worst experience; because Grayce and I were always jumping out and taking chances, we managed to avoid a lot of grief. It's the same with societal pressure; sometimes you get farther by talking back to society than by trying to suck your way to success.

By the late thirties we had moved to a bigger house, near Spring Valley Park. I tricked the family into getting it. We couldn't buy it until we had sold our old house, so I took a gamble and pretended that we had, because I knew they'd be too nervous otherwise. I lied and said we had a buyer; I was sure we'd manage one way or another. Spring Valley had been a white neighborhood which later became "Boogie (bourgeois) nigger," although we didn't call it that—we called it a "big-shot neighborhood." So now we were living in a block of big houses with real yards, near a beautiful little city park, like white people.

I also had a number of "big-shot" lawyer friends, one of whom was Carl Johnson, the head of the Kansas City NAACP. I came close to having an affair with him—it was certainly a heavy crush—and I used to go to NAACP meetings. Then I got hold of something from the Socialist Party in New York, and also read about Adam Clayton Powell for the first time, in an article in the *Saturday Evening Post*, and when the Coca-Cola bottling plant refused to hire Black truck drivers we organized a boycott. That was my first real political action.

And then I had my second health collapse. I had what we thought was a very serious intestinal flu and was desperately ill. It later developed that I had a congenitally small ilium (small intestine), and I got an intestinal blockage and had to go to the john in a bucket—I didn't realize it, but I was hemorrhaging—because I was too sick to walk downstairs. I went into the hospital, where they wanted to do an exploratory operation, but my parents wouldn't let them, so they said, "Well, if you won't let us do an exploratory, then you might as well take her home, because there is really no hope and she might as well be comfortable." They all thought I was going to die; I weighed only eighty pounds. But Zella gave me vitamins and Daddy coaxed me to eat, and gradually I started to gain weight and came back to life.

While I was in the hospital the woman next to me, after eating her dinner, threw up, and died. I called the nurse and told her, "I don't think the lady in the next bed is breathing." They thought I was scared, but although I remember being scared of a crazy man who lived over on Howard Avenue, I've never really been afraid of dead people—I realized that was just too tacky. When I was little I would look at Zella when she was asleep and think, "God, what would I do if she died?" And I would feel so sad, but now, even though I can be sad thinking about my own funeral, I don't have a sense of horror at the thought of dying.

Society has a neat trick of convincing you that the inevitable ought to make you unhappy, but I hate the church so much that I simply refuse to let it make me nervous about dying. I think we should look forward to death more than we do. Of course everybody hates to go to bed or miss anything, but dying is really the only chance we'll get to rest, and I don't think it would be as sad as it is if the church didn't get in there with its bullshit and make everything mucky. It's part of our job not to cooperate with the prevailing attitude about death.

Our family has never been terribly introspective; I hardly ever think about what I think, except maybe politically, until things really start to go bad, like being sick in the hospital and expecting to die. And even then I used to say, "Well, at least I don't have to get up and go to work in the cold." People learn to cook and sew and play tennis or the ukelele, but the average person never asks himself, "How can I learn to live in such a way that I can avoid being miserable no matter what happens to me?"

I try to use my troubles as a way to distinguish between pain and suffering. There's no way that I know of to avoid pain absolutely, but suffering is the interpretation we choose to place on the pain we encounter. If you lean down and come up bumping your head on the open door of the kitchen cabinet, you get a pretty sharp blow, but your feelings about it are different from when you have a fight with a friend or when a lover hits you on the back of your head as hard as he can with a big book or knocks you down and makes you hit your head on the television set. The suffering is increased when someone you love or trust causes it, and the difference is one way of separating pain from suffering.

Pain is the objective reality of the damage you suffer from a trauma, and suffering is the additional element you bring to what you've just experienced. I think it's extremely important to make that distinction, because if we subtracted the suffering from the pain, we could more easily forget and be rid of our bad experiences. But we tend to repeat the indignities we experience, social, mental, or physical—we keep them alive. "Injustice collecting," I call it; we like to fondle and display our injuries and elaborate on them in every possible boring detail. Of course I do this myself; I'm very big on reminding everybody that I'm 60 years old and fragile, but my real feeling is that whatever I've failed to accomplish in my 60 years, I've probably done as much as anybody in my situation could be expected to do. Death to me is like a period at the end of a sentence. I don't say I couldn't have done more, but I feel that if you've had a fairly lucky life, you should look forward to death because you're ahead of the game, and I've been so lucky it really would be greedy to complain.

After Zella had her operation we were very cool, very happy and gay, and went to the hospital very cheery. She lived maybe two years after that, in good condition; then she started feeling terrible and went to a cancer specialist who asked her if she was afraid to die. I hated his guts, and I still do. What would he have done if she had said "yes"? We were looking up all kinds of remedies in books and found one that recommended a grape cure, which we tried, but she was just too ill. She went into a coma within a week after she saw the doctor and died very gracefully, although in agonizing pain.

I had been working on the elevator in the Altman building, and when I came in they were all just sitting there stunned, but the minute I walked through the door I started to cry and so did everyone else, in a chorus, as if on cue. After a few minutes of that my nose got stopped up and I thought, "What is this shit?" (except that I wouldn't have said "shit" in those days). So I said, "Now, wait a minute. If Zella was sick enough to die, then we are crying because we want her to be alive, to be sick in all that pain just so we could say we had a mother, but you know that doesn't make any sense. Some people don't even have one year of a mother as good as she was, and we had her all this time. So what is all this crying business?"

We stopped cold, and never cried any more until after the funeral. At her wake we simply refused to adopt a grieving attitude and horrified a lot of people who, knowing how crazy we were about Zella, expected to come and find us all in a heap in some corner waiting to be consoled. Instead we acted almost as if we were having a party, and would talk in a normal tone when they were all speaking in whispers. "Why didn't you tell us?" they would ask tragically. And we would say calmly, "Well, she was in a coma, and we had done everything possible—there didn't seem to be anything else anybody could do." Daddy was more pitiful; he was crying. But Joy and Faye, who were just little bitty kids, began giggling at the funeral, which got me very mad, and I almost didn't speak to them after we came home. Later we decided they were doing it out of nervousness.

New York: De-niggerization and Re-niggerization

After Zella's death we started to drift away. The kids stayed home with Lynn, but Grayce married a serviceman from Hampton, Iowa, named Leonard Bayles and came to New York. I followed her to be with her and share an apartment—her husband was stationed in Camp Lee, Virginia—and then later on Joy and Faye

Grayce and Leonard, my sister and brother-in-law—wedding picture

came, which is ironic because if Zella had had one dream back in Kansas City, it was to come to New York, and now we're all here, and she's dead back in a Kansas City graveyard.

I've always known what was the right thing to do, although I don't dream about it in advance. I've never been the dreamer type—I don't think about things that can't be done, because by the time they occur to me, I am usually in a position to do them. I never was one for sitting around in the wheat when I was a little girl and thinking about how great it would be to go to New York, because by the time I got around to saying it, I would be saving up money to get there. I knew I hadn't the money to go to college, but I always said to myself that if I ever did have it I would go. I can project into the future where I should be at a given time, and by that time I normally find I am on my way there—but in the meantime I don't suffer. I don't have a lot of respect for people who moan and whine about things they can't do, because I don't think anyone can dream a bigger dream than she can make come true, and if I do, then I am being unreasonable in my dreams.

Knowing what you are entitled to is a part of happiness. I am never going to be young and beautiful with a 23-inch waistline, and if I am unhappy because I am not, then tough shit on me—that is assholery, especially since I know a lot of 23-inch waistline beauties who are miserable, including but not limited to Marilyn Monroe, who was so miserable she killed herself. I happen to realize that being a 23-inch waistline Miss Black America is not the best of all possible circumstances.

It was in 1942 that Grayce and I came to New York. Everybody told us we'd never find an apartment in Harlem; they tried to get us to look up in the Bronx, but I said, "I am going to look for an apartment where I want to live and nowhere else, and I don't want to live up there. That ain't no place for me." And although we had no money, we found an apartment at St. Nicholas Place on Sugar Hill, the best part of Harlem, when none of the Army people with lots of money could find a place there. The minute we got into the building we sued the landlord to make him paint, which made him very upset because in order to get the apartment we had agreed he wouldn't have to, so of course he hated us and we got great glee out of that.

Both Grayce and I worked. First I was at the Veterans' Administration at 346 Broadway. Then I took the civil service exam and became a government clerk, Grade 2, in the U.S. Treasury Division of Disbursements. I got fired from that job. After that I had jobs at the Museum of Natural History and at Gimbels. I made maybe $100 a week working seven or eight hours a day, which would have been easy, except that I was going to school too.

I didn't really come here to go to school, but the schools were here, so I went. And typically, everybody said, "Obviously, your goal will be City College." But I said, "No, Columbia, because it will be tough enough going to school at all, and I'll be much better off if I really do something difficult than if I just aim for a half-assed school and have to work almost as hard." It was like later on, when Joy lived in a horrible apartment up in Harlem—she was as often behind in the rent as we were in our new house, living where we wanted to. I find that the higher you aim the better you shoot, and even if it seems you're way beyond yourself when you set up your goal and take your aim, it always turns out that you can do a lot more than you thought you could. I've always felt that you should never try to do anything tacky, because it might take as much effort as to do something you liked, and the extra effort required to do something like going to Columbia instead of City College would be more than made up for by the energy you get from doing what you want to do.

I had no trouble getting in, and I started at Columbia in 1944, taking a night course at University Undergraduate, later called General Studies. I registered immediately as a pre-law student, which I guess was unusual for a Black woman at that time, but I didn't feel particularly Black, and I'd always wanted to be a lawyer—not only to right wrongs, but because most of the people I knew who were lawyers were better off than the others. When we were kids and we had a candy wine ball in a pickle, we would try to make the other kids think it was horrible so they wouldn't want any, and I realized that the people who were telling me I shouldn't try to be a lawyer were using those same tactics.

All I had to do was to look at lawyers and then look at mothers to know which I would rather be. Who with any taste and brains would want to be changing diapers all day? And very early in the game I said that if I ever did get married, I would have a cooky jar I wouldn't tell my husband about, where I would save money, and I would have that money set aside very handy, close by, so I could get a divorce right away if I wanted to. I wasn't going to get caught in that trap. I never bought the okeydoke, and when you don't buy the okeydoke you're free to look around to see what you should do, because you've established what you don't want to do, understanding that it's a crock of shit. And from there on it's very simple to realize that if you don't get caught in the trap you may not do all that well, but at least you're free to make a change.

Everyone told me I should be a nurse or a teacher, but I thought anybody with the brains and energy to become a teacher ought to want to become something better. And lately, since I have been going to college campuses, I have been bringing down the wrath of all the nursing schools because I can't see why anyone in college would want to be a nurse instead of a doctor. I've gotten into deep trouble with some very good people who get very pissed. But I say, "Don't start up with me. If you're going to deal with shit, why don't you become a proctologist?" Why would anybody want to earn that little money and deal with that much shit?

So I decided to apply to Columbia Law School; I wanted to combine my last undergraduate year with the first year of law, and I was refused admission. The Associate Dean, Willis Reese, told me I had been rejected not because I was Black, but because I was a woman. So I wrote him a letter saying that whatever the reason was, it felt the same to me, and that some of my more cynical friends thought I had been discriminated against because I was Black. That was a smart tactical move, because just at that time Black people were beginning to sue the graduate and professional schools for their racist admission policies, and when I went to see the Dean I was so cocky I made him nervous—he didn't particularly want a lawsuit.

I said, "If you have admitted any white man with lower grades than mine, then I want to get in too." That was probably the first time I used what I call the "testicular approach." I've found that when you apply the right kind of pressure to the appropriate sensitive area, people become even more concerned than you are about your progress and happiness and contentment. So when I told him it felt like racism to me, he got worried, especially since this was 1948 and I was wearing my Henry Wallace button, so he knew I must be crazy. That's another trick I find very useful: when you think you are going to lose, you might as well lose partly biting and not sucking. I figured if I got thrown out of his office, it wouldn't be from a kneeling position; I would at least be sitting up. And the irony was that in the end he let me in and kept out my white friend from Barnard, Pat Jones—she never did become a lawyer.

There were only about eight women in law school altogether, and I was the only Black in the class. They generally have a token Black, and I was it. I was graduated from law school in 1951, bottom of the class, although I managed to get through in three years while working part-time in the library. I don't really have a legal head; I was very good in college, but law school is a kind of obstacle course. They want an almost mathematical mind, the kind of person who can walk past a pool of blood and think, "what a beautiful shade of red"—they call that "objectivity." They want to divorce you from your nigger status, to de-niggerize you, but they think being de-niggerized means living in your head and not in your heart or your soul or your body.

I thought I'd like criminal law, but they managed to shit-cover even that chocolate. Psychology and law are inherently interesting subjects which they manage to make totally boring, as part of the obstacle course. They don't really want you to get through, so they make it so difficult and boring you're ready to blow your brains out.

Law school made me see clearly for the first time how the law was used to maintain the bullshit rather than to change things, that justice was really a crock of shit. In negligence law, for instance, we had a Dean Smith, a Southerner, who made a big point of not being able to pronounce the plaintiffs' names if they were foreigners. And there was the Palsgraff case against the Long Island Railroad, which established the principle that the plaintiff may not recover even if injured. I used to laugh and say that the kid couldn't recover because her feet were too big for her age—if her legs had been shorter, her foot wouldn't have been on the track and the train couldn't have run over it. Anything that could possibly be twisted into putting the blame on the victim was part of the accepted theory of negligence law, as we were taught it at Columbia.

But I had a wonderful sociology professor, Bernhard Stern, who edited a Marxist publication called *Science and Society*. He was small, with a sharp nose and twinkly eyes and a wonderful sense of humor, and he had a big influence on my understanding of the socialist world and the racist world; he predicted that a race war would probably break out, with Russia lined up against China. (This was in the 1940's.) He was a first-rate teacher, and his course was a real turning point. Even then I was dividing teachers into finks and good people, and he was the best. And then in law school I had Walter Gellhorn, who taught administrative law and whose sister, as I recall, had been in the labor movement.

So it was very easy for me to figure out who had their shit together; it was just a question of choosing the right direction, which for me was left. I had no great dramatic revelation that I can remember, but when there was a choice, I would always choose the anti-Establishment way. Most people seem to overlook one reason why so many people are leftists: the country has been so fucked up by the people in power. It isn't only that poor people are abused, but that the Establishment makes such a mess, a total asshole mess, of everything, and I don't know how anybody with any brains could be anything but more and more anti-Establishmentarian as they learn more about what's happening. In my history courses I would always be pulling for the anti-Establishmentarians; the Wars of the Roses, for instance, was a wonderful situation because the top governing hierarchies were fighting each other.

You don't need to be terribly smart to tell the difference between a lemon and a peel or a nut kernel and a shell. You may never have eaten a walnut before in your life, but no one with any sense would try to chew on the shell. So as I've gone through life, in politics and in everything else, there have been opportunities at every turn to go with the Establishment or against it, and to me it simply boiled down to the question of whether you eat that tough bottom rind or the bacon slices. I never had the slightest sense of being a revolutionary, it was just a question of selecting what was palatable and leaving aside the rest.

Now of course in a whorehouse society you get paid because you are fucking someone you don't like, and the system pays you for doing unpleasant things. I certainly did my share as part of my work, but politically I never did—in my whole life I never needed anyone to tell me what was fit to accept intellectually and what was not. I didn't lead the civil rights marches, of course, but I sure as hell knew where my sympathies lay in the fifties. I didn't go immediately, because no opportunity presented itself; I've never gone looking for anything, although now that I have a little more money and time and influence I sometimes initiate things. But in 1964, when I was invited to go to Mississippi, naturally I went. I have never sought out revolution, but I certainly was always prepared to move in that direction.

When I got into law school I was drawn esthetically, at least, to the anti-Establishmentarians because the Establishment was such a crock of shit, and also because there are always more of them. I'm always inclined to go where there are fewer people, whether it's because the others don't have the brains and imagination to be there, or because I just feel the people there need help, and it seems to me that what they're doing is at least as important as going to Radio City. I simply can't understand thousands of people standing in line every week to get into Radio City. The things that most people do seem to me dull and boring and artificial; I can't see why a person would rather go on a ski slope than a picket line. A picket line happens to be more fun, and the fact that it is also politically astute is just a bonus. I'm not at all sure I am political so much because I want to do good for other people as because I want to live the best life I know how and not be bored to death. I think the reason the bars are so full and they push so much liquor on the airplanes is that people are breaking their asses to have fun because they don't know where the fun really is.

When I got out of law school in 1951 I didn't start practicing right away; the first job I had with a law firm, Hartman, Sheridan and Tekulsky, was as a clerical, helping the bookkeeper. Several of the laywers there, especially Irving Bergman, and occasionally Burton Turkus, Paula Moore, and Mildred Mebel, let me do legal chores and encouraged me to see myself as a potential lawyer. I flunked the bar exam, both parts, the first time I took it, but passed the second time, with a lot of help from Lewis Ullman, a member of the firm, and was admitted in 1952. (Lew ultimately committed suicide, poor dear.)

By 1954 I had my own office at 295 Madison Avenue. I did mostly matrimonial work, and a certain number of assigned criminal cases. (These were not Legal Aid; I had begged to work for them but was repeatedly turned down by the then head, an ex-District Attorney named Florence Kelley, who later became a judge.) The kind of cases I got were assigned to you as a private attorney by the judge, and you represented the client without pay, for the experience—at least, that was the theory. It was very tough at first, but I managed, barely. My clients always had a hard time paying legal fees, and one Christmas I had to work at Bloomingdale's to pay the rent.

I was exhausted, and in 1955 I had my third big health crisis. After the one back in Kansas City I would periodically get attacks of what I called "the mollygrabbles," from which I always recovered, but this time I ignored the pain to the point where I got gangrene and wound up in Mother Cabrini Hospital, where I had three feet of intestines removed. Mother Cabrini was a small Catholic hospital in Washington Heights, at the upper edge of Harlem. They were having a lot of trouble keeping out Black people, who were encroaching on the neighborhood, and at first they tried to throw me out, but Faye told them, "If you put her out, you had just better watch your ass." Everyone expected me to die, but I didn't know it, so I naturally didn't. Later I found out that the doctor would come in every day to ask, "Is Bed Two dead yet?" But I was sick for a very long time, and all kinds of people collected money to pay for my hospitalization and the office rent, people like Betty Ormont, Harriet Hannelin, and Leonard Cohen, a good friend who was then leader of the West Side Democratic Club and is now a civil court judge.

The Young Democrats were part of the new scene, "reform," they called it then, which I was involved in, although I was older than most of them. But I was disappointed at the meetings, which tended to focus on procedures. People were not, it seemed to me, interested enough in issues, but much more in how to raise money and run the organization. I think that's still the case, and that's one of the reasons I am not more enchanted with organizations. Funding and running

With Ted Kupferman and Shelley Slepian, c. 1950. Ted was then a candidate for judge; now he's on the New York Court of Appeals bench

an organization takes so much effort that the substantive issues it was set up to deal with often become totally submerged in the procedural problems of maintaining it. The Young Democrats were fairly typical in that way, but I was glad to be part of them; I had the feeling it was as good a scene as any around.

In the late Fifties I acquired a partner, Don Wilkes, and a husband, Charlie Dye, both of whom ultimately proved disastrous. I married Charlie in 1957, when he was 31 and I was 41. He was a Welsh science-fiction writer, and a drunk. Joy always teases me about marrying Charlie, because for all my talk against marriage, the fact is that he was one of the very few men in my entire life who at all seriously suggested we get married. She thinks I would have married whoever came along, that my whole rap against marriage is a crock, and that I am really a secret romantic. It's true that when I was younger I used to get crushes on all kinds of people, mostly beyond my reach, but maybe that's wiser, since marriage means getting a crush on someone within your reach. Anyway, I married this dude.

He had come to a party we gave, where he fell for a friend of ours, Eleanor Martell. Ellie probably took one whiff of that stale liquor breath, spotted him for what he was—his teeth by this time were decaying and he wasn't all that appetizing—said, "No, thank you very much," and split, whereupon he got a tremendous crush. He would go into a tailspin over anyone who rejected him, and would come around sniveling and crying to me, and I'd try to get him together with Ellie. And then it developed that he had also been rejected by another friend of ours, Stella Halpern, a classical pianist. Supposedly she had broken his heart, but I remembered that she had once called me to report that he had met her after they'd broken up, and had brought her an Easter bunny. When

Charlie Dye, my Welsh husband, in a sober moment

she refused to go back with him, or even out with him, he pushed her down the subway stairs and threw the chocolate bunny after her. I had helped her threaten to arrest him, and stopped his assholery, so I realized that he was a crock and I should have been warned.

It turned out that he was the type of person who will latch on to people to whom he feels somewhat superior, and then when they reject him, thereby establishing his inferior status, he goes into fits of depression and rage. Charlie used to go up to Stella's house and try to get her to let him in, and she told me she was getting scared of him. I don't know if he was anyone to be afraid of, but he certainly managed to make a terrible nuisance of himself most of the time.

So this was the prize. Fortunately, I never took marriage very seriously; it just seemed to me that he wanted to be married more than I wanted not to be married. I never thought it would last very long, but finally, I guess just to see what it was all about, certainly not with any idea of a serious marriage, I gave in. We were married in the sunken living room in Leonard Cohen's apartment by Judge George Stark, a friend of his. Charlie was blind drunk. We couldn't get a cab from his apartment on Second Street and Avenue C, but he wouldn't go by bus, which was exactly across the street—he forced me to walk to the subway, and I got soaking wet. And of course none of these things persuaded me not to go through with it, so I guess I am not as immune as I like to think from society's brainwashing about marriage.

That very night we had a party up in Harlem where he got still drunker and grabbed crotches and did whatever else he could think of that was totally outside the pale. Joy thinks if I could marry a creep in that condition, I certainly had to be in love with him. Maybe a lot of women marry men they don't think any more of than I did of Charlie, but I certainly had no illusions about being in love with him. Don't ask me why I did it—that's just how it was.

I more or less moved in with him, still spending a certain amount of time at my place, and periodically, after I'd get tired of his drunken nonsense, I'd take all my clothes that I couldn't get into a cab, leave them at a cleaner's on Second Street and split, after he had gone to the bank. He worked at Irving Trust Company down near Wall Street as a security guard, which meant he carried a gun; but fortunately he didn't bring his gun home, because drunk and crazy as he was, I am not at all sure he wouldn't have shot me in one of his rages. And the idea of a man in his perpetually drunken condition working as a security guard gives you an idea of the kind of people we trust with guns.

On the plus side, though, he was a wonderful story-teller and he could be very amusing. Not amusing enough for me to put up with the rest of him, obviously, but anyway I did. When I first knew him, he would laugh at me because I got dressed, as he put it, to go to bed—he didn't think people should wear anything to sleep in. One Christmas I got him a pair of pajamas because it did occasionally get fairly cold in the apartment, and when he put them on he loved them so much he would hardly take them off for me to wash them. That was the way he was: he would say one thing and then be just the opposite when it came down to the wire. I also bought him a really beautiful pair of shoes, because I enjoyed shopping for him and he was such a ragamuffin when I first met him; that is, I called him a ragamuffin, but he thought of himself as an elegantly seedy author.

He didn't like to take baths, so much so that he would go in the bathroom and turn on the water in the shower without getting in. After I caught on, I'd make him come over and let me feel his skin to check up on him. He got cleaner and neater the longer we were together, but it always amuses me when people talk about the special odor of women, and their special problem. When I married Charlie, his socks were practically standing up in the closet. (It is funny, though, that neither Charlie nor my Dad, who also wasn't crazy about bathing, ever actually smelled.)

Although he drank constantly, he was not always mean when he was drunk. He drank Gallo muscatel for the most part, but sometimes Thunderbird, which was another of my names for him. Just about every night he would drink a quart, and more than a gallon over the weekend. At night he would sit on the floor, usually with no clothes on, and play his records. He was a big jazz fan, and whenever he sold a piece to a magazine, even if we had broken up, which we often did, he would call me up and we would go to Birdland. He was smart enough to stay away for weeks at a time, though, after I'd left him.

He had a tiny studio apartment, just one room with a little kitchen and bathroom and a small clothes closet where he kept his pornography collection. He said it was worth $1,500, which it well may have been, but it wasn't worth anything at all to me, and I threw so much into the incinerator after he died that I put the fire out.

In spite of everything, he was interesting to me because while he was terribly damaged merchandise, he had been at some point a quality person, and he was a peach all through my crisis with Don Wilkes's larcenous abandonment.

Wilkes had been the great white hope of one of the major Wall Street law firms. He thought he was so smart he could represent poor people as successfully as he had conducted the multimillion dollar case of Ford against Ferguson. But what he didn't know, which I understood very well, and which really flipped him out, was that there is no justice for Black people, or nigger-loving lawyers. We took on four or five big negligence cases, and in order to hurry them to trial he waived the jury, and to his shock always got dismissals and/or minimal damages.

We had a case where a woman was crushed between two cars when she got out to help a car which had stalled on the Long Island Expressway. One leg had to be amputated and the other was virtually useless, and Wilkes took the case to the judge without a jury, because he refused to believe me when I told him you could actually lose such a case. But of course it was fixed, and the judge tried to browbeat us into accepting minimal damages and ultimately gave us, as I recall, a verdict of maybe $20,000. The insurance company paid the limit of the policy, but that amounted to only $10,000, so this legless woman in a wheelchair with one leg gone and the other useless only got a pittance, which was heartbreaking.

Wilkes's work with the Wall Street firm had been brilliant, but he didn't have the strongest character in the world, and what he didn't understand was that his brilliance meant little or nothing in the crooked courts of New York, and that he would lose not only that case—in effect—but also a case where a woman slipped in water from a clogged drain in her own basement and suffered a fractured skull and damage to her eyesight. But there again, thinking he had a sure shot, he brought the case to trial without a jury, and again we got no recovery, although there was a statute that clogged drains were a no-no, and complaints had been made to the landlord. They called it contributory negligence on her part, as though she could have walked four inches above the floor.

Then there was the Moriarty case, where a man who worked for National Gypsum had been driving one of those go-cart arrangements around the factory. It got out of control and he was smashed to death. It was established that there was some sort of mechanical defect, but again

With Joy and Faye by the swimming pool in our house in Orange, New Jersey

there was a judgment for National Gypsum and the Butler Bin Company, which made the go-cart.

The pressure of these defeats finally drove Wilkes around the bend. He'd been spending money the firm didn't have, based on what he assumed was coming in, but he was so naive he didn't realize how racist the courts here were, and when he lost one case after another he finally flipped out. He ran away with $57,000 of the firm's money, leaving about $5,000 in the bank to cover bills amounting to over $50,000.

This was the worst crisis I had to face, and it was then that I developed my theory that you never have problems bigger than you can handle, and if you just don't panic you will make it. Two or three weeks after Wilkes had absconded, someone came in and offered me $100 for an electric typewriter I had recently paid $600 for. But I thought, "If I sell my typewriter I won't be able to type up any papers, and the $100 isn't going to do much good anyway. This is not a distress sale, and I am just not going to take such a loss." And that's when I began to realize that the great disaster is panic, and that it was my business not to panic—that was my job, at that moment. If I could just keep my little boat from toppling over, I would probably be able to weather the storm, and that's what happened.

All through this bad period I owed a lot to Charlie; after Wilkes ran away Charlie came into the office and typed and answered the phones, and generally

Selling tickets for the Malcolm X benefit with Joy

kept my spirits up. Actually, during that time he drank less and behaved better than he did at any time before or after; apparently it was easier for him to be decent when I was on my ass, because when things got better Charlie began to go to pieces. He got very sick, and the doctor told him he had a bad liver and would have to give up drinking if he intended to live. Naturally I mentioned Alcoholics Anonymous, but he wasn't interested. I was very much into laissez-faire, and took the position that if he wanted to drink himself to death, okay, as long as he didn't treat me too badly or try to complicate my life, which of course he did. So whenever my cup got too full, I would just leave.

That summer we took a place on Fire Island, where he had constant tantrums and insulted everybody and was generally impossible, and finally I got to the point where I decided that was it. I left him on Fire Island and moved all my stuff out of his apartment. When he came back in September he would vacillate between crying like a helpless baby and invading the office, drunk as a lord. Finally I called the police, who took him to jail, where he stayed overnight. The next morning when I had to go to court he looked so pale and pitiful, I felt really sorry for him. Soon after that he died, which I suppose was as good a disposition of the case as could be expected.

I sent his body to California to his mother, and heard from her later only in connection with his Social Security, which she got. I was dead broke at the time and entitled to it, as his widow. But she wanted it, and I figured that with all the hassle, it would be worth about as much as fishing around in an unflushed toilet to recover a ballpoint pen.

One of the last cases Wilkes and I worked on together was that of Eleanora McKay, whom you know as Billie Holiday. Her agents, Associated Booking Corporation, had neglected to advise her that a federal statute required persons who had been convicted on narcotics charges to register when they left the country, and the U.S. Attorney was threatening to indict her when she returned from a European tour. We were approached to defend her, and Wilkes was able to persuade the U.S. Attorney not to indict.

Billie was grateful; she invited us to her birthday party, but it proved to be her last. Not long afterward she was taken to Metropolitan Hospital. While she lay there, desperately ill, a nurse claimed to have found heroin in her room. It was obviously a setup; I don't believe that if heroin had been smuggled into the hospital it would have been left sitting in a Kleenex box, which was where Nurse Figueroa claimed to have found it.

I can't say in whose interest it was to bring it in, but both Billie Holiday and Charlie Parker, whose estate I also handled after his death, were highly exploitable by the publishing and record companies because of their addictions. I have no doubt that if the companies had not benefited by their being on drugs, and therefore highly dependent and vulnerable, they would have kicked the habit long before. Louis McKay kicked Billie off drugs many times, but somehow whenever the companies had a new contract for her to sign she would be picked up by the police.

When she was arrested in the hospital, Wilkes came up with the strategem of offering to have her testify before the Grand Jury. This tactic saved her from being indicted for the felony of possessing narcotics, which would have meant moving her to the prison ward. But she was still under arrest, and a police officer was in her room at all times. There was very little we could do, except save her from the prison ward, for she was dying.

She was still rather beautiful right up to the end, especially when she smiled.

The **TRUE** Story of

BILLIE HOLIDAY

By WILLIAM DUFTY

© 1959, New York Post Corp.

ARTICLE IV

Billie and the Author

"They called it The United States of America versus Billie Holiday and that's just the way it felt."

In the raw economy of phrase with which she spoke and sang, Lady Day herself thus once described the forlorn Philadelphia courtroom scene that cost her a year in jail for violation of the narcotics laws twelve years ago.

But the U. S. vs. Holiday was a drama with a 1947 beginning and no end. Vigilant law enforcers were still breathing down Lady's neck early this winter when her fatal illness set in.

Billie came back from Europe in January of 1959 full of bounce and vitality. A European tour always had a tonic effect on her. They had loved her in Milan; she'd had a ball in Paris with expatriate friends from the old days uptown and a new breed of admirers that gassed her as much as she excited them: tough, cosmopolitan leaders of the African nationalist movement with whom she felt a stirring and bitter kinship.

She was scheduled to return to London for a one-shot TV spectacular in the spring. She couldn't wait. She had just about given up hope that the New York police would ever permit her to sing in New York clubs again. One of these trips, she vowed, she would settle down permanently in London, and commute by jet to the States for concerts and TV, instead of the other way around.

Suddenly, one afternoon, she telephoned. I could tell from her voice that something serious was afoot. Lady never hollered "Uncle" until she needed one bad. When I got there, all her

bounce was gone. She was scared. She had just gotten a telephone call from a man who said he was Inspector McVeigh from the U. S. Customs Service. The man said he had been looking for her for a week. He asked her to come to the Customs House the next afternoon for questioning. She said he invited her to come alone, without a lawyer.

She had no idea what it was all about. Neither did I. I called the Customs Bureau to make sure there was an agent named McVeigh. Lady promised me she wouldn't move an inch without a lawyer. She had done just that in 1947 and had paid bitterly for it ever since.

I called a lawyer friend of mine, Flo Kennedy, of Wilkes & Kennedy.

Nobody in the law firm had heard of any special regulation requiring travelers abroad to register with Customs. As we talked, I had a sudden recall of an old story I had read in the papers about a pair of narcotic addicts put under arrest for failure to register with the Treasury Dept.

The lawyers checked, and sure enough they found that the Narcotics Control Act of 1956 (18 U. S. C. 1407) provides that "no citizen of the U. S. shall depart from the U. S. if he is addicted

to or uses narcotics as defined in the Internal Revenue Code of 1954 unless such person registers with Customs prior to departure and upon his return to this country. Penalty for failure to register will subject the offender to fine and imprisonment."

Alas, the statute also covered retroactively anyone "convicted of violation of the narcotic or marijuana laws of the U. S. or any state, the penalty for which is imprisonment for more than one year."

Lady's 1947 federal sentence had been a year and a day. What a difference a day makes. Twenty-four little hours was the hooker that made the 1956 law apply retroactively to her.

She had done her time, and had been punished for 12 long additional years by revocation of her police permit to sing in New York clubs. Now she could be punished again.

The thought of it made her lawyer ill. It made me ill. And it made Lady ill.

When she was worried about going back to jail again, you could always tell. She called the liquor store and ordered full quarts of Gordon's gin, and she started looking for a home for her dog.

We tried to tell her it couldn't
Continued on Page 22

Continued on Page 22

She had a very sweet, almost childlike smile, but she was a very, very tough lady. There are all kinds of stories about her temper tantrums and her behavior in bars, which I never observed personally; I never knew her well, although she was very political. The first time I ever saw her was up in Harlem, where she sang "Strange Fruit" at a benefit for Emmett Till, the young Black who was lynched in the South for whistling at a white woman.

She was so exploited all her life by the record companies, her agents, and the unions that it was actually in the interest of any one of those groups to disgrace her in the final weeks of her life, so that there would be less public sympathy for her. After she died we had a really dreadful situation, because through the stupidity or cupidity of her agency, headed at that time by Joe Glaser, she was not affiliated with any of the performing rights societies, which meant she had no regular income from ASCAP, the American Society of Composers, Authors and Publishers, or BMI, Broadcast Music, Inc. That was criminal, and somebody should have brought an action against the agency for failing to advise her on that; but even worse, they had never collected on the contract for her last European tour.

I'm sure there are two sides to some of these stories, but I can't imagine what possible explanation there could be for their not even having collected on her American Guild of Variety Artists union benefits. Billie Holiday never got her sickness and death benefits, which she had paid into for probably 25 years; they all went down the drain or into some pig's pocket. I have no way of knowing whether the agency was too stupid, too corrupt, or just didn't give a damn, but if they didn't know, they were criminally ignorant, and if they did they were exploitative and racist.

All my experience runs counter to the myth which obtains in jazz circles, that these agents are so in love with and protective of their clients; and Billie Holiday's posthumous situation was a perfect example. An attorney she knew who had painted the floor of her apartment out of devotion to her, and in general had acted like a groveling worm, turned into a total vulture the minute she died, and started suing the estate for all kinds of fees, which were honored by the court, although in most cases no bills had been submitted.

All the people around her who had sucked her dry while she was still alive turned into grasping, scrambling animals the minute she was dead, and this is typical of the tawdry people who surround celebrities. I'm sure it's not limited to Black musicians and dancers, but the pathology is much more noticeable where they're concerned, because the people who circle around them to pick what little flesh is left on their bones or financial structures are the crummiest types.

When I began to see the enormity of the situation—by that time I was handling Charlie Parker's estate as well—I started to fight for the rights of these artists, which unfortunately was easier to do once they were dead. I couldn't have fought for a live artist the way I fought for Billie Holiday or Charlie Parker; if I had, the record companies would just have cut off their livelihood. It's the perennial problem of artists fighting the people they must continue to do business with, and between their agents and the record companies and publishers, many gifted people are ripped off in a million different ways.

One of the first things I did was to affiliate both artists with BMI, and we were at last able to get a few thousand dollars as an advance, which of course was an outrage, because these artists had made millions for the record companies and music publishers. These companies had almost entirely stopped paying

---

The TRUE Story of
BILLIE HOLIDAY

By WILLIAM DUFTY

Continued From Page 4

happen. But nobody could be sure. She found a home for Pepi, her tiny Mexican Chihuahua, she stopped sleeping and started drinking again.

On Thursday, January 15, Billie showed up at the Customs House, Room 455. Flo Kennedy went along as her attorney. Two Treasury Agents, Martin McVeigh and Mario Cozzi, were waiting to question her. They advised her that anything she said could be used against her. Then they put her under oath.

Playback of the Past

She told them her name, occupation, address; verified her passport, her date of birth, and her flight to Paris in October, 1958.

Then Agent McVeigh asked, "Have you ever been convicted of any narcotics offenses . . ."

"Yes, I have," Billie said.

"Did you plead guilty?"

"I wanted to go away for a cure," Billie replied, "and they gave me . . ."

"I have a copy of your record from the FBI," McVeigh broke in, "which indicates that on May 28, 1947, you received a sentence of a year and one day at the Federal Reformatory for women at Alderson, W. Va. Is this true?"

"Yes, that's right," said Billie.

"Were you arrested at Philadelphia by Federal narcotics agents?" Cozzi asked.

"I wasn't really arrested," she replied guilelessly. "They were sort of like you people, they were very nice to me."

They asked her if she were familiar with the new 1956 regulations on registering.

"I didn't know anything about it at all," she replied. "I went there to sing, to do concerts . . . myself and my piano player. My agent gave me tickets. He told me where to go and who to meet but he told us nothing about registering. I never saw any sign. I didn't know. I went to the doctors, I did everything else I should have done, so why shouldn't I have done this? I didn't know."

They asked about her accompanist, Mal Waldron. They asked her again if she had registered.

"Nobody asked me to," she insisted. "I never did it before. This must be something new, because wouldn't they ask me?"

"No," said Cozzi, "it's not the government's responsibility to ask every individual passenger or person leaving the U. S. if they have a narcotic record . . . you'd be insulting a lot of people. . . ."

"Oh," said Miss Holiday, "I suppose so. I didn't see any signs, I'm awfully sorry about it."

'Nobody Cared Enough'

So they showed her a small sign, 7 inches by 11.

She denied having seen it before. "If I had," she added, "I would have went and done something about it. Really, I didn't know. . . . They took pictures of me standing on the ramp with a little bag, the newspapers. . . . I couldn't have been trying to sneak away. . . . They kept me out there in the cold for half an hour."

Was there anything else she would like to add to the record? the agents asked.

"Yes," said Lady bitterly. "There's a lot I would like to add but I'd have to write a book."

When they persisted, she made a forlorn little plea:

"It seems like such a little thing and nobody cared enough about me—my agents, the managers I got for this and that—to tell me about it. I've been trying my best to be a good girl and a little thing like this happens and I have to come down here and go through all this . . . It's terrible, that's all. Once you get in trouble for narcotics, it's the end. I think it's the worst thing that could ever happen to anybody in this whole wide world, that's all I got to add."

Her lawyer's statement was anti-climactic. Although ignorance of the law is no excuse, the lawyer emphasized, Billie was not alone. There was her agent and her attorney who apparently did not know of the new regulations.

"I, personally," Miss Kennedy added, "was not aware of it. Although we were not representing her at the time, had we been representing her we would not have brought it to her attention either because we did not know of it. . . I think it can be seen that it has been Miss Holiday's intention to abide by the law."

Miss Kennedy then requested that the hearing be wound up as quickly as possible.

Solemnly, the Treasury agents announced that the record would be referred to the U. S. Attorney for the Eastern District of New York. "I necessarily will be guided by his decision," said McVeigh. The federal men were courteous and considerate.

Billie came out of the hearing shaken. It had been a long day, she felt, but she was still scared. Miss Kennedy complimented the singer on being an excellent witness.

"I should be a good witness by now, honey," Lady snapped. "I've had enough experience on the damn stand."

Don Wilkes, Miss Kennedy's associate counsel, arranged that a subsequent proceeding would be held in his office. Billie met the Customs men there, read the record of the hearing, initialed each page and authorized it as a true and accurate copy.

Then the waiting began. The next session would be held in the office of the U. S. Attorney in Brooklyn. The days dragged on. Billie had never walked into a Federal Building since 1947 without expecting to need bail. She stopped sleeping. She started drinking. She started losing weight. Finally, we were able to persuade her to see a doctor.

Alarmed at her loss of weight, the doctor started visiting her daily. Billie listened to him on every subject except gin. He begged her to cut down, but she couldn't. "If he had the government breathing on him, he'd be drinking, too," she said.

Billie knew her liver wasn't up to par. Her heart had seen better days.

But the threat of going back to jail was a complication Billie didn't tell her doctor about. It was something shots and pills couldn't get near anyway.

Finally, in early February, a date was set for the informal hearing before the U. S. Attorney. The lawyers notified Billie. She said she was ready. But each time the day arrived, she panicked and begged off.

She was sick, the lawyers knew. But the date at the Federal Building couldn't be put off. Finally the two lawyers literally had to make her go. They both went to her house, waited for her to dress, trying to assure her they had every chance of getting the charge dismissed. But Billie couldn't believe it.

They got her in the car, finally and started up the West Side Highway. Near 42d St., Billie panicked once more and asked them to stop the car. "I just won't go," Billie sobbed. "Let them come get me."

Don Wilkes started filibuster ing in his most soothing Southern tones. Flo Kennedy, whom Billie called a hip kitty from Kansas City, kept chattering—change the subject.

Somehow, they got her to the Federal Building. Lady walked in like the Queen of Song walking toward an ovation at Carnegie Hall.

Three Assistant U. S. Attorneys were there—representing divergent points of view. One was in favor of prosecuting. One was in favor of dismissal. The third was an unknown quantity.

One More Chance

In describing her attorney's performance afterwards, Lady said he was better than anything she'd ever seen on TV. "He topped Orson Welles," she said matter-of-factly. Welles had been a friend of Lady's since 1940. She'd never missed one of his pictures.

After an hour and a half of pleading, the U. S. Attorney said quietly that the government declines to prosecute. Lady could hardly believe it. The day was Feb. 12, 1959.

She dragged the lawyers into the nearest bar and they all had a drink. Instantly, her old bounce began to reappear. She came home a different woman. That night, she told us, she slept like a baby. Her doctor was amazed at the way she seemed to be responding to his treatment. Billie never told him, or anybody, the six-week ordeal she'd been through. She thought it would be good for the doctor's morale if he felt responsible for her recovery.

She began rehearsing and planning for the one shot spectacular she was scheduled to do in London. Well in advance, she filled out Customs Form 3231 of May 1958, listing herself as a "violator" as the law required.

When Lady's fighting heart gave out last Friday, heroin, as usual, got too much credit.

Nobody knew how much the unending saga of the United States of America vs. Billie Holiday had cost her.

Continued in tomorrow's Post.

49

AT Chambers of the Surrogate Court
held in and for the County of New York
at the Hall of Records, 31 Chambers
Street, Borough of Manhattan, City of
New York, on the _____ day of_____
196

PRESENT:

Hon._____
                    Surrogate

- - - - - - - - - - - - - - - - - -X

In the Matter of the Application of
DORIS PARKER, as Administratirx of
the Goods, Chattels and Credits of
CHARLES CHRISTOPHER PARKER, JR.,
ALSO known as CHARLIE YARDBIRD
PARKER and CHARLES PARKER, Deceased,
for an Order to Discover Certain Monies and other Personal Property
belonging to Decedent.

Index No.
A 670/1956

ORDER OF
DISCOVERY

- - - - - - - - - - - - - - - - - X

On reading and filing the Petition of DORIS PARKER as

Administratrix of the Estate of CHARLES CHRISTOPHER PARKER, JR.,

also known as CHARLIE "YARDBIRD" PARKER and CHARLES PARKER,

Deceased, verified the _____ day of _____, 1962 and

it appearing to the satisfaction of the Court that certain

royalties, monies, emoluments and other personal property which

should be delivered to the petitioner is in the possession,

under the control of or within the knowledge or information of

BEVERLY DOLORES WOODS a/k/a "CHAN" WOODS; A. ALLEN SAUNDERS MAXWELL T. COHEN;

the Musicians' Clinic; The American Federation of Musicians;

Local 802, American Federation of Musicians; Local 47, American

Federation of Musicians; The Music Performance Trust Fund of

the Recording Industriws; Samuel Rosenbaum, Trustee, Music

Performance Trust Fund of the Recording Industries; Continental

Records, who withhold the same from the petitioner.

NOW, on motion of FLORYNCE R. KENNEDY, attorney for the petitioner, it is

ORDERED, that an inquiry be had respecting said royalties, monies, emoluments and other personal property before our said Surrogate's Court of the County of New York at a term thereof to be held in Room_____, Hall of Records, 31 Chambers Street, Borough of Manhattan, City of New York, on the _____day of _____, 1962 at _____o'clock in the forenoon of that day, or as soon thereafter as counsel can be heard, and it is further

ORDERED that BEVERLY DOLORES WOODS a/k/a "CHAN" WOODS; *A. ALLEN SAUNDERS* MAXWELL T. COHEN; THE MUSICIANS' CLINIC; THE AMERICAN FEDERATION OF MUSICIANS; LOCAL 802; AMERICAN FEDERATION OF MUSICIANS; LOCAL 47, AMERICAN FEDERATION OF MUSICIANS; THE MUSIC PERFORMANCE TRUST FUND OF THE RECORDING INDUSTRIES; SAMUEL ROSENBAUM, TRUSTEE, MUSIC PERFORMANCE TRUST FUND OF THE RECORDING INDUSTRIES; CONTINENTAL RECORDS Attend the said inquiry personally and/or through their proper offices and be examined respecting any royalties, monies, emoluments and other personal property of said CHARLES CHRISTOPHER PARKER, JR., also known as CHARLIE "YARDBIRD" PARKER and CHARLES PARKER, which should be delivered or paid to the petitioner herein

_____
SURROGATE

royalties to them or their estates. What the companies did instead was affiliate themselves with ASCAP and BMI and collect performing rights royalties as publishers without alerting the composer or artist. This was virtually criminal. And of course the record companies brought out memorial albums, on which they made good chunks of money. We did finally manage to collect a fair amount from the record companies, but the story of the exploitation of Black performers by the people who make fortunes from them has yet to be told.

In the Charlie Parker and Billie Holiday cases, I elected to do something with the law that had not been done before, because I could not see any way within the limits of my financial situation to sue all the companies that I knew owed royalties. I looked in the law books and found the Order of Discovery, which is normally used to find out which tenants owe money on a piece of real property, for example. I couldn't see any reason why that could not be applied to a situation where fifteen or twenty publishing and record companies owed money to the estate of a jazz artist, and I used it that way. It horrified everybody and made all the court officials know I was there, and of course they didn't like me very much. But along with looking after the interests of the estates, I was also using my profession to strike a blow against the Establishment. I still encourage law students to study this aspect of the law.

I'm getting my token revenge on those record companies now, through working with Jan Berger's Young Activists Now. YAN successfully picketed Atlantic and Columbia, smashing records on the sidewalk to get them to hire some of the Black and Puerto Rican teenagers, who supply so many of the dollars that make them millionaires, in after-school and summer jobs.

Kicking Ass

Handling the Holiday and Parker estates taught me more than I was really ready for about government and business delinquency and the hostility and helplessness of the courts in rectifying the imbalance between the talented performers and the millionaire parasites who suck their blood. These experiences, together with Wilkes's takeoff, marked the beginning of a serious disenchantment, if indeed I ever was enchanted, with the practice of law. By this time I had learned a good deal about the justice system, and had begun to doubt my ability to work within it to accomplish social change. Not only was I not earning a decent living, there began to be a serious question in my mind whether practicing law could ever be an effective means of changing society, or even of simple resistance to oppression.

Another turning point in my attitude came in 1963, when Kennedy was assassinated. I was on my way uptown to the beauty shop, which I call the "ugly shop," when I heard he'd been killed. I remembered that when I had visited friends a few days before, a newspaper man had told us about the KKK (Kill Kennedy Klubs) in the South, and how he had heard that there was a plot to kill him in Florida. Kennedy was persuaded not to go, but there was going to be trouble in Texas, the man had said.

When I heard the news, I was immediately suspicious; I knew that it had been a government action. I knew that unemployed drifters like Oswald did not carry $700 around in their pockets, that even Texas landladies did not rent rooms to total strangers without charging rent, and that if Russia was supposed to be our enemy, Marina Oswald would not be getting such a light kiss-off. I knew it was a fix, and that was when my suspicions about the delinquency of the government and the cooperation in that delinquency by the media, by business, and by society—the "good people"—was confirmed.

By the mid-Sixties nobody seemed to be doing anything about racism at home—the major focus was on the war—so in 1966 I set up the Media Workshop. After an anti-war demonstration a number of people—including Jim Haughton from "Fight Back," some of whom are still working with me in CARS (Coalition Against Racism and Sexism)—came back to my apartment. We were talking about the war in Vietnam, and I was saying that it was very important to oppose it, but that I thought it was equally important to deal with racism in media and advertising, and that we should go to some ad agencies.

I had acquired some understanding of the financial structure of the media through handling a case involving the Ann Sothern Show, and I knew how much a half-hour of TV time was worth, how much the advertisers pay, and how the advertisers and the networks co-produce. I realized why we had such terrible programs, and on the spot I set up Media Workshop.

Within a week or two we confronted Benton and Bowles. They refused our request for information about their hiring and programming policies, so we went to their building at 666 Fifth Avenue and picketed with signs saying, "Is there a bigot in your market basket?" "Leave Bold Unsold," and "Jim Crow lives on Madison Avenue." After that they invited us upstairs, and ever since I've been able to say, "When you want to get to the suites, start in the streets."

While we were picketing, a friend of mine, a man who was a vice-president of another ad agency, went up to the third-floor window of the building across the street and took wonderful pictures of us. I always use that as an example of how you shouldn't reject people who don't

---

ONCE UPON A WEEK

By Florynce R. Kennedy

THE SATURATION POINT - Somebody's going to have to do something about the little Sir Echo news coverage which has come to rival the little Sir Echo commercial to drive people out of their minds and up the wall.

I first noticed the super-saturation of no-news coverage when all the ritualistic, tear-making, insignificant, pomp and circumstantial details of the overthrow of the Kennedy administration by assassination were spread across the news media again and again at the expense of new, hard news and developments in the aftermath to the assassination.

My suspicion that the super-coverage was a super-cover-up was confirmed by the dead, desperate silence that fell upon the embarrassed media, when they had worn their re-plays thin. After that, the best way to assure media attack and to be dubbed a trouble-maker (Like Mark Lane, who has established Committees of Inquiry on American campuses, in American cities and all over the World or Joachim Joesten, who wrote "Oswald, Assassin, or Fall Guy" or like Englishmen Lord Bertrand Russell and historians Trevor Roper and Arnold Toynbee) was to consider the who-killed-Kennedy subject, without following the "party line".

Then, somewhere along the line come the blow-by-blow, death rattle by death rattle coverage of ancient General Douglas MacArthur's terminal illness and death, and the viewing of the casket in New York, and the New York funeral and the Washington memorial services, and special spectaculars on reviewing the life of the dead gentleman.

Later, there was repetitive, stale coverage of poor, rich ex-President Hoover's lingering illness and death. As the end came the media became pre-occupied with last gasp by last gasp, precious lead story coverage, especially noticeable in TV and radio "news" casts.

Now comes President Johnson's bad cold, his cough syrup, his raspy throat and his temperature, none of which, of course, ahs the slightest connection with his super-manning all day Inaguration Day in the January cold, without top coat, overcoat (or even a B-movie trench coat) I'd rather hear more about Lucy Bird, (or Banny Lou, or whatever her name is) and her interest in the Catholic religion, and a Catholic escort. To me, that's news!

I knew the wall-crawling time had come when a Channel 2-CBS-TV program was interrupted to give a SPECIAL REPORT to the effect that Sir Winston Churchill had NOT died! Well the poor old soul finally obliged. Again, I would have found more interest, certainly more news in coverage of his daughter, Sarah's purported romantic interest in an ex-patriot Negro Artist. But maybe it's too much to ask that news be news, and consideration be given to topics of interest to those of us who have little interest in octogenarian heads of armies nonogenarian ex-heads of state and their dying days and deaths, and funeral and memorial services.

Most of us have heard too much about those who are on top of us and too little about how to get their feet off our collective necks.

"THE CAT AND THE CANARY"-DRAMATICCOMEDY to SCREAM AND GASP BY - At State 73, one of the new East of Broadway, uptown little theatres, the audience is almost as interesting as the performance. On my first visit to Stage 73, the audience gasped and screamed, then laughed with embarrasement, fitting to their sleek sophistication, at having been taken in by the fast-paced, frankly dated, mystery with squeaking doors, hidden panels and claws attached to unseen bodies. But taken in we were, perhaps by the closeness to the threatened, believably attractive Annabelle West, played by AdAle O'Brien, whose goodness always missed the cloying point. The tiny theatre made you feel the dark hand or plunging bloody body might well land in your very lap. Helen Martin stalks the stage like a dark Zombie, now threatening, then benevolent, always regal in apron and turban. Altogether the Whodunit Company has a very good show.

have the same commitment as you do, or who for various reasons must protect their own interests. You should use them and let them do as much as they're willing to, rather than get hostile and make fun of them. Obviously, if you are a vice-president of an advertising agency, you can't fight in the same way as someone heading up a union of Black people who want to get in on the construction industry or television unions.

Later, in a dispute over sexism, the women of NOW, the National Organization for Women, which I have been mistakenly credited with helping to found, held a similar demonstration in front of the Colgate-Palmolive building on Park Avenue, where again we ridiculed them. Kate Millett set up a toilet stool on the sidewalk which she had used as part of a sculpture and we poured "All" detergent and other Colgate products into it. Earlier we picketed the *New York Times*, led by Ti-Grace Atkinson. Feeble as these protests were, they seemed one of the few effective means of focusing public attention on racism and sexism in the media.

We picketed WNEW-TV when the station manager, Lawrence Fraiberg, refused to see us. After we announced the picket line he became available to meet with us, but we went ahead anyway. We were picketing in front of WNEW Radio, just off Fifth Avenue at 46th Street, and William B. Williams, the disc jockey, came out and asked, "Why are you picketing over here, Flo? The TV station is up at 67th Street." "Because there's more traffic here and it's more convenient to my office," I said, and they laughed and sent someone down and put us right on the radio. So you see how easy it can be to apply pressure in what I call the testicular area.

Picketing the *New York Times* with actress Susan Gailey ▲

With Ti-Grace Atkinson, Kate Stimson, and Kate Millett, picketing the *New York Times* ▶

This media protest led to our going to CBS. We demanded time on the news because a Negro minister in Chicago, who was not Black in the political sense, had made some crack to the effect that if Martin Luther King came to Chicago they'd tell him to get the hell out of there. Reverends A. Kendall Smith and Robert Kinloch had called me to join them, and we had chicken and waffles sent up while we were sitting-in in one of the offices, I remember, and got syrup all over the executive desk. When we would not leave, they arrested us and wheeled us out, still sitting on the secretaries' chairs, to the paddy wagons.

I refused to act as attorney; I told the judge that to get equal justice we needed a $75,000 attorney equal to the attorney retained by CBS. There was a three-judge panel on the case, and they had to stop and have meetings about this. Finally A. Kendall Smith took over the role of defense attorney.

We played it totally crazy; at lunch time our supporters would go out and demonstrate in sheets with signs about the one-eyed Klansmen sitting on the bench. During the trial Kendall Smith, with great dramatic flair, left the bar and came and sat with us in the audience. "Where are you going?" the judge asked. "You are acting as attorney in this case, but you are also a defendant." "I just wanted to sit with the people for a while," Kendall said. He came back and sat down and stretched his arms across the back of the bench, and just relaxed for a few minutes. Then he went back up. Harry Arouh of CBS testified that Kendall had called him "Boy" and "Whitey," and we fell on the floor with laughter. And Bob Kinloch, who a few years later went blind, played elder statesman and made wonderful political pronouncements.

In the end, not knowing what else to do, they acquitted us on a technicality. CBS actually withdrew the complaint, as I remember, but I think actually they just wanted us out of that courtroom.

In 1966 I planned a bus trip to Cambridge, Maryland, to protest the criminal charges pending against H. Rap Brown. He had been charged with fomenting a riot, even though a Congressional investigation had previously absolved him of any blame for the disruption which took place after he spoke there.

We left New York about four A.M., and soon there seemed to be cars following us, although we couldn't be sure. When we got to Cambridge, people kept directing us wrong, so we just kept going straight and found ourselves heading out of town. When we tried to back up, the bus driver discovered there was no reverse gear, and we had to go on until we found a road that curved inside a golf course on its way back into town. So there we were at ten in the morning, circling around in the middle of a deserted country club, with four strange cars right behind us.

When we finally got to the City Council's office, we were supposed to have a meeting with Maryland's governor, Spiro Agnew, whom no one had ever heard of at that point. We got the Attorney General instead. After he came in the room, one of the people with us jumped up in front of the door and wouldn't let anyone else in. While we were arguing with him, the Attorney General started to hit me, but the Black guys who were with us started for him, and he cooled it.

Later that day we took a tour of the Black community in Cambridge. The really poor Black people showed us how they lived: they had no sidewalks, no lights on the streets, and most of their houses were what we would call chicken coops; they were so low you had to stoop to get into them.

When we were ready to leave town, the cops tried to come on the bus with us. I was wearing a button that said,

A MESSAGE FOR WHITE RADICALS

The following is an interview with Florynce Kennedy, one-time lawyer for H. Rap Brown. Two reporters from RECONSTRUCTION interviewed Miss Kennedy during her stay in Lawrence as a guest speaker for Wesley Foundation's seminar on white racism.

RECON: To what extent have you, as a lawyer, been involved with H. Rap Brown?

MISS KENNEDY: I represented him a few times, but I wouldn't call myself his lawyer. Theoretically, I don't do criminal law. The only way I get into a case is if it's so important politically that no other lawyer will touch it, then sometimes I'll do something on it. But the courts are so racist and so bigoted. As a lawyer, you're looking for justice for people, but if you know there's no justice, what are you going to go looking there for? There's absolutely no justice for anybody I'd want to defend.

RECON: What are Rap's present activities?

MISS KENNEDY: Rap is writing a book. He's out of the news, obviously. What the media do is render a person a boogey man and then attack him with impunity and theoretically kill him. So now the Black Panther party has taken over.

RECON: What is the present state of leadership within the struggle for black liberation?

MISS KENNEDY: The thing about leaders of oppressed people is that they don't have the confidence of the people they purport to represent. It is essential to oppression that the oppressed people have very little sense of worth themselves. Only as they feel more worthy, do they tend more to trust their leaders. The attitude of the black community toward us and all the rest is one of latent suspicion. Within every group there are certain people who have infiltrated it. What probably happens is that there are various levels of committed people and the committment varies with the individual.

You know if there's going to be liberation, there has to be spying. No establishment is going to LET itself be changed or overthrown or permit directional change that it can avoid. There will be espionage forces within any liberation group. It's a question of being paralyzed by that. If you do enough to make a change, you can't do it all off-the-record. I prefer to avoid masochism and to try to stay within the legal limits. There's a lot of fighting that you can accomplish that is likely to cause a confrontation with police. I'm more worried about the masochistic element than the espionage element.

I regard the espionage elements as messengers to the establishment. That's the way I tell them what's going to happen. The more rational and less masochistic the plans are, the greater the threat to the establishment. They have to prime the community against me before they can bring me down.

The suspicion of oppressed people induces a kind of paranoia in those who have been particularly traumatized. The moment you join a liberation struggle you are endangered by the establishment, those not in the struggle and other areas of the liberation struggle. If you're going to be where it's at, you'll have to be somewhere on the horizontal level of the liberation struggle. It's the most exciting game around, quite apart from the politics of it.

RECON: Is your primary identity within the black revolution as a lawyer?

MISS KENNEDY: Not really. I have so little faith in our system of justice that I almost flatly refuse to be involved with any legal proceedings with people involved in the struggle. I do what I think every middle-aged black woman should be doing. I'm very peripheral, but if you're two inches tall and everybody else is a quarter of an inch tall, you seem tall. I'm really sort of a dillettante. I'm more frivolous than political, but I'm interested in politics becuase that is where what little bit there is, is. In a thoroughly corrupt and oppressive society, ther just isn't anything else to do.

RECON: Do you feel that we're seeing the beginning of a serious black underground movement?

MISS KENNEDY: I will simply hope that there is such a thing. And I would hope that they would never reveal any plans to the press or to me.

RECON: As a lawyer and as a black woman, how do you feel a black person should respond to the nation's legal system?

MISS KENNEDY: Eldridge Cleaver, for example, has addressed himself to the problem in a way different from some other Panthers. He simply failed to respond to a summons to a criminal proceeding to put his tail in jail. Other people have responded by returning to jail. I am delighted to see someone with a more creative approach to a criminal summons than to go stand there and pay lawyers to get his ass out of the ringer. Once you are absolutely persuaded that justice is absolutely irrelevant to criminal proceedings in this country, then you have no requirement to respect the summons. I am personally persuaded that there is no justice for any kind of liberation struggler. Therefore, the Black Panthers, being an important part of the liberation struggle, cannot expect any kind of justice in any criminal proceedings. There would be no reason for anyone to expect that a political person or anybody involved in liberation would get a fair trial in the racist courts of this country.

RECON: To what extent can white radicals identify with black liberation strugglers?

MISS KENNEDY: If you test the fences of this society and dare to influence the direction of this society, they know you mean business by the extent to which you identify with the black revolution. The sub-conscious recognition of the importance of change can be guaged by the tendency to identify with the black determination. If you want to absolutely communicate the depth of your determination to bring down this society that is committed to racism, then indicate determination to frustrate racism with a coalition with the black revolutionary struggle.

When students on the campus identify with black students they are free to be niggarized. At Columbia, the black students were not niggarized while the SDS and white students were. The students who were in the supporting buildings around Hamilton Hall were beaten and maced. That is niggarization — treating white people as if they were niggers. The amazing thing is that the parents haven't said a word in unison about the beating of their children. That is the extent to which this society is committed to oppression. They have accepted the establishment stipulation that these people are dangerous and must be treated as niggers. The black community did support the strikers, and I believe some of the white parents would have helped up to the point where the cops came in.

My concept of oppression is that there is no oppression without the consent of the oppressed. The consent of the oppressed requires that when people depart from the programming and go to the fence, then they must identify with the person who erected the fence. Each oppressed person has an idea of the direction of the fence and most of them never go near it. Even if they insist that there is no oppression, they know approximately where the fence is, and you can't drag them in that direction.

RECON: Do you see the struggle for black liberation as the same as our struggle for liberation and if so can we form a coalition?

MISS KENNEDY: This is what I think is crucially important. It will require some adroit maneuvering. I frankly think that the only time white people will be welcome in the black movement is when there is a crisis for them (blacks) and it's a matter of survival. As long as they (blacks) are swimming, as long as their boat is drifting, they will be very reluctant to make alliances with white people. I think, however, when they are taking a stand, when the crisis is actually here, then support will be welcome. It will have to be a crisis where they are literally going down.

I think that the thing for the white radical or the white struggle to do is to keep its powder dry, keep its finances high, watch the development of struggle everywhere. You see, black people will trust white liberation strugglers when they see them attack the establishment. The way you can get the confidence — you will never really get it — but any kind of confidence, is the extent to which you challenge the white establishment. Now, this is why there is such contempt, in my opinion, in the black community and even in the black youth community, for the so-called hippies.

The hippie is a drop-out; he has rejected the values of the establishment, but he has not taken them on. He almost invariably fails to reveal such information as he might have about his slumlord uncle. In other words, he will admit that the real-estate board is racist, that the slumlords are anathema, but he doesn't give the name and address of his uncle or his uncle's friend who is a slumlord. He's not telling what he knows about corruption in his community. And until that happens, the black guy knows that he is covering his ass. He can always turn and run back to the establishment, and while he may catch hell at home, he can still shave his face and he' be covered.

This is why I urge white radicals to fight the media, to challenge every aspect of his environment that he clearly knows better — he knows which pillow the gun is under in his old man's bedroom and he knows which one in his family is a member of the American Independent Party, he knows which house the Nazis meet in, which plantation the Klan meet at. Every white person knows something, and if he doesn't know it, he can find it out.

The way for the white liberation struggle is that of espionage, so to speak, and you've got to be pretty mad at somebody to spy on them. It's one thing to accept somebody's hospitality and it's another thing to accept that hospitality ar turn on them. You are a traitor to a degree. If I were advising black movement, I would say always suspect a traitor becau if he flipped to give you information, he could flip back give them information. So you see, it's going to be extreme difficult for white radicals in contemporary times to have really close line with the black struggle. But because the blac people will have to survive as they struggle, there will be tim when they will accept a rope thrown by anybody. If you' going down for the third time and a KKK member throws yc a rope and you know damn well he's going to shoot you whe you come out of the water, you're going to grab the rop probably. You'll grab the rope hoping that by the time you g to the shore some of your allies might have come.

The young (black) people are far more hostile, much mo destructive with the white community. They really are bitt and they really want no part of a white radical with emp hands. In short, if you want to cure malaria, you don't get bed with the malaria patient. You go spray the swamps. And you want to cure poverty, you don't show your sincerity b climbing five flights of stairs and adding complications to th person with that tiny budget when your four dollars doesr even mean that much. There's no room for you, and if you on the floor, it just means somebody will have to step ov you to get to the bathroom.

I'm suggesting that if you want to cure poverty, go whe the money is. If necessary, don the uniform of those who ha the money or get with a cousin who has the uniform and ca get in the police department — if you don't want to get there, find out what the pigs are up to and then screw the And don't even bother to tell the black people. If your job good enough, it will come to their attention because your a is getting kicked and that is when they begin to trust yo They know that when they see the toe on your ass that yc are a possible ally. Even then there must be a certa parallelism rather than integration. I don't think that's abo to happen and I don't see why it should.

RECON: So you think then that the white liberati movement should be intensified?

MISS KENNEDY: I think students on the campus a sufficiently radical to be an ally. Don't forget, if you're so enough, a caress is painful. If I had a boil on my cheek ar you come over to show you love me, and touch me on th boil, it's painful, and I don't want no part of it. So if yc respect a potential ally, you don't touch him. You know he sore from one end to the other. That's the way the bla people are.

Young black people are sore from top to toe. The painf trauma they have gone through, to have seen their parents d everything in the world to be part of the white communi and being rejected and pushed into corners. There is not part of their ego that has not been bruised. All you can do give them balm and time to heal. Part of that balm for healir will come from watching somebody else get niggarized. Don expect sympathy. Do not feel that if a gift is made to ther that they will respond as if they have received a gift. Th chances are that they will regard it as a very small payment o a long-overdue debt.

With Gil Banks of Fight Back, singing at the MAMA March, 1975 ▶

Officials Say They Lack
Authority To Drop Charges

MISS FLORYNCE KENNEDY

Cambridge City officials yesterday told the spokesman for a group of New York civil rightists that they lack authority to drop riot and arson charges against H. Rap Brown.

Mayor Osvrey C, Pritchett and City Attorney Charles E. Edmondson made that statement to Miss Florynce R. Kennedy, a New York attorney and spokesman for the group of some 16 Negroes and whites who came here Tuesday by bus to request that Cambridge drop the Brown charges "in view of the President's Commission on Civil Disorders."

The Cambridge officials pointed out that Brown has been indicted on three charges by a Dorchester County grand jury and they have no jurisdiction in the case.

Meanwhile, in Odessa, Del., two Brooklyn, N.Y., men remained in jail on $2,000 bond each today on concealed weapons charges after their arrest Tuesday on a trip south to protest indictments against Brown in Cambridge.

Brown is under indictment for counselling to burn a school, rioting and inciting to riot in connection with Negro rioting last July and is currently fighting extradition from Virginia to Maryland to face the charges.

As a bus carrying 16 Negroes and whites went through Odessa Tuesday, a pickup truck trailing the bus was stopped for speeding. Inside the truck Police said they found a .30-30 rifle, 20 rounds of ammunition and a knife.

Charged with concealing deadly weapons are Robert R. Williams, 20, and James E. Jones, 18, both of Brooklyn.

The passengers in the bus continued to Cambridge, where they talked with city and Dorchester County officials in a meeting marked by harsh words and bitterness.

"Your town is going to smell like you when we get finished," Miss Kennedy told State's Attorney William B. Yates of Dorchester County.

Miss Kennedy said before the meeting that the group wanted to persuade Cambridge officials to drop the charges against Brown, chairman of the Student Nonviolent Coordinating Committee.

At the meeting she cited a staff report to the President's Advisory Commission on Civil Disorders, which said Brown wasn't responsible for the rioting. She urged Yates to drop the charges or make any additional information implicating the Black Power advocate available.

Yates countered by saying that the staff report was made up of lies and didn't constitute evidence.

Several members of the group surrounded Yates at one point in the discussion when he started to leave after saying their questions were unreasonable. He returned to his seat without being touched and continued.

As the discussion proceeded, Brown was in a New Orleans jail, awaiting payment of the final $10,000 on his $30,000 bond there. He's being held on two federal charges, intimidating an FBI agent and carrying a weapon between New York and Louisiana while under the Maryland indictment.

"Warning: Your Local Police Are Armed and Dangerous," which tickled the shit out of them. They thought it was very funny, but as they were laughing about the button they tried to force their way in. "You can't come on the bus unless you have a search warrant," we said. Then they told us that some people from CORE who had been traveling with us in a pickup truck had been caught armed and got busted in Delaware, and they wanted to check the bus for arms. We told them they'd have to arrest us all, that we would never retreat, and that they would have to move the cars in front of us.

I hustled and made some calls to find out what had happened to those fellows, and the minute we got back to New York, at one in the morning, we went straight to WBAI and went on the Bob Fass Show to tell about the trip and the arrests.

In 1967 I was up in Montreal at an anti-war convention, and I got very mad because they wouldn't let Bobby Seale speak. He was more radical than the rest of the people there, and wanted to talk about racism, instead of limiting the discussion to the war. When they tried to stop him, I went berserk. I took the platform and started yelling and hollering. As a result, I was invited out to Washington to speak, for a fee of $250 plus expenses, and that was the beginning of my speaking career.

The day Martin Luther King died, a friend called me and said, "What are you going to do?" We thought the best thing would be not to try to plan anything elaborate but to do something immediately, and we decided to hold a rally in Central Park. The first thing I did was get a loudspeaker from the Parks Department; I called the city and announced that we were going to have this demonstration, no matter what they said. "We'll be there," we told them, "you just be ready or not." But nobody gave us an argument; everybody we asked was very eager to help, which taught us that when you're hot, you're hot, and when you're not, you can't give it away.

It was announced on the radio, and we got repercussions so fast we thought somebody else must be organizing it. The next morning when we went to Central Park we couldn't believe the number of people; there had been only a few of us making phone calls. Dorothy Pitman Hughes was there, I remember, and when the people next to us were singing "We shall overcome," Dorothy in her beautiful voice sang instead, "We shall overthrow."

I got pissed at the crowd because they were mad that some white people were with us. "Where were you when Rap Brown was in jail?" I yelled back at them. Richie Havens just walked to the mike and said, "Dig yourselves," and then they all started sending money up. It was a tremendous moment.

I attended all four Black Power Conferences, including the planning stage of the First National Conference on Black Power, which was the beginning of the downfall of Adam Clayton Powell. I don't think the decision to de-ball him had anything to do with kissing secretaries or divorce; it was because he became peripherally involved with the whole concept of Black Power, allowing some of the people to use his office and so forth. The device used to de-ball him was a woman, who he claimed was a bag woman for numbers racketeers to pay off police in Harlem. Now of course what they do with people in his position is first challenge them to prove what they are saying about the corruption of the police, and then when they do, sue them for libel. So Adam Clayton Powell was right down my protest alley, and when someone called me, of course I went. Reverend A. Kendall Smith and Reverend Robert Kinloch, who later were with me when we got arrested at CBS, helped to organize the action, and we took a bus to Washington to protest the efforts to remove Powell from Congress.

The first Conference on Black Power was held in Newark in 1967, the second in Philadelphia in 1968, the third—an international conference—in Bermuda in 1969, and the fourth in Atlanta in 1970. There were also Black political caucuses in 1968 and 1972, both in Gary, Indiana, and I didn't miss those either, but I was disappointed in both of them, in 1968 because they failed to support Dick Gregory, and in 1972 when they failed to support Shirley Chisholm.

I've always thought it a bad idea to wrestle over control of an organization, and when I went to meetings where they would spend endless hours arguing over whether to have red cabbage or white for the slaw, I would just think to myself, "I can't waste my time on this bullshit," and go off and set up a committee. I founded the Feminist Party after NOW got to be so boring and scared; I can't see leaving my house and getting into a subway or a cab to go to a meeting where everybody is more terrified than I am.

I went to the very first meeting of NOW, in New York. It was a terribly cold night, and Marge Barton, an assistant director suffering from film union discrimination, and I went out in the freezing cold to a town house on the East Side. When I said something about the war—how women ought to oppose it—Betty Friedan and Muriel Fox, who had set up the meeting, went bonkers. They thought I had gone crazy—"We are not here to talk about the war, blah, blah, blah." Then I brought up the fact that women had control of so much money—although less than men—and did most of the purchasing, and suggested that we bring consumer action against the media and against the war (I guess I didn't dare mention the war again, but certainly against the media). And of course Muriel Fox, who was

vice-president of an ad agency, almost had a nervous breakdown over that, so I recognized, although I stayed on for another few years, that this was no place for me to spend much time. I saw how they hassled people like Ti-Grace Atkinson, who was most straightforward on abortion, lesbianism, and prostitution, as well as on participatory democracy, and who was prepared to risk a head-on challenge to sexism. I saw the importance of a feminist movement, and stayed in there because I wanted to do anything I could to keep it alive, but when I saw how retarded NOW was, I thought, "My God, who needs this?" so when Ti-Grace left I went with her. A few years later, in November of 1971, I founded the Feminist Party.

Like the Media Workshop, it came out of a response to a specific need. I had just finished making a speech out at Queens College and was talking with some of the faculty and students about the electoral process, and someone said, "I wish the feminists were represented." On the spur of the moment I set up the Feminist Party, whose first big action was to support Shirley Chisholm for the presidency.

I also attended the Atlantic City Beauty Contest protest, which was the best fun I can imagine anyone wanting to have on any single day of her life. It was very brazen and very brash, and there were some arrests—Peggy Dobbins was charged with releasing a stink bomb. No bras were burned, though; that was a media invention, and that's when I lost what little respect I had left for the media—they were such clumsy liars. When Gloria Steinem and I would lecture together, all the dumb male media monkeys could talk about were the "bra burners." I called it the "tit focus."

In 1971 we had the Coat Hanger Farewell Protest on the steps of St. Patrick's Cathedral, over the abortion issue. Diane Schulder, Emily Jane

ISIS
all women
rock group

NOV. 24, 1972 · 8:30 - 11 pm
just for women, donation $1.50

independent
FILMS
by women
gunvor nelson
barbara linkevitch
sharon hennessey
anne severson
chick strand
dorothy wiley
connie beeson
and
freude
donation $1.00

SAT, NOV 25th
7:30 pm

FEMINIST PARTY
CONVENTION
for women & non-sexist men.
WORKSHOPS
SEMINARS
demonstrations, press conferences
lead by FLO KENNEDY, TI-GRACE
ATKINSON, MARGO ST. JAMES,
JOSETTE MONDINERO, SUSAN
MARGOLIS, ETC. $1.50/day ADM.
meals by HOUSEHOLD TECHNICIANS.
crafts exhibit & sale.
621-4660 for further information
W.A.S.T.E.
Women Against Supporting their enemies

FRI & SAT, 9am - 12pm, NOV 24 & 25

Goodman, Carol Lefcourt, and several other lawyers had sued on behalf of several hundred plaintiffs to have the New York State abortion law declared unconstitutional, and it was that whole setup which taught me not to rely completely on the courts for anything. WONAAC (Women's National Abortion Action Coalition) held a huge march, and the following day we were told there would be a legislative change in the law to make it less obnoxious.

That was a clear victory, but it was like a successful bath; you don't expect not to take another bath, so why don't we understand that we're in danger of being swamped by the anti-abortion movement? Countermovements among racists and sexists and nazifiers are just as relentless as dirt on a coffee table or under your arms or between your legs. Every housewife knows that if you don't sooner or later dust and wash clothes and change beds the whole place will be dirty again, but anti-Establishment politicians are always moaning and groaning about how tired they are and how few gains they've made, as if by waving a magic wand social change ought to be accomplished once and for all.

I think a lot of people get disenchanted with these various movements because when they go to meetings and try to live up to all the sisterhood bullshit, they find that their "sisters" are usually unhappy, and therefore very unpleasant people to be around. I refuse to work with people I don't like; it isn't just the political association that people should be looking for, and one of the reasons people don't like politics is that they've got to join a bunch of strangers. That's another reason why I encourage people to make their politics a part of their life; when you give a dinner party, if you're supporting Fred Harris's candidacy, for instance, make everybody pay five bucks and send the money to Harris so that he has matching funds and doesn't have to collapse so soon.

After all, we expect all our people to stand up strong and not sell out. We're disappointed with Shirley Chisholm when she puts her stamp of approval on Rockefeller, and yet when she needs

Marching along the boardwalk at NOW Miss America protest, Atlantic City, 1974

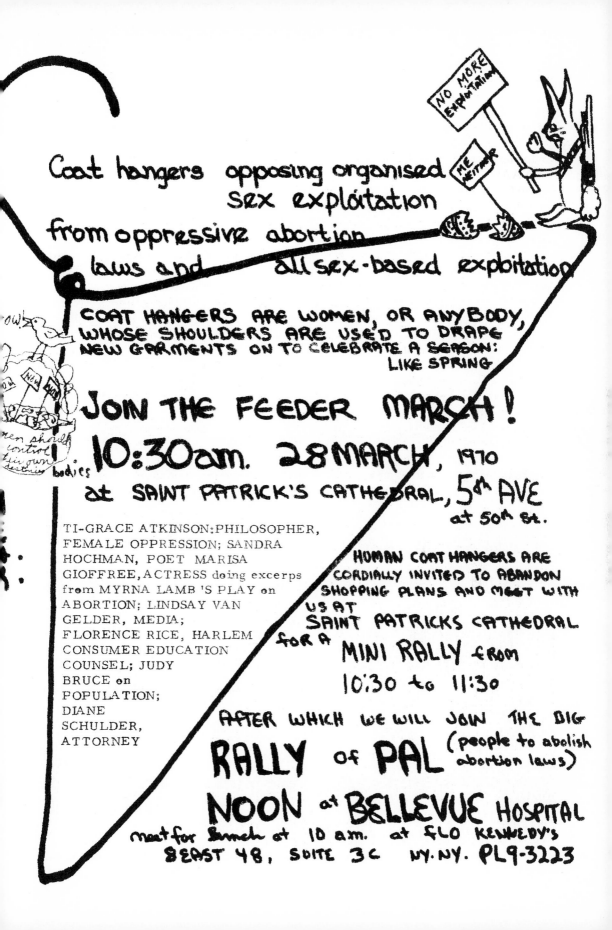

Coat hangers opposing organised sex exploitation from oppressive abortion laws and all sex-based exploitation

NO MORE exploitation

ME NEITHER

COAT HANGERS ARE WOMEN, OR ANYBODY, WHOSE SHOULDERS ARE USED TO DRAPE NEW GARMENTS ON TO CELEBRATE A SEASON: LIKE SPRING

JOIN THE FEEDER MARCH!
10:30am. 28 MARCH, 1970
at SAINT PATRICK'S CATHEDRAL, 5th AVE at 50th St.

TI-GRACE ATKINSON: PHILOSOPHER, FEMALE OPPRESSION; SANDRA HOCHMAN, POET MARISA GIOFFREE, ACTRESS doing excerps from MYRNA LAMB'S PLAY on ABORTION; LINDSAY VAN GELDER, MEDIA; FLORENCE RICE, HARLEM CONSUMER EDUCATION COUNSEL; JUDY BRUCE on POPULATION; DIANE SCHULDER, ATTORNEY

HUMAN COAT HANGERS ARE CORDIALLY INVITED TO ABANDON SHOPPING PLANS AND MEET WITH US AT SAINT PATRICKS CATHEDRAL for a MINI RALLY from 10:30 to 11:30

AFTER WHICH WE WILL JOIN THE BIG RALLY of PAL (people to abolish abortion laws) NOON at BELLEVUE HOSPITAL

meet for lunch at 10 a.m. at FLO KENNEDY's 8 EAST 48, SUITE 3C NY. NY. PL9-3223

$300,000 to pay her campaign debts, nobody's around. I'm not saying Rockefeller paid her campaign debts —although I hope he did—but it's unreasonable to expect so much purity and commitment from people without giving them much loyalty in return.

My public and personal lives have always been complementary; my political actions and involvements are all carried out under the flag of close personal friendships. With people like Sandra Hochman, for instance. Sandy, a film maker, poet, and novelist, represents the kind of person the average feminist would snub. She has money, she's blonde, she went to Bennington, and she likes good things, but she also likes to slop

around a little bit. Sometimes she's immaculately put together with every hair in place; other times her hair is streaming down and she's wearing sneakers. She's a swinging person. Some people might call it neurotic, but I call her a swinger—she swings from one end of the spectrum to the other.

I first met her when I went to a party at her house, a fund-raiser for Norman Mailer and Jimmy Breslin, after Gloria Steinem got me involved in Mailer's campaign for mayor of New York. "I'm going to be a feminist," Sandy told me, and she's become one. "You're a poet who goes from bed to verse," I always tell her. Now she goes from verse to film making to novel writing.

In 1972 I had temporarily had it with

66   With Pat Goz and Diane Schulder at abortion rally, New York, 1972

At "Celebrate Women" demonstration with Alice Sant'Andrea and Sandy Hochman ▶

living in New York. My apartment had just been burglarized for the third time, and I was living barricaded behind gates at the windows, with an alarm system and a gun. One day in May I found myself at the end of the lecture season dragging my ass en route from the San Francisco airport to the Mark Hopkins Hotel, where I intended to reward my bone-tired carcass with a few days of decadent luxury. It was such a beautiful day that as I rode along in the cab I suddenly decided to move out there. I took a house on Potrero Hill, which immediately got robbed, after which I took an apartment in the Golden Gate Center, which Susan Margolis found for me.

Sandy came out to see me in San Francisco. She has since published a novel, *Happiness Is Too Much Trouble*, about her experiences in Hollywood, which we call "Suck City," but at that time she was undergoing them, and was very upset about one of her love affairs. She was threatening to commit suicide, and I remember telling her, "Now, listen, Sandy, if you're talking about suicide, I want you to pack your little bag, make your reservations, and get your ass out of here. I don't want no blonde dead people below my terrace here in the Golden Gate Center, and I don't need those security men coming up here and asking me what this millionaire's blonde daughter is doing dead beneath my terrace. You just get your ass right out of here." She had been dead serious, but after I said that we laughed so hard we went crazy.

Sandy has a great sense of humor and is one of the best street fighters I know. One of my favorite recollections is the scene of Sandy in a long shocking pink peignoir dancing in the middle of 57th Street across from Henri Bendel's, on the picket line we set up in front of Avon International, protesting their failure to put money into the "Celebrate Women" program. Ultimately we did get

a couple of thousand dollars from them.

"Celebrate Women" was a three-hour TV program which Miriam Bogert produced during Celebrate Women Week, which the mayor of New York proclaimed from February 1 through 8 of 1976. It was based on the "Yes, We Can" show which Raysa Bonow had done up in Boston about two years previously. Miriam tried for a year without success to raise the money for a similar program here in New York. Then we conceived the idea of picketing companies like Avon, Clairol, Mobil Oil, and Chemical Bank to coerce them by shaming them publicly into contributing enough to cover our production costs—which amounted to such a tiny fraction of their advertising and publicity budgets—and we raised the money in two days of picketing.

Raysa Bonow is another important person in my life. I first met her when she was producing a TV seminar on television and racism. Raysa had one of the top jobs in Westinghouse Broadcasting. She conceived the "Not for Women Only" television show, and has worked with David Susskind. In 1968, when she was working for NBC, we went to Chicago for the Democratic Convention. We took a room in a motel, and agreed that we were not going to go out and get gassed. Instead, we turned our motel room into a sort of emergency battlefield first aid station for the people who were out in the streets, and Robert and Carol Lefcourt and Annie Garfinkle would come running in to wash their faces and try to get the gas and the mace out of their eyes.

The Lefcourts have been friends of mine for many years, ever since I started sharing summer houses with them and Diane Schulder out on Fire Island in the mid-Sixties. Diane and I had the idea of taking a house there, and Robert Lefcourt and Gerry, his brother, and Robert's wife Carol wanted to share one

Miriam Bogert and I giving Joe Franklin of WOR-TV, New York, a Media Workshop award

with us. I sent them out to look first—whenever I'm starting to think about looking for a summer house I always send my white friends out to find it—and they found a tiny one right next to a tennis court. It's like when I want a cab—I send a white person out to get it, because if the driver sees a Black person he thinks you're going to Harlem, which occasionally I am, to go to the ugly shop. But most of the time I'm not, so I don't rely too much on the fairness of Americans. Of course once the house is rented and we're settled in nobody minds, they're not that racist, but when

they see you coming they sometimes get a little nervous. So it just simplifies things to send the others on ahead, especially since I'm also very lazy.

Robert Lefcourt is the editor of *The Law Against the People*, to which I contributed an article based on a speech I made at Columbia University on the whorehouse theory of law, because I was so in love with that concept—I fall in love with my ideas a lot, as you can imagine. *The Law Against the People* was the direct result of my browbeating Robert. He was always writing articles for the *East Village Other* and other "radical," or relevant,

FIRE ISLANDERS!   NEW YORKERS!

WITHDRAW YOUR CONSENT
TO THE
CONSPIRACY OF SILENCE
WHICH ALLOWS THE CONTINUATION OF THE UNAESTHETIC SPECTACLE OF POINT O' WOODS AN
EXCLUSIVISTIC, RACIST ENCLAVE ON FIRE ISLAND, COUNTY OF SUFFOLK, STATE OF NEW YOR

FREE THE (SURELY, BY NOW BORED) KLANNISH, INCESTUOUS, W.A.S.P.
POINT O'WOODS PRISONERS,
ESPECIALLY THE YOUNGER GENERATION FROM THEIR OCEAN FRONT
CONCENTRATION CAMP (PARTIALLY SUPPORTED BY YOUR FEDERAL,
STATE AND/OR LOCAL TAXES).   SELF-RESPECTING JEWS AND/OR
BLACK PEOPLE MAY OR MAY NOT CHOOSE TO PASS THROUGH, VISIT,
OR ENTER THIS OBVIOUSLY DULL LITTLE COMMUNITY (how have they
stood themselves so long, without ventilation or fresh flesh?).

BUT THE PITY, INDULGENCE, PRIDE, CONTEMPT AND LUXURIOUS PERMISSIVENESS
IN AND FOR THE EXPRESSED AND IMPLIED KLANNISH ANTI-SEMITISM CONSTITUTES
BLEMISHES WHICH NEITHER AMERICA, NEW YORK, NOR FIRE ISLAND CAN ANY
LONGER AFFORD OR SUPPORT ------

J
  O   THE OPEN HOUSE BEACH-IN, TEACH-IN ON THE P.O'.W. OCEAN BEACH
    I
      N   AT HIGH NOON, POINT O'WOODS, SUNDAY, 3 AUGUST, 1969

DO YOUR OWN THING, BY ANY MEANS NECESSARY, BY PLANE, BOAT, BEACH TAXI, BIKE,

WAGON OR BAREFOOT   --   JOIN US TO ANNOUNCE, FILM, PROCLAIM AND CELEBRATE

THE BEGINNING OF THE END OF THIS IMMORAL, BUT ESPECIALLY UNAESTHETIC COMMUNITY.

MEDIA WORKSHOP
8 East 48th Street
PL-9-3223

---

newspapers around town, but rarely got paid for them, and I thought his ideas should be more widely disseminated, and that it was time he started making a little money.

Then Diane, as a member of the legal team which worked to change the New York State abortion laws, was approached by McGraw-Hill to do a book. She didn't want to write it by herself, so we planned projects together out on Fire Island, where we had the greatest fun in the world, laughing and giggling all the way through. I've always thought your work should be as indistinguishable from your pleasure as you can make it, and so far I've always managed to combine them.

Diane was our lawyer when Ti-Grace, Ruth Simpson, Ellen Povill, Merle Goldberg, and I got arrested in 1972 at our anti-Nixon demonstration, and she was even more brutalized than we were. I should let her tell that story herself:

It was a day off from work, a nice sunny day, and I wanted to stay home in my apartment and finish cleaning up after a party. Flo

With Paul Krassner protesting racism at Point O' Woods, Fire Island, 1969

had invited me to the W.A.R.N. (Women Against Richard Nixon) demonstration, but I had said, "No, thank you." Then, sitting peacefully at home, I got a call: "Hello, they've arrested Flo Kennedy, please rush down to the precinct." I took a taxi right down there, and sure enough, there were the women. About half a dozen of them had been arrested.

There was some kind of threat of keeping them overnight, and I thought it was my job at that point just to see that everybody got out safely, particularly since I had received reports of brutality. So I spoke to the officer in charge and he invited me to come in, and as a matter of fact I did help the police quite a bit, because some of the women at first refused to give any information, including their names. I played the conciliator, urging the women to identify themselves; they hadn't wanted to speak to the police at all until they had a lawyer. So I set up

a line of communication between the police and the women, and they both seemed very happy that I was there.

At this point the women had been taken upstairs, and it wasn't clear whether they were going to be getting out that night. I had an appointment which I wanted to cancel, so I left my coat upstairs, telling the officers and the women that I'd be right back, and went down to make a call from the public telephone. When I got there, a Sergeant Rooney stopped me and asked who I was. Apparently they had just changed shifts, and he didn't know me, but when I tried to explain, he became very belligerent and hostile. I was a good foot shorter than he and 200 pounds lighter, and he was armed, but he was treating me as if I were the menace.

He told me that I'd have to leave the precinct at once, and when I told him that I

With Ti-Grace Atkinson in the police station after "Women Against Richard Nixon" arrest, New York, 1972

had worked out an arrangement with the police and the women, he simply did not want to hear what I had to say. I went out to make my call, and apparently he instructed an officer to order me to leave, and if I refused, to arrest me. So I called the Civil Liberties Union instead, and spoke to Paul Chevigny, who said, "Just stand your ground. You have every right to stay there. Don't leave, the ACLU will help you."

I went to tell the women gathered outside what was happening, and at that point I was knocked to the ground by a couple of police officers, arrested, finger printed and searched. I was released shortly after my clients. My initial inclination was to sue for damages. The DA's office was anxious to discuss the case against me, but they bargained the dropping of the charges for a stipulation not to sue any police officer. Ultimately, charges against me were dismissed, and I brought an action

against Sergeant Rooney within the police department which "censured" him for his actions.

I remember that Irene Davall, still wearing her witch's costume from the demo, went to the Democratic Headquarters and told them what had happened, and they put it right out on the AP wire, and we made the *New York Times* and the *Daily News* as well. When the trial came up, we had a very strange situation: there was a female judge, female lawyer, and female defendants. The only men in the whole court were the court reporter and the cops who were testifying. There had even been a female photographer, whose pictures we threw up on the judge's desk to show that there had been barricades and that we weren't blocking traffic. The judge threw the

Ti-Grace Atkinson (in the hat), Gloria Steinem, and I leaving the police precinct after "Women Against Richard Nixon" demonstration, New York, 1972 ▶

whole thing out of court, saying, "I think the courts have got more important things to deal with than this."

That demonstration was one of Sandy Hochman's great moments. When they tried to arrest her, she told them, "Look, I've got an appointment with my dentist, and I simply cannot be arrested now. You'll just have to meet me at my place at 3:30." And they left her alone.

I think it's important to understand that our crowd is not just a bunch of people whom I'm leading, but that we inspire each other. Florence Rice, for instance, is my favorite example of a person who was using cannon to kill rabbits. She was head of the Harlem Consumer Education Council, and was directing the power of that organization against schlocky furniture stores and butcher shops, until I persuaded her to turn her attention to the New York Telephone Company and Consolidated Edison. The result was that Flo was recently described by Clinton Cox in an article in the New York *Daily News* as "the poor man's Ralph Nader," and "the leading street fighter in the consumer movement."

I'm not always the instigator of the things I do, though. It was my friend Peg Brennan's idea that we buy some property together in Nova Scotia. Peg is a communard who lives in a house in Brooklyn which she shares with a shifting number of people. One of her sons has a huge tract of land in Nova Scotia, about 200 acres, and he gave us ten of them to build on, in exchange for part of our land, which is right down on the waterfront. So far we have only the land, but we still like to go up there.

What usually happens is I am too old and too weak and usually too tired to drive all the way up to Halifax, so normally I fly. The others take an overnight ferry to Halifax, and the next morning they drive off the ferry, pick me up and we drive to Truro. We have a

huge teepee on the land and I go out there with them, but I don't sleep there. I stay in a motel run by the Mic Mac Indians, and only leave it for as long as I can go between shits, since there's no john yet on our property. If we're spending the day I don't eat anything in the morning before I go, because with my three missing feet of intestine I don't have much storage space.

So obviously I'm not much of a camping enthusiast; I did it mainly because Peg liked the idea. I do a lot of things because other people like the idea, and I think that's a good way to be. My mother was like that; she would do things she thought we wanted to do, even though she wouldn't have chosen to do them herself.

Sometimes I find myself in opposition, politically, to people whose side I am usually on and who are also close friends, and then I find myself living out some of my own concepts, such as horizontal hostility. The brouhaha over Jane Alpert was one of those issues. She was an underground activist in the late Sixties who got arrested, jumped bail, and then in November of 1974 voluntarily surrendered, after a conversion, she claimed, from the left to radical feminism. After surrendering she reportedly made statements which may have endangered her brothers and sisters who were still underground. Ti-Grace, Susan Sherman, Joan Hamilton, and I wrote a petition denouncing her, to which Gloria Steinem, Kate Millett, and Jean Boudin wrote a reply, defending her and denouncing us.

But the point is that although Gloria and I still do not agree about Jane Alpert, we've remained very good friends. When I see people around town who signed that letter whom I hardly know and don't care anything about, I almost don't speak to them; I have definitely cooled on anybody who signed it. But if my good friends signed it, then I feel slightly

Network television, radio broadcasters, photographers and reporters covered
the Press Conference at the entrance to 199 Church Street, at 9:30 a.m., on
June 24th. Consumers voiced their objections to the tactics, poor service, and
demands of the New York Telephone Company. Speeches, songs and skits were also
part of the activities and drew passers-by's interest.

Consumers and Reporters waiting for the hearing to begin.

Chris Ross, Photographer   Photo courtesy of the New York Press Service
     At 10:30 a.m., in the hearing room, to the great astonishment of the New York
Telephone Company's representatives, and probably the staff-employees of the NYSPSC
(no commissioners were present to be astonished), the room was overflowing with consumers and newsmen. Although the broadcasters (WNBC-TV, WCBS-TV and WBAI radio) left
after being denied permission to broadcast the PUBLIC hearings, reporters from the
New York Times, the Daily News, the New York Post, Newsday, the Associated Press and
United Press International remained throughout the session.

     THE HEARINGS RECEIVED FULL COVERAGE IN THE PRESS AND, THANKS TO THE WIRE
SERVICES, NEARLY EVERY RADIO STATION IN THE NEW YORK CITY AND STATE AREA RE-
PORTED ON THE CONSUMERS' OBJECTIONS TO THE RATE RISE.

different. Everyone who signed the letter protesting our position on Jane Alpert lost, let's say, five points. But people like Gloria had 97 points to begin with, so now she has 92 points, and nothing is going to change my feelings toward her, although when she joined the other women who attacked us, then of course that took her down a notch.

There are also times when I am on the opposite side of the situation from Ti-Grace, but when I differ politically with a good political friend or ally, or just a close personal friend, the friendship normally survives, unless it's a vicious attack on me and/or my associates. But since the letter of the pro-Jane Alpert crowd was personal, and pretty directly an attack on us, I felt that it divided the flakes and lumps from the people I could really respect. Most of them are people I don't care anything about anyway, and if they lost five points, they'd be off my list of people even to speak to. Most people

in the feminist movement are only five-point people; I don't know them, I've never worked with them, and I think of them as cowards of flakes from the gitgo.

I want to make this point, because it seems that some people out in the hinterlands think of me as a kind of Big Mama Earth, when in fact I'm not loving or dovying at all. I'm not free from horizontal hostility; I'm not free of the various symptomatologies peculiar to the pathology of the oppressed, the oppressor, the good people, the niggerizers, the nigger nobles, or any of the rest of them. It's from looking at myself that I get all these names in the first place; it's by examining myself that I learn about de-niggerization, re-niggerization, good niggers, and bad niggers.

That's why I don't have any interest in and am not particularly nice to people who call me up and ask me to address myself to their personal problems; it's

Gloria Steinem and I on the lecture circuit at East Texas State University, c. 1970

The Issue That's Splitting Feminists

BY JUDITH COBURN

Were the recent arrests of three underground radicals based on tips given to law enforcement authorities by ex-undergrounder Jane Alpert? No one has been able to prove that charge yet, but newspaper speculation about the terms of Alpert's surrender last November and the recent arrests of three undergrounders have begun to polarize the women's movement in New York into supporters and critics of Jane Alpert. Three petitions are now circulating, one of which specifically charges Alpert with informing on her former underground colleagues, one of which is critical of Alpert indirectly, and one of which, in response to the other two, strongly defends her.

Alpert pleaded guilty to charges of plotting with three others to bomb eight government and corporate targets at the height of the Vietnam protests in the late '60s. Alpert, her boyfriend Sam Melville, and John David Hughey III were arrested in 1970, while a fourth member of the group, Patricia Swinton, remained at large. After the three pleaded guilty, Alpert jumped bail and Melville and Hughey went to prison. Melville died in the 1971 Attica uprising. Hughey was paroled after serving two and a half years. Last November Alpert voluntarily surrendered to authorities, and in January was sentenced to 27 months in jail.

Newspaper reports have fueled radicals' fears that Alpert might inform on the underground. She is one of the few underground members who have voluntarily surrendered and renounced their former activities. At the time of Alpert's surrender, her lawyer, Michael F. Armstrong, a former Queens district attorney, was described by New York Times reporter Lucinda Franks as saying that "although his client had given extensive details of her fugitive existence to federal investigators, he had instructed her not to release them publicly before she was sentenced." The New York Post has quoted U.S. Attorney Paul Curran as saying, "She fully cooperated with the government." Alpert has denied the allegations, and told the Post at the time of her surrender that "she didn't know the whereabouts of any other fugitives."

In an August 1973 Ms. magazine article explaining her "conversion from the left to radical feminism," Alpert described a series of encounters with members of the Weather Underground, including Mark Rudd. The article provoked heavy criticism on the Left and charges that Alpert was compromising the security of those still underground.

The signers of the petition defending Alpert assert that, after her conversion and the publication of the Ms. piece, "Alpert severed her slight contact with the underground and remained unconversant with any information about it. Her conduct

'Three petitions are now circulating; one charges Jane Alpert with informing on the underground.'

Jane Alpert

Petitioner Steinem

Petitioner Kennedy

under enormous pressure was and continues to be that of a woman with great integrity and strong feminist commitment." The petition is signed by a score of well-known feminists, including Gloria Steinem, Kate Millett, Rita Mae Brown, Phyllis Chesler, Karen DeCrow, Jill Johnston, Grace Paley, and Margaret Sloan. Another signer is Jean Boudin, poet and mother of Kathy Boudin, a Weather Underground member who is still at large.

Pat Swinton, whose arrest March 12 after five years of underground life escalated suspicions about Alpert, says she doubts Alpert has turned informer. "It could be something she said in conversations with the FBI that gave them a lead. But I'm sure that whatever was said was done unwittingly."

The petition most directly critical of Alpert says it has been written out of the "conviction that Jane Alpert should not be welcome in the feminist movement since according to a report in the New York Times she is 'cooperating fully' with FBI investigators." The petition goes on to say that her 1973 open letter to Ms. "divulged information about both men and women activists . . . informing on sisters and brothers is not part of the feminist movement." The petition is signed by more than 50 women from New York Women's Union, New York Women's School, Women's Health Forum, East New York Alliance, National Lawyers Guild, the Prairie Fire Distributing Committee (which distributes the Weather Underground book "Prairie Fire"), and a variety of other leftist and feminist organizations.

The other anti-Alpert petition, almost a prose poem in form, is signed by four women, Florynce Kennedy, Susan Sherman, Ti-Grace Atkinson, and Joan Hamilton. The petition reads in part, "It is not war that destroys us, but betrayal . . . Jane Alpert is not important, what is important is that women stop playing games, dangerous games . . . There are two kinds of justice in this country, the system of justice for people like Jane Alpert, and the system of justice for people like Assata Shakur. Is this what we want the women's movement to represent? The kind of movement Jane Alpert represents. A movement based on class privilege, on white privilege."

Some of the newspapers have characterized Alpert's "conversion" as a shift *from* radicalism *to* feminism, a distinction that it is doubtful any of the participants in the controversy surrounding Alpert would be likely to agree with. But the question of the relationship of feminism to left radicalism is at the heart of the controversy. It is a question that has troubled the women's movement since its inception, and—whatever Jane Alpert did or didn't say to the authorities—it will continue to do so for a long time to come. □

work to be done, and I have enough to do working on myself. Otherwise I'm only interested in working on the pathology of the society as a whole, because it takes as much time to get one ass out of the wringer as it does to try to stop the wringer.

So my motto is, "Kick ass in '76, and keep on kicking." In 1975 we held the MAMA March, the March Against Media Arrogance. We decided to have another one in 1976 and planned to give toilet paper awards, as we did in 1973 at the Hollywood Toilet Bowl Caravan, where we took twenty folds of bathroom tissue three squares long and presented it to pigocrats in media like "Marcus Welby."

I think the way I live is the very best way anybody could live; I don't know anybody who has more fun. And the most fun you can have is when it's relevant, and not a fake struggle like basketball or football or hockey, where people suffer more injuries and mayhem than from any kind of demonstration or political protest. So that's the first thing—and the second is that real struggle pays off. Number three, it's fun to use the power you've got, and number four, it's tacky to let flaky people be in charge of anything, whether it's giving a party, producing a show, putting out a newspaper, or running the country.

People who behave as though there's something wrong with wanting to improve things are to me pathological, and I can't believe that anybody with taste and brains would want to join them. Whoever they are, in art, ballet, golf, piano playing, movie making, or buildings building, they are not esthetic or meaningful people, in my opinion, unless they're doing something about making this a better place to live in.

I just don't know what people think they're doing if it isn't some form of what I'm doing, and to do anything less makes no sense to me. When I get all these mailings about sending money to little starving children in Africa, I can't understand how anybody smart enough to write that stuff can be so dumb as not to realize that's not the way to make the change. How can they think that the way to deal with starving children in Africa is to have people who have already paid their taxes write checks, when all that tax money goes into the imperialist wars that bring about the misery in the first place?

I'm just a loud-mouthed middle-aged colored lady with a fused spine and three feet of intestines missing, and a lot of people think I'm crazy. Maybe you do too, but I never stop to wonder why I'm not like other people. The mystery to me is why more people aren't like me.

Speakout for Chilean women prisoners, New York University, 1974

BEHIND THE SEEN by GREGG HEACOCK

The Hollywood Toilet Bowl Festival

Flo Kennedy and her sisters of the National Feminist Party drove to LA for the Hollywood Toilet Bowl Festival where they plunged away at the media and the White House in an effort to clean house. Appearing at the LA Press Club (where the walls are lined with pictures of white, male journalists), they protested the treatment of women by the media which fails to hire women or to serve them respectfully as an audience.

Jacque Schwartz, who is demanding reparation for women by the studios of $150,000, accused the media of ripping off actresses: "The best an actress can hope for is to play a prostitute or a mad woman." Otherwise, they are stuck playing mindless dollies.

The Affirmative Action Program developed to encourage media hiring of women and minorities is tokenism at best. In Marin County the person responsible for keeping women out of the industry has just been appointed head of the Affirmative Action Program for Women. (Is it male logic to put the fox in charge of the chicken coop?)

Even cable television is ruled by prejiduce. Liz McDonald, who had just finished filing 32 suits against companies for not hiring women, said she came to LA to relax and work for cable TV. Theta Cable told her they had one position open in sales but they were not interviewing women because "Women can't sell media." Ms. McDonald is about to level her 33rd suit.

As Flo Kennedy has said before, "There are very few jobs that actually require a penis or vagina. All other jobs should be open to everybody."

If hiring is awful, viewing is worse. Using the force of straight talk, Flo criticized television for giving women for their daily viewing "no budget, low budget, apolitical bullshit. It's either chocolate covered manure or manure covered chocolate. You don't get anything straight --ever. And on Saturday morning women are assaulted by three hours of cartoons, many of which are racist and sexist, followed by five hours of sports--Saturday's preoccupation with balls. Not that sports shouldn't be on TV, but there should be some alternative programming for women."

A media man asked how women would react if soap operas were taken off the air. Flo never flinches at "typical round-eyed media questions": "Alcoholics love scotch. And some diabetics would like nothing better than a marshmellow diet. Brain washed people want what their brains have been washed in." All the more reason for change.

When you add up the specific crimes of the media the total effect could not be more if there were a conspiracy against women.

Television tries to make the male power structure unimpeachable. Doctors are represented by the good Marcus Welby while news shows never tell us how doctors and medicine damage women daily. The use of amphetamines and diuretics on pregnant women to reduce their appetite and water content has been responsible for malnurishment of fetuses and the increase in retarded and hyperactive babies whose nervous systems are already damaged by the "speed" given to their mothers.

FLORYNCE KENNEDY

Flo extended her attack to newspapers. "They give only two pages for so-called 'womens' news, while feminist news ends up on the nigger page."

Oppressed people are oppressed for a reason. Those with power control the money. They are so happy to protect women by keeping them from earning more than $10,000 a year--if women would earn $11,000 their femininity might be destroyed. We are fighting a national economic battle. "I'm concerned with money," says Flo, "because in a whorehouse society that's one of the things it is all about. If women knew child care was being denied for a lack of $35,000 while one cartoon on Saturday morning cost $80,000 to produce, they wouldn't stand for it. We need economic guerrilla warfare to change where the money goes."

All money matters are kept secret so people won't know how they are being ripped off. The media has allowed such secrecy.

The epitome of secrecy and disregard for the public is, of course, found in the White House. "The White House is an out house!" shouted one woman. Flo puts it where no one can miss it: "I wouldn't leave my baby with a babysitter who was as crooked and corrupt as the men chosen by Tricky Dick to run this country. A crooked creep who has no better judgment than Nixon has no right to ask me to protect the presidency. Flush him out of office!"

In explaining why the Feminist Party was holding their Toilet Bowl Festival, Flo said, "I don't think we can turn the Atlantic into syrup by pouring in a cup of sugar. But if a car is on your ankle, you should at least be able to scratch the paint a little."

Feminist Party convention

Urinary Politics

by Ellen Frankfort

CAMBRIDGE, Massachusetts—Pied-piper-like in the drizzly rain, the Feminist Party (quite small in number if one could discount the immeasurable spirit of its founder, Flo Kennedy) walked through the streets of Cambridge, past the Square, into the Yard, beyond the large new Design School and the older immemorial Memorial Hall, picking up people all the way who joined with those in front of Lowell, a crowd of the curious who had come to see the event announced that very morning on the front page of the Crimson without so much as a blush—a Pee-in at Harvard Yard.

"If God meant women to have pay toilets, we would be made with exact change," read one of the banners shielding the bodies as streamers waved in the dampness and Flo chanted loud and clear: "To pee or not to pee, that is the question . . . pee on Harvard Yard"—as if that were the answer, using illogic to prod into consciousness the undercover connections between the wastes of the body and the stench of the body politic. The connections continued to surface when Marge Piercy's poem, written for the occasion, was read. "To the Pay Toilet" : "You strop my anger, especially when I find you in a restaurant or bar and pay for the same liquid coming and going . . . Sometimes a woman in a uniform's on duty black or whatever the prevailing bottom is getting 30 cents an hour to make sure no woman sneaks her full bladder under a door . . . While a row of weary women carrying packages and babies wait and wait and wait to do what only the dead find unnecessary."

And as the figures were presented on the highly disproportionate number of men's to women's rooms (especially if one considers that institutions such as Harvard, designed as they were by and for men, nevertheless have more women, if one counts all the secretaries, who, faceless and nameless as they may be, still are born with bladders), and the crowd moved closer to watch, the cameras started to click.

"Unless Lowell Hall gets a room for women as well as men so that women taking exams don't have to hold it in, run across the street, or waste time deciding whether to pee or not to pee, next year we will be back with the real thing." And while the mere threat of peeing in public seemed to titillate the students and Cambridge luminaries who stood by much amused, Flo Kennedy continued to explain how bathrooms were always an easy way to make people feel niggerized, that that was the way it was in the South not too long ago when there was a different one for coloreds and whites and that things were not very different for women. For a man can urinate in urinals even when the stalls require change or go off to some corner and inconspicuously pee whereas a woman always has to pay in public places unless she chooses to use the sink or that one free toilet that either has no door or no paper or a puddle or something just to remind you you're a nigger.

But the Pee-In was merely the prelude to the New England Feminist Party Convention's weekend of workshops, including two that were fascinating to me—Diane Schulder's "Marriage and Divorce" and Lou Shields's "Sexuality and Celibacy"—demonstrations, dances, a soul-food supper at the Ritz, children acting out "a more realistic version of Cinderella than you are likely to find elsewhere" opening with the line "Once upon a time there was a horny old man," an unusual church service conducted by a theological student from Harvard, a member of Women's Inspirational Theological Conspiracy from Harvard (WITCH), where men were asked to leave for a brief time toward the end which turned out to be a moment for self-criticism, and then reunited for the burning of sexist Bible quotations, all done in the Charles Street Meeting House on Beacon Hill, amidst Boston's Brahmins, many of whom were the early feminists.

One of the most interesting analyses I heard all weekend came out of a panel on "Women, the Media, and Watergate." Diane Rabenold of Boston summed up the fate of three women who had been deeply involved. Dita Beard had been "one of the boys" and played by their rules. But when her role was discovered she was "thrown to the wolves and when at last she suffered a heart attack, even her own doctor said she was disoriented." When Martha Mitchell stopped being an amusing indulgence for her husband or a dancing dog for the press and made one of the earliest recommendations that Nixon resign, she too was labeled insane and actually carted off to a mental hospital for an overnight stay. But the most final fate of all was that of E. Howard Hunt's wife, who, with her husband, had been part of a dual spy team as far back as the Bay of Pigs. Although they had worked together as a partnership, it was Mrs. Hunt who was killed in a plane crash which, according to Rabenold, is surrounded by much evidence that suggests sabotage.

"What you gotta realize, honey," Flo Kennedy said, "is that the government and the delinquent elements work together after a certain point. The government crooks always have their connections together after a certain point. The government crooks always have their connections in the media. But what we've gotta see is that a woman like Martha Mitchell who thought she was getting out of her tacky white Southern trash background by sucking her way up winds up with her old man going to jail, just like every other nigger woman has to worry about because, honey, if you're born to suck, you ain't gonna become anything but a noble nigger. What we don't realize is that in a prostitute society, the sucking line is so long, you can't get anyone to bite. Why, it goes all the way from here on the Hill beyond Copley Square. Now, of course, you always have those, when the shit is hitting the fan real hard, who get busy measuring the size of the turds to make sure you don't over-state the oppression. They're the researchers and the straight media. And you need them, I suppose. But all these women were suckers, that's the point. And we've got to learn how to be biters. We're all earthworms and when we begin to get a few hairs, the piranhas scream 'ego trip.' Now what's wrong with an ego trip. The very phrase is a pathological symptom. Every time someone gets out of jeans, the others become suspicious. I mean this mentality—I work for an underground railroad, therefore I'm on top—has just got to go, baby. Hi there, Tampa, and here comes Maine, come on in, baby. You see, I'm so tired of this whole question of whether or not Nixon knew. I'm

much more worried if he *didn't* know. Then he's like someone playing the piano in a whorehouse who doesn't know what the bumping above is. How dumb can you get? But we're termites and we got to do what they do in terms of biting. Bite now, suck later, bite when no one can see you and the whole house is

coming apart. That's why we can't afford any horizontal hostility with each other. And that's why you don't take on anyone but the big ones. And if you can't confront, then sabotage or fantasize sabotage, at least, in your head. I don't want to hear anyone whining—I can't do it, I got too many kids, I'm too old, I'm too sick, too poor. Look, I'm old and I got this bad back and I just remember that when I want help to get my boots back on. We got to use all our weaknesses we've accumulated. You can't change from weakness to strength overnight without getting the bends or the shakes. So be sneaky and weak if it's for political advantage. Because we can't afford not to. We may know how to tell the chocolate covered shit so we don't eat it any more, but honey, we haven't figured out any other diet. and we're starving. Just take this whole thing on co-optation. That's just more loserism. Every time you step forward, someone tells you you're going to be co-opted. You can't move then. You can scream all you want about capitalism but it still is good to see Haldeman shaking in front of the cameras rather than telling them

Continued on next page

FLO
IN BLACK
AND WHITE

"Show the power structure that you're prepared to kick your mother and father, and they'll find you relevant, because business and government are *in loco parentis* to the oppressed individual."

From a speech at Boston University, October 20, 1970

I've just come back from a little swing of the country, and what I'm finding is that the round-eyed schools are catching up. It's like somebody who goes to a party and finds that everybody else is five drinks ahead, so they just drink, drink, drink real fast, and pretty soon, if they got there two hours late, they're only a quarter of an hour behind. And that's what's happening.

On Monday I went to Billings, Montana—are you ready?—and it must be admitted that I do plant a few seeds of rebellion, but they're ready for it. I do not get round-eyed questions, women do not have to put the men down any more, and self-esteem has had its effect all over the world. It's a funny thing—for the same reason that oppression is contagious, and accepting it, so also rejecting oppression is contagious. And what happens is, when one group of people reject oppression, other people catch on, they get involved with a freedom itch, as it were, and so what's happening now is that round-eyed schools are having their first seminars and are getting the kinds of crowds that the swinging schools were having a year or two ago. Eastern Montana had a big, big room—all white, of course—people, not the walls—and they just went everywhere, all over the place—a few little black raisins here and there, but practically all white, and it was full. Eastern Montana, can you imagine? And the other room was video, and it had about 200 more, and there was a third room that didn't even have a video, just sound, and *that* was full, they said.

So in other words, without taxiing the field, this thing was going. And I think further evidence of how fast it's going is always to be judged by the thermometer of the pigs. Now of course we regard it as co-option because we have a loser pathology, part of our oppressive pathology is a loser orientation, so that if we influence the culture, they've co-opted us—we're always losing, no matter how you figure, we're losing. "Too many people come in, we're getting commercial." Success is very embarrassing, right? We complain because nobody will let us go on TV; then, when we do get to go on, we don't trust ourselves, we must be doing something wrong, because we're influencing people. Everybody says, "Right on," and we think, "Oh my God, this is terrible!" So there' a little bit of that, but for the most part people are really just into it, everybody's totally high on this whole thing.

I think that schools like this really have to move, you have to call boycotts or do something around your issues. I don't know what the media are doing here in Boston, but I think the main thing you have to do is project beyond the campus, you have to move up ahead to lift everybody else. And one of the things you've got to do is try to get away from the snobbery of the movement towards the middle class and the so-called "upper class" (women are never upper-class). And I think it's very important that people understand that when they say "power to the people," they don't only mean power to the dirty, grimy Black, Chicano, Indian people—they also mean power to the rich, dumb people who have been educated beyond their intelligence—and that's most of us, that's what education is into. To the degree that a society is oppressive, education is into having you suspend the exercise of your intellect.

So we must begin to understand that losing is a part of the oppressive pathology, and while it isn't necessary for everybody to be into winning, some people ought not to be embarrassed by winning, by success, and by the realization that to cure the poverty of women, just like to cure the poverty of Black people or G.I.'s or anyone else, you have to go where the money is. The idea that we should relate only to those people whom we regard as beneath us is very bad. The women's movement is alway saying, "Could you recruit some Blacks?" They don't want to admit that there's a problem of horizontal hostility between Black and white women, so they feel more comfortable if they have more Black women, but the Black women are very often not into the thing, and they're skeptical, for very good reasons. The Black community any number of times has been invited—"Come on, sister, come on, brother"—as long as the shit is hitting the fan, and then the minute it slows down and it's time to use it for fertilizer on the land they've conquered, they say, "One of you can be a foreman and all the rest have to groove on the vicarious thrill of eeny-meeny-miny-mo." So I think it's quite understandable that Black people are not so anxious to get into struggles that are not on their own timetable and in their own priorities.

But when you want to examine the pathology of the oppressed and figure why women consent to oppression, you must find out what the *quid pro quo* is for accepting and consenting to oppression. And when you do that you begin to understand for example why back in 1968 you'd get all these round-eyed questions: "I'm not oppressed," you know.

Now, of course, if you don't bite the bridge mix you can deny it's chocolate-covered bullshit. You see, the Establishment comes around and gives you bridge mix—"You're a little girl and nobody's gonna hit you" bridge mix, "You are gonna be loved and you're gonna wear a pretty little dress with frills" bridge mix. Bridge mix is chocolate-covered candy with nuts and raisins and mint and caramel inside. But the Establishment keeps saying, "Don't bite the bridge mix." They say, "Marriage is a contract," but they don't have you read the contract before you're married. Gloria Steinem likes to quote the people who say, "You really ought to take a test before you get a marriage license," and then she says, "This makes sense; you have to take a test to drive a car, and your marriage is at least as important as driving a car." And that would be equal to biting the bridge mix. But the point is that the bridge mix, according to women in women's liberation, is not chocolate-covered cherries and nuts and raisins, but it's actually chocolate-covered bullshit.

So you're told not to bite it, and you don't mind—they say the loveliest smell after Chanel No. 5 is the smell of a dirty diaper. All right, so groovy. And in the movies they're always talking about love, and getting the man, and winding up with the big blast at the end where you go driving off, waving out the back window; and all the songs, "I love him," "I love you," "Call me, I'll be there," "Hit me, beat me, knock me down, he treats me mean, I love him just the same, he kicks my ass and it feels so good, I can't sit on it but it's wonderful, chase me out, throw me out the window, let me follow you"—you know, everything, anything.

Then somebody comes along and says, "If you bite through the chocolate, you know what's there." But you still don't bite it. "He didn't tip the waiter, but I know he loves me," and of course naturally he's not going to give you any money when you get married, because he didn't tip the waiter and that was your cue, but you didn't look. He opened the door and didn't slam it on your hand, so what does it matter if he didn't tip the waiter? But in times like this, sooner or later somebody starts slicing one piece of bridge mix after another. And they keep telling you it's an isolated incident when you bite one and find it's not really a nut. So after a while along comes the Women's Liberation Movement, and you say to the world at large, "It's all, or mostly, chocolate-covered bullshit." And then that's when they say, "The Communists are telling you that." But then more and more people start to write about it, and they bring historicity and pathology and all kinds of economic, political, religious, media evidence before you, and you just go back and say, "Look, I've got this evidence—this, this, this, this. And every time I bite one, that's what it is." And then they say, "The Communists are always trying to ruin your teeth."

So one thing about the liberation movement is that everybody's biting the bridge mix, and everybody's reexamining all these wonders of women that we've all been into. And the reason the men aren't asking the

"Win With Women," 1974 Women's Political Caucus benefit with Liz Carpenter and *Ms.* magazine editors Pat Carbine and Gloria Steinem

round-eyed questions is that they're beginning to understand that one of the reasons they were skeptical about the oppression of women was that women had been among the oppressors of *them* in personal contexts. It's really hard for people to understand that oppressed people are very oppressive, for reasons of horizontal hostility.

It's women's sense of their own lack of worth that makes sibling rivalry and horizontal hostility so easy. If you have a sense of your own worthlessness, then somebody else from your class or race or religion is clearly not to be looked up to. This is one of the bases for the pathology of women saying, "I don't get along with women, I get along with men; they're superior, so if I get along with them *I'm* superior, but I've left all my class behind." Or the one and only: "I'm the one and only woman in the executive suite; I'm the one and only woman in the medical school; I'm the one and only woman here and there." Now that used to be a source of pride, but we're understanding politically that this is unacceptable. Black people used to say, "Only Black family on the block." That used to be a source of pride. No more. All the way down the line: "I don't want to be the token; I don't want to be the show nigger; I don't want to be the house nigger; I don't want to be the corporate nigger."

And this is why the political implications of the women's movement are so important; because more than any other group imaginable, the women are everywhere. Ti-Grace Atkinson always says, "Sleep light—you may be fucking the revolution." Every so often, send the food over to the poison control lab and check it out. It's sort of a joke, but that's where it's at. . . . It's really important, quite apart from sympathy or left politics, for people to begin to examine the philosophical basis for maintaining guilt in this society, in terms of the ways in which the rules change when you begin to withdraw consent to oppression. And the reason it's important for women in the women's liberation movement to do that is because you're next. Because you're so important, and your niggerization is such a shock to you that you're not going to behave well. You see, the Black people have not all been ennobled by niggerization, but they've gotten very smart, they know how to survive. And one of the ways to survive is to sort of pull in your head and get under the shell. But that's something that women are not really so ready to do, because they've been encouraged to be outspoken—read Scarlett O'Hara, read Jezebel—"Oh, you little devil, you." Now of course you're also an angel, you're also a madonna, so there's a lot of confusion. But the fact remains that they weren't aware they were oppressed, so there's a whole generation of people who are beginning to feel that they've been in a trick bag all this time, and many of them in the squarest places, round-eyed people, 1942 haircuts, everything—they're just ready to go! They're ready to move!

So what's happening is that the women are beginning to plan all sorts of regional actions. And I think to the extent that I've been influential, it's in helping them to pass the masochistic state—they're going to bypass all that. . . . It's like with the Black movement, the way for you to get Black people to do anything is to show them that you know where it's at. And believe me, the vigiling techniques, and the research, and getting into bed with the malaria patient, and trying to cure poverty by going into the poor

the HERALD

Serving New York,
New Jersey and
Connecticut

Week of
October 10, 1971

35c

The Gospel According to St. Flo

They come to attorney Florynce Kennedy for leadership and courage and chili

by Katherine P. Wyatt

Flo is frightening. Incapable of being labelled, classified, or boxed, hers is a saintliness of the lunar age. So let the scripture read:

"Any action against racism has two possible thrusts, what it does for me and what it does against the racist."

"Liberation means freedom, widening the choice is what it's all about."

"If people are not into fun, it's their image; the greater the variety the greater the fun."

Amen, or perhaps – Women.

One knows one has arrived at Saint Flo's 8 East 48th Street shrine from the three signs by the door: Florynce Kennedy Attorney, Estate of Charles C. Parker. Jr. and Estate of Billie Holiday. Stepping in from the dingy corridor one smells incense – typically succulent chili, or Moo Goo Gai Pan and fried rice.

This is Flo's apartment, which is also her office, which is also a god-awful mess. But Flo wears her hair shirt of compulsive messiness with grace and pride.

"The 'filthy room' has so much dirt in it that there's no place for you to sit," she says to a young man who has entered her bedroom, or the "filthy room." (The front room is officially designated the "dirty room.") He joins Flo, reclining on her unmade bed of nettles, and a few women meeting to establish a new organization, Women's Rights, Inc. As usual the chicest among them is Flo, wearing a black halter top, brown pants and *le dernier cri* in jewelry. On the floor, peeking out from the moguls of paper by her bed are two Louis Vuitton bags that have lain there for a week.

A talk show playing on the portable television -- standing on top of the console TV – prompts Flo to speak:

"We ought to be ashamed just criticizing the foolish questions women are asked on TV. We ought to have our own program. Four hours of football every Saturday, and it's women who do all the buying. Cooking is women's work until it pays $35,000 a year, then a man with a blazer becomes the cook on TV!"

Among the chosen, she is justly invincible. Flo is entirely free of a victim mentality. She has no fear of racism, because, as she has justly observed, "I don't believe anybody could use me faster than I could use him." Hence she has the security to bypass lamentations and concentrate on visions:

"We got to stop crying rape when there's no trouble. We got to get our s— –t together and stop whining. We can boycott. We don't have to buy General Foods and Proctor & Gamble. Yardley soap doesn't cost any more than a bar of Zest."

It seems she has but one Fear, more marriage: "You can go in and out of a closet a million times, but the moment the door locks, I get nervous."

And one Tragic Flaw: refusal to recognize her potential.

LARGE FOLLOWING

Certainly within the ranks of issue-oriented reformers there must be many who see Flo more as threat than saint or mother. And though she's black, beautiful and far beyond liberation, Flo is far too volatile to ever become the darling of the safe establishment press. But Flo's clout in black and women's circles is significant, and her standing is high too among a wider host of individualists who can spot a true original.

Sandra Hotchman, poet and author of the much praised novel, *Walking Papers*, has only good words for Flo: "energy of an artist . . . common sense of a very mature person . . . lots of guts . . , a single-handed dynamo against oppression."

community, is not where it's at. Go to the banks, go to the insurance companies, go to the television networks, and begin to become relevant to the power structure! Show them that you're prepared to kick your mother and father, and they will find that you're relevant, because business and government are *in loco parentis* to the oppressed individual.

"Silence is collaboration, and rape without struggle is no rape, it's just a bad screw."

From a speech at Salem State College, Massachusetts, October 9, 1974 (This speech was also used in the film Flo Kennedy, *produced and directed by Dr. Barbara Kaster.)*

I got some questions: Number one, what's with Boston? Number two, what is this shit? And number three, where is everybody? You know, the story of Boston is the story of the pathology of oppression, so don't feel that I'm not with the subject, because whether you're talking about women as niggers, niggers as niggers, homosexuals as niggers, students as niggers, prison inmates as niggers, city people as niggers, American taxpayers as niggers, consumers as niggers—niggerization has a certain symptomatology. And the story of Boston is the microcosmic story of niggerization.

And I think it's important for us to examine it. I think we're really lucky that we're getting this filmed, because we'll want to bury this bone (or shit, whichever you prefer to call it), and I think we shouldn't be permitted to do that. South Boston has everybody sick, but it isn't enough to be sick unless you find out why you're sick, and move to try to get well. One of the symptoms of pathology is the desire to be elsewhere, but unfortunately there's no place to hide, and so in a sense you're almost fortunate to have the pathology of oppression right here, in your immediate area, because it gives you an opportunity to do some analysis. So instead of being sick, think real hard as you watch what's going down, and do something. Tell a small truth, make a small noise, make a defiant gesture (where it's safe—I don't want anybody getting killed).

Although I'll tell you. I was due here this morning, but I came up yesterday, and I usually try to get there the night before because I'm very tired, very old, very weak, very sick—three feet of intestines missing, fused spine—so I move very slowly and with great effort, unless I get evil, and then I can move a little faster, not much, but a little bit.

So I came up yesterday, and I told my sister—we're buying a house this weekend—"if I don't come back from Boston, it's okay." 'Cause this was the last big thing—there are five of us sisters and everybody had what they wanted, more or less, our modest needs had been met. So I set everything up about the house, and then I said, "Look. Nobody apparently is ready to give these people blood, which is clearly what they want." And I noticed that it was sort of orgasmic, when they finally got this one Black guy and tore his clothes and beat him up, and you could almost feel a kind of release in the pathology, without even knowing the people from South Boston that

Lecturing at Florence, Alabama, 1975 (note cupcake teeshirt)

were involved, ripping at this symbol of their fear and anxiety. And you felt that that blood had helped them a lot, so I hoped that the crowd would have had their thirst slaked sufficiently that they wouldn't still be in the street yesterday afternoon, but I had to take that chance. 'Cause I had thought about it, and I couldn't think of a better person to give them a little more blood, if that was what they needed, than myself.

Fortunately, by the time I got here the blood had apparently done what I had hoped it would. But in thinking about the possibility that something would happen to me, I reached a lot of conclusions, because I recognized that to die in South Boston would have been no worse than to die because of an automobile accident. And people smoke two and three packs of cigarettes a day knowing that 52,000 people a year die of lung cancer, and other people drive at 60 miles an hour on a wet highway, understanding that many, many people die and are maimed by automobile accidents. And it occurs to me that political people—women, men, students, Black people, consumers, taxpayers—need to get away from the tremendous fear that we attribute to the fear of being hurt or dying. Because I think that there are probably more industrial accidents, more motorcar accidents, more sicknesses brought on by people overeating, overdrinking—I know third-generation alcoholics, and I imagine around

Boston you may even have some fourth-generation alcoholics. I was married to a Welsh drunk and my sister is married to an Irish guy who digs his beers, so we really have a great respect for people that like to drink. And our whole society does—one of the first things they do on an airplane is to turn off the "No Smoking" sign, so you can begin on your cancer, and the next things they do, before you can get your soft drinks they gotta go around and push the liquor. So you see, our society is really not that much into seeing life as precious. That's one of the pathological myths that obtain—that our country is concerned for life. But we complain only if your giving of your blood or your life is for an anti-Establishmentarian purpose. In other words, you are supposed to be nonviolent, if you're trying to get your freedom. The women in the movement, the Black people in the movement, the Wounded Knee activists, are all supposed to be nonviolent. Somehow you are supposed to have yielded the right to violence to your government, and your government is supposed to be violent on your behalf, should it become appropriate.

Now you see, it's very interesting how the pigs' prerogative is exercised. Sports is one of the major preoccupations of our society—I call it "jockocracy"—and it's fascinating to note the preoccupations of our society with balls. Tennis balls, footballs, basketballs—there shouldn't be a season without some balls to focus on. Who got the ball, who signed up to carry the ball, who broke his hip getting the ball, who's refusing his contract—you cannot go to sleep at night with the radio or television on without learning what happened to the Oakland A's, what happened to the Miami Dolphins, and in great and excruciating detail. And it's very interesting, because should you want to know what happened to the Equal Rights Amendment, you might experience considerable difficulty. I occasionally go into a state and I really don't know if the state has passed the law or not. I was amazed, for example, to find that North Carolina had not passed it, and not at all amazed to learn that the Stop Equal Rights women had passed out homemade bread and apple pie to the legislators, to show them that women really didn't want to be equal. Now I'm not sure how they made that leap of logic, because I happen to dig homemade bread and I can go with apple pie, but for some reason there are those people who still prefer to use the cupcake survival technique, and I'm the last person in the world to put anyone down for figuring out a technique for survival. But you see, the cupcake survival technique is a form of nigger nobility, and in South Boston, which as I say is a sort of microcosm of the macrocosmic institutional oppression that we're into in this country, you have what I think was an excessive nigger nobility.

Nigger nobility is reacting to oppression in a better way than you would if you weren't oppressed. In other words, the worse you're treated the more noble you become: "Oh, just ignore it." And unfortunately for me, I really have quite a crazy family, although my sisters are not nearly as crazy as I am—none of us takes any personal shit, but politically my sisters run the gamut. But it's really incredible that people like Reverend King, for example, whose wife was killed in Atlanta, says, "Nobody can get me to hate anybody"; I can get pissed if someone steps on my toe and doesn't say "excuse me." And I know there's something lacking in me, but honey, I

W74
Win With Women
THE FOUR SEASONS
W74
Win With Women
W74
Win With Women
W74
Win With Women

want you to know I wouldn't have it otherwise. And I think there's something very unwholesome about eating shit and calling it chocolate. It isn't quite as bad as it sounds, you see, because our society is really expert in the matter of making the bridge mix. The bridge mix is chocolate-covered manure. Now some of my language is a little strong, and a lot of people can't take it. You know, I'm always a little bit amazed at our sensitivity to language—after all, this is the language of the White House, this is the way the President talks. In fact, he had some new ones I didn't even know—how many people know what a "candy-ass" is? That's one of his specials—I never heard of candy-ass, and I just learned it's a prison word for homosexual.

So the other thing I notice is, a lot of people get upset when you say "shit" or something like that. But do you realize that almost our entire country sat still while they barbecued people in Los Angeles, firebombed a house, burned the people to death? They didn't even know who was in the house, because it took them 24 hours to identify the ashes and the carcasses and the bones and the fried skin. And you see, this is a part of the pathology of people who are so sensitive to some kinds of stylistic offensiveness, and so callous to real cruelty and brutality. And everybody, from cab drivers on, every kind of person I've talked to tells me how sick they are about what's happening in South Boston. But apparently the respect for those racists is so substantial and the terror at the possibility of getting damaged is so awful that I'm confident in this area 80,000 people are repelled by what's going on in Boston, and yet 8,000 people are really dominating the situation.

Now of course the government decides when violence is appropriate, and one of the questions I would like somebody to answer is, what happened to the tear gas? What happened to the last order of tear gas? Because I'm confident that if a few Black student movements from several colleges had decided to demonstrate over loan applications, honey, they would have found the tear gas *eo instanter*, okay? And therefore I believe they were restrained in using the tear gas because it was white racists that were misbehaving. So I want to know when, if ever, we're going to begin to react against the double and triple standards. We have all this compassion for Nixon—he's suffered enough. They're only quarreling over whether to give him $250,000 or $800,000. He's got a $60,000 pension, he's got all the tax loopholes, he's got all that money he stole from Internal Revenue from years back, and I don't see where the suffering is. It appears to me that *we* have suffered rather considerably.

So you see, this nigger-noble acceptance of the pigocratic values is one that I think we may have to watch, because we must take some responsibility. The good people cannot allow the government—because you see it's really the government that's involved here—to sit back, buy all that tear gas with your taxes, and then save it for you. That ain't cool.

Now the next thing we have to ask is, where are all those howling students from Harvard that used to love to go to the Boston Commons and protest the war in Vietnam? I have been on many a protest against the war in Vietnam—why is it that when it's just a short ride, or even a walk, to South Boston, nobody that I know of has been reported as having made

even a token march on South Boston? Those people aren't even armed—they've got bats, and I imagine a few of them have guns, but we marched in Washington against the troops of the Army, and where are the people that used to go to Washington? South Boston is less expensive, and I really think it's a greater menace to us individually. The war in Vietnam was terrible on our financial fiber, it was death on our moral fiber, but the difference is that these people in South Boston can become your rulers. The Vietnamese were not very likely to come over here from North Vietnam and take over the Boston House of Commons, or whatever you call it. So the threat is quite immediate, and we have to understand that we cannot have the luxury of just sitting by while this sort of thing happens. And I think the howlers of Harvard should get their shit together and do a little bit of howling, otherwise I have to assume they're hollow on the inside, and I really think that a hollow Harvard student is nothing to follow, and it's important for us to recognize that. I want to know where the Yalies are, that used to yell against the Southeast Asian atrocities. I think it's a much greater atrocity, having urged people to send their kids to school, to niggerize them when they try to go. There's something quite pathological about that, and typical of the tendency to change the rules when the oppressed begin to learn the rules. In other words, they urge you to study, to be twice as good as your oppressor, to impress your oppressor, but then when you learn the rules they change them. . . .

So I think the next move for the people in the Boston area is to begin to feel responsible in some small degree. I was very happy to see that the Black legislators and community people had a press conference yesterday and made their announcement that they were, by any means necessary, going to see that those young people who are trying to go to school in South Boston will do so. And I shall hope that the feminists who've been wondering where their sisters are would see this as an appropriate chance to deal with the racism of their sisters. They've tried long and hard to get Black women to deal with what they saw as the sexism of Black men, and I always told them that that was undiplomatic, tactless, and thoroughly unpolitical. Because the relationship between Black people, in the first place, is much more of a sister-brother relationship—Black people don't have white children, and white people don't have Black children. So the best that Black women can be to white women is good friends. But if, as many white people like to say, the Black women are sisters of the white feminists, then I would certainly think that feminists could at least call a press conference and announce that the racist women who are active, not just in South Boston but in Detroit, Irene McCabe; in New York, under Rosemary Gunning; and here, under Louise Day Hicks, are unacceptable as sisters. And I think even white women who are not feminists should dissociate themselves from this mob, because believe me, when I see them on television, they look just like a mob of feminists; and the only difference is that I know that racism is lower among feminists.

But—*but*—I'm wondering where are those women who are so ardently concerned about the lack of Black representation in the feminist movement? I had a cynical feeling that they needed them for scarecrows to frighten the white men, and when I listened for a word on the Boston situation from the feminist community, and I get this hollow silence, then that cynicism is reinforced. And I'm hoping that in the upcoming weeks we will see some press activity—I don't expect people to go into South Boston and be torn apart like that man was, but the very least that should happen is that the feminist movement, the student movement, the anti-war people should stir their bodies to get on the line, at least rhetorically, and make statements to the press indicating the lack of support for that scene. Because silence is collaboration, and there's no rape without struggle, it's just a bad screw.

There's a little story I've been telling about strategy, and it applies to the church, to the media, to the police, the government, business, everyone. It's the story of a woman who's at the dentist, and she's leaning back in the chair. She's a very square lady, and I don't mean Kimberley knit square, I mean house dress square. So she's leaning back in the chair and the dentist has worked on her for about three minutes, and all of a sudden he realizes that she has managed to obtain a very tight grip on his testicles, and she's squeezing just short of agony. So he stops and says, "What is this?" And she says, "We are not going to hurt each other, are we, doctor?"

Now after five years of feminism and twenty years after the Brown versus the Board of Education decision, I'm urging you to assume the testicular approach, not just in rape but certainly in rape, and recognize

96 With Wilma Scott Heide, ex-President of NOW, International Women's Year Conference, Mexico City, 1975

that anyone that's close enough to hurt you can be hurt. And I really think that you've got to seize the time, and the time is now. And you must move through your votes, through your dollars, and through your bodies to confront and get on the record in this particularly pathological situation. Even if it's over today, you must pay some kind of dues for the racism that you've permitted, and the oppression. See, this is not just for Black people, this is a bid for power, and it's question of who is going to lead you in the Boston area for the decades to come.

So your job is to watch the leaders of this anarchy—in the real sense the greatest anarchy we've seen in this particular area. It is not unique—after all, the American Nazi Party went to school board meetings in San Francisco—so it is happening all over the country. But use your dollars, use your votes, don't underestimate your power as students and as people. And if they tell you you're not ready, you just say, "Ready or not, here we come." Thank you.

"Most people are not taught to understand that the two o'clock orgasm leads to the three o'clock feeding."

From the keynote speech delivered at the Second National Hooker's Convention, San Francisco, June 21, 1975, Margo St. James, chairperson and presiding madam.

Yeah . . . Give 'em the fist, give 'em the finger, okay, thank you all. . . . Now I've been around a few times, and most of you have heard what I have to say—I just want to say a couple of new things, and split. But I have to say some of the old things too, 'cause they're soooo important. I don't want a single human being not understand some of the basic formulas I rely on when I talk about prostitution.

When I talk about prostitution, I'm talking about the symptoms of a pathological society. The treatment of whores is just part of the symptomatology of the pall of guilt that is used to make them think there is something wrong with them!

The chocolate covering on the shit of housewifery and the shit covering on the chocolate of prostitution is part of an oppressive society. It's absolutely necessary in order to control people, and get them to want to take the shit you dump on them. You must make them think they are not *entitled* to freedom from corruption or freedom from oppression. One of the ways you do that is to extend the pall of guilt. You must select something that is common to all people to establish the pall of guilt. Even though sex is not fungible, it is identifiable in each type of person. If you can use sexuality as a *modus operandi* for oppression, you've got a rather simple way to get at the people. So if you think about it—you're pregnant, you're guilty! Although they tell you you are most beautiful when you're pregnant, all the models who epitomize beauty have skinny waistlines. So they're shitting you right from the start.

This fucking business is supposed to be a really great thing. Here in

America they try to make the college person, or the person who isn't married, that hasn't made his or her choice and is still drifting, think this fuck thing is so beautiful that you've got to go out and buy perfume. You've got to get a girdle, a bra, spray under your pretty little arms and between your pretty little legs, and so forth.

Now you see, that is a crock. Most people are not taught to understand that the two o'clock orgasm leads to the three o'clock feeding. So they lure you into a situation where they can control you better. If you have the three o'clock feeding, the diaper service, the screaming meemies all day and all night, then obviously you can't get out there and fight the fuckers. Okay? This thing has you isolated at home, in a little cubicle, and the way they got you there is to make this fuck thing so beautiful.

Of course, in the meantime, after the first two or three screaming meemies, you start getting kinda down on the fuck. In the meantime, the same guy that got you so hot that you thought marriage was going to be anything but a crock of shit is now ready to split. You're ready to split, you don't wanna fuck 'cause you don't want any more kids. Then they try to block off the only way out, which is being a whore.

George Hilton, the economist, gave a very good speech in which he said it was a question of control. The way you control people is to keep them poor, keep them isolated, keep them ignorant, keep them in the dark, and put plenty of shit on them like you would a mushroom. Now in order

With Reverend Cecil Williams, Margo St. James, and Robin Tyler at COYOTE's First Hookers Convention, Glide Memorial Church, San Francisco, 1974

to do all these things you've got to trap them really good, and marriage is about as good a way as any.

The common denominator being sexuality, it's good to make it bad from the start, make it the guilt area. It smells. All right? Now we could say Chanel No. 5 smells bad, and if that were the case they wouldn't sell any. But they say your body smells bad, at the same time saying that all the thrills and beauty come from this area—but the smell is terrible. Now the smell is endemic to the organ, so you can place guilt on the odor, 'cause that would be consistent with every person. And so, y'all be scrubbing and rubbing and if you've got vaginal jelly you gotta be careful what you do, 'cause it may not taste good.

But the point is, besides the practical aspect of all these little problems, you've got to make such confusion in terms of media, government, business, church, until nobody knows what the fuck is going on. So what you've got to do is render one alternative to the missionary position, the marital thing. You've gotta fix it so there is a way out. And the way you do that is turn the victim into the villain and the villain into the victim. So they say the whore is being oppressed by the pimp. As far as I'm concerned, if the women want them to help transact their business, it's their choice. It's like a partnership. If a whore wants a pimp, it's a business arrangement and I kinda like the idea—even if the pimp takes all the money, I kinda dig the idea of the woman being the one to have the money to give to the motherfucker. The fact is, she is controlling finances. Everybody says they get beaten up and everything else, but the fact is, plenty of housewives get beaten up. . . .

Radicalism's Rudest Mouth: "Women are not necessarily good—oppression doesn't make people better."

From Some of My Best Friends Are Men, *the first national television series created by women, produced by Margo Lane for the Canadian Broadcasting Corporation, July 4, 1975*

Carol Gault: A lot of people I talk to today seem to think that the "issue of women is something that they're getting tired of—they're looking for some new way of hearing about it, or they think that they've heard everything already.

Flo: Well, nobody ever gets tired of jockocracy. We have a tremendous preoccupation with balls in your country and in mine, and no one ever says, "We've done football," they say, "We've done abortion"; they don't say, "We've done baseball," they say, "We've done prostitution." So you see there are certain subjects that no one seems to get tired of, and I'm always suspicious of people that get tired of truth. The only people who are tired of hearing about women's issues are probably people who wish for another half an hour of sports scores.

I think that the feminists of your society and mine have been covered with manure, the way we covered pacifists with manure. We make war attractive and we make people who are against killing unattractive, so people want to disavow connection with the bad niggers. And I'm not just talking about Black people, I'm talking about oppressed people being niggerized. But they want to disassociate themselves: "This one is ugly—she's a witch"; "This one is cute—she's a whore"; "This one is loud in her demands for fair treatment—she's a big mouth"; "This one is quiet—she has no sense of humor"; "This one is intellectual—she's a bluestocking"; "This one is not intellectual—she's a militant." She doesn't own a gun, a B-52, or napalm, but she's a militant.

They're trying to please Daddy; almost every family of four or five children has one Goody Two-Shoes, and the Goody Two-Shoes among women are the nonrebels. And they're also made very nervous; if we are right about the right to choose whether you want to become a mother, think how many mothers fell into the trick bag, and what are they going to do now? It's easier to get mad at the feminists than it is to get mad at your husband; he's bad enough as it is.

Every woman is not a feminist; in my country a Louise Day Hicks is already in politics, and I think of her as a monster—she's certainly no sister of mine. And we've got people like Irene McCabe. The women's movement is not only feminism in the States, and I'm sure there are many pathological women's groups up here. In the States the largest group of political women are preoccupied with keeping Black youngsters from sitting with the white trash, and they're walking the streets of South Boston.

So it has never been my thesis that women are necessarily good. I've never thought that oppression makes people better; oppression, in my opinion, is not good for you. And women are sneaky and hostile, and oppressive; they beat up their kids, they scream at the butcher, they mistreat their parents—they're just as pathological as anyone else. Otherwise, it would appear that people are improved by oppression, and I don't believe that. We must be very careful about the women we select; don't forget Phyllis Schlafly, down in the States.

And your poor little Miss Trudeau, unfortunately, occasionally makes statements that seem to be disconnected from her brain, or maybe she is not a very keen observer, or maybe she's trying to polish apples. And of course her circumstances aren't bad, although I gather she's somewhat nervous, but at least she tries. But even she seems confused. So I don't have any critical attitude about women.

Carol Gault: Let's take the stereotyped trapped suburban housewife who wants to change her life or improve it in some way—how can she, and others that she organizes with, most effectively do something to get some of those changes?

Flo: Oh, but they're doing it. Women are defeating men all over the lot, and I'm surprised that so few women are running for office, relatively speaking, here in Canada. But I think, in the upcoming elections, after we've seen how difficult it is to get abortion legalized and to decriminalize it, there will be more women running. I think women should run for office. It doesn't matter that they won't win, because as they run—especially if they offer a program like drawing all of your money out of commercial banks, like not voting unless you get a commitment from the person running for office that he or she will favor the decriminalization of prostitution and/or abortion—I think the politicians, who after all are in many ways like prostitutes, will begin to service the women's community.

But I don't recommend to suburban housewives the same testicular approach that I might recommend to a bunch of angry feminists, or women on welfare with very little to lose. If you ask what would *I* do, I think we should seriously discuss castration for rape. We should expose the background and foreground and sex habits and all the other unpleasant habits of judges who send people like Dr. Morgenthaler to jail.

Carol Gault: What about the woman who says, "I'm quite satisfied. I don't need any of these changes"?

Flo: I'm not even talking to her. I am not talking to anybody that's satisfied. And I think that Johnny Carson and Dick Cavett and the various women's shows are talking to all kinds of women. I talk to a specific group of people. I'm not running for office, I'm not trying to recruit anybody—I don't mind if the Indian woman doesn't have any interest in sexism and doesn't feel abused. Again, it's like a honeymoon night and a rape—the difference is consent. . . .

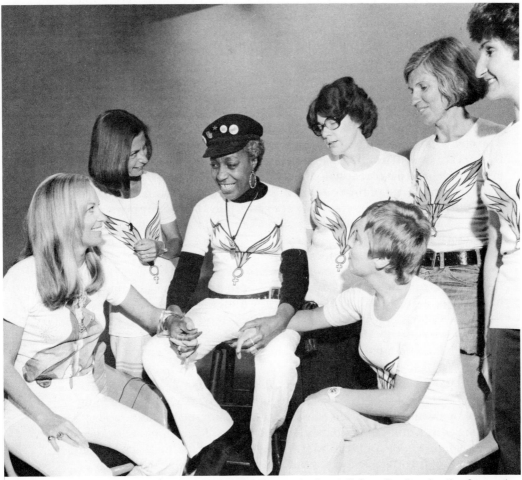

With Margo Lane and the *Some of My Best Friends Are Men* production staff, Canadian Broadcasting Corporation, Toronto, 1975

"It's a question of whether you want to eat manure or starve. I just think that there ought to be an alternative."

From a discussion with Norman Mailer and Black journalist Marian Watson on Midday Live, WNEW-TV, *New York, July 22, 1975, recorded by Alice Sant'Andrea*

Flo: I think of you as a professional jockocrat and I'm just so annoyed at jockocracy; that's a society where the aristocracy is based on sports. Just look at the media coverage and the six-figure book advances. I also put the space race and the whole Soyuz-Apollo scene into the jockocratic framework. And I see a clear relationship between militarism, jockocracy, and sexism.

Jockocracy involves the body bit, whether it's sex, sports, or dancing. You have a society where there are changes being demanded and people want in on the pie or the corruption or both. Then you have the problem of where you're going to let them in, and sports is a safe place because they make a lot of money, get to be very big stars. The demands are satisfied and yet they have no part in the controls of society or government, business or banks, or any place where there could be serious social change. And for women to become as interested in sports as men are, I think is part of the trick bag, tracking women through HEW Title IX interpretation into sports seems to me sort of a repetition of what happened to Black people. It's a safe place to put them where they can make a lot of money.

Mailer: I think the question is more complex than that, Flo. Why not take off after the entertainment business or the record business? Everything in this country is a hustle, so why settle on sports or jockocracy? Sure, sports is a hustle. What goes on in a ring when you have two men who are the best fighters is a human drama on a grand scale. It's down in all that corporate mire, down in all the corruption of this country. But if you are going to talk about the corruption of this country, there is nothing to talk about but that.

Sports contests of a certain sort are marvelous. I think for people who follow boxing, it [the Foreman-Ali fight at Zaire] had a separate value of a special sort. It had a lot of value for me. I identify with Ali in a lot of ways. I never had any illusions that there was the least bit in common between us except for one thing. I have thought of Ali for many years as a great artist. Here's this artist who's slightly over the hill—can he come back? Because to me it meant a great deal in terms of my own life.

Marian Watson: You made a very disgusting remark yesterday on the *Today* show. You said Muhammad Ali in most probability would be running for president of the United States. You don't know anything about Muslims.

Mailer: I didn't say that he would probably be running. I said he might be running and that if he did, I would vote for him. I'm quite aware that to the degree that Muslims are what they are at this point, he would not be running. But I think there may be huge changes. I was thinking of the huge changes in this country and it is quite possible that the Black Muslim movement will go through profound changes, too. They have already.

Holding a jock strap at the NOW Atlantic City Conference, 1974 ▶

Marian Watson: It does not surprise me that anyone would say that Muhammad Ali should run for president. But I don't think you were serious.

Mailer: I don't go around making remarks like that without being serious because I put my bottom in the fan. I said it because I really believe it. I think he really would make a good president. I've seen the way he handles people. He's got a marvelous judgment of people. He's got a marvelous head. He's a tremendously intelligent person. I've seen him grow in twelve years. About running for president, I didn't say tomorrow. In eight or ten years, if he continues to grow, he's going to be an extraordinary figure. I also wanted to give people a bit of a shock because there's a tremendous tendency to think of the people who are in the presidency as having to be divinely suited for it by becoming lawyers and serving thirty years in Congress.

[On the issue of men and women competing against one another in sports:]

Flo: Yes, because that's part of the whole body bit. The CON game, the Control of Niggers. Get everybody body-to-body in one way or another. You can focus a whole society on bodies in action, this drama of bodies fighting bodies, making love, bodies in the movies, bodies dancing. But women fighting men will be great box office and we will naturally have it.

Mailer: Everything Flo says, I half agree with. At least I agree with the part that it is a hype and it's being used. And it's a hustle. Actually, I think this culture is too oriented toward mind. There's nothing wrong with leaning over toward body. This country was built with bodies, not minds. And what's the alternative to these bodies? It's the computer. About the time that people divorce themselves from their bodies, the computer takes

At the International Women's Year Conference, Mexico City, 1975

over everything. As between the two, I'll take all this phoney hyped-up super-sports.

Flo: Well, it's a question of whether you want to eat manure or starve. I just think there ought to be an alternative.

Mailer: No, it's a question of whether you eat goat turds or owl stuff.

Flo: When you tell me this is all there is, if you go from bodies, you go to computers, then I agree that things are pretty bad. But what are we doing about the American Bar Association, the American Medical Association, the real estate community, the bankers who are throwing the city of New York to the wolves? Mayor Beame, the uniformed services, and half of the citizenry should be on their way to Washington to say, "No, we don't want a $1.2 billion Navy ship that Smiling Whitey Ford wants. We don't want $35 billion to go into armaments every year."

The more that we are involved with who's going to win the fight, what's your astrological sign, how does you hand read, what dance are you going to do, the more the Stennises and Smiling Whiteys and Tricky Dicks are going to take the bulk of the money and give the whole society pentagonorrhea.

[On violence between men and women]

Flo: I think there has been a one-sided fight that goes on between men and women. Assaults on women are much more widespread—for example, rape, which is terrible and of great concern to me. It's also a matter of racism. If you're going to get raped, try to see to it that it's your Black or Puerto Rican super, if you want the world to take it seriously.

In my opinion, women getting ready to defend themselves is important. I think the jockocratic aspect of fighting professionally and making money is good, even if she gets knocked out. Many women were getting knocked out when I was doing matrimonial law. I do hope that some women can defend themselves in marriage and against rape. . . .

"No matter how high you fly, when they want your ass they'll bring you right back down into the gutter."

Hurricane Carter is the former middleweight boxer who, with his co-defendant John Artis, is out on appeal from a life sentence for murder, after serving ten years, on the basis of an alleged prosecution frameup.

On January 13, 1976, I went to visit Hurricane Carter in prison in Clinton, New Jersey. I had heard Hurricane Carter on the Bob Fass show on WBAI, this eloquent Black man—and believe me, there's a shortage of eloquent Black men who have suffered and understand, and still have courage and some part of their balls left, after the motherfuckers have tried their damnedest to grind them and their balls into hamburger. So here's this man talking from prison with much more vigor and enthusiasm and understanding of the political reality than most of us out here who are living like worms.

So I called up Hurricane Carter, whom I'd never spoken to, but of course I'd been hearing about his case, and frequently when you can turn somebody into a super-nigger you can get a little justice for him. The necessity to turn people into super-niggers before they can get justice is one of the reasons I stopped practicing criminal law, and ultimately stopped practicing altogether, although as a hustle I still practice it when I want to, for politics. Because I realized that the law was not set up for justice for anybody that I cared about—it may be justice for the landlords and the banks and the television networks and the telephone companies, to get multimillion dollar rate rises, but when it came to the people I cared about, justice was nonexistent. And the only way you could get justice for them was to prove yourself a super-lawyer, to work like a son of a bitch practically around the clock for virtually no money, or else to make your client a super-nigger—and a nigger doesn't have to be a Black person.

And so if you can turn them into a super-nigger, and work like a super-lawyer and become niggerized by all these judges, then maybe you can get justice for them. But now that my hustle is different, lecturing on campuses, I find that every so often I've got to go back into the law because someone's ass got caught in the wringer.

We met in Carter's "office," a cell which prison officials permit him to use to work on his appeal.

Flo: When you came in, I said, "hurry," because I try to shorten everything, being kind of old and trying to save my breath. I was shortening your name—I wasn't trying to rush you. And all of a sudden I realized that that is what we've got to do about getting you out—*hurry.* We done stalled it long enough.

Hurricane: You ain't old. For those who love deeply—and you love deeply, because that's what you've been doing, fighting these fights all this long time—those who love deeply, they never grow old. Oh, they may die of old age, but they die young. So you ain't old—you're young, man.

Flo: Well, I'm a johnny-janie-come-lately, and I'm not trying by any means to take this over, but what I want to do is in this one day set in motion something which I hope the citizens would carry on. What I'm prepared to do is announce a national committee to recall Governor Byrne and to urge an inquiry leading to a determination whether or not impeachment is the appropriate remedy regarding all the public officials involved in your case: the trial judge, Varner, who had the initial jurisdiction over the trial in the first instance; the prosecuting attorney from Passaic County; and the Essex County prosecutor, who is now the governor, and who therefore doesn't have access to the innocence and ignorance trip that a normal racist, innocent, ignorant governor would have.

Now within the next four weeks I will be speaking in four states. I'm going to Alabama, Georgia, Florida, and California, and I will bring you back a minimum of ten names from each of those states supporting this recall, because the campus people that I talk to would be prepared, in the worst school I would ever go to, to give me ten names—I may bring fifteen, I may bring twenty. When I say a "national committee," I mean that literally. So I would like you to authorize me to get this petition together and announce it and then carry it with me when I leave, do New York before I leave, so that with all the people in CARS (Coalition Against Racism and Sexism), I could leave here with five or six hundred signatures at the very least.

Because I think all the good people who tried to do it the reasonable way, with letters and petitions and requests and radio programs and concerts and fund-raising and lawyers, should by now be ready for somebody crazy. And that's what I would like to supply, the crazy element to this, which is to get this son of a bitch's ass!

Carter: Well, I don't know if that's crazy, or intelligent. If we keep knocking at the door, and yet we know that door can be opened and the people standing behind the door won't open it, then you've got the right to take that door off the hinges. It's time to bring people together, all kinds of people, because people are certainly ready.

Flo: I usually hide from this kind of thing, because I've got too much on my plate already, so I hide and think, "Well, it's going to be all right somehow," and then the motherfuckers won't do it and won't do it, and finally, running and hiding, I just feel myself completely cornered. So I think the time is now, and when I get cornered and can't be innocent any longer, when I finally have to admit that the shit has done gone on long enough and I get tired, then I can't be patient any longer.

It's against my principles to go to the raped victim—when I see somebody getting raped by the major Establishment, my choice is whether to catch the rapist or apply Vaseline to the rapee's ass. Coming down here is taking some of the last little bit of Vaseline I got left, and I want to go after this son of a bitch's ass. So you can't really stop me. I'd like to get your formal permission, or at least your acknowledgment that you don't have any objection to my doing this thing, but I don't ask permission to get the motherfucker, 'cause you're a hostage—they've got you as a hostage from the Black community. And that to me is really serious, because that means they're taking our best and most articulate people and putting them in prison, to destroy them, and to destroy us! When the vice-president of ITT is being held hostage in South America, the authority of the whole company is diminished. My authority, my freedom, my lack of inhibition is limited as long as you are a hostage, but as long as I can pretend, "Well, he's going to be all right, they're going to deliver him home any minute now, he's got Bobby Dylan, he's got Ali, he's got Ellen Burstyn," well, I'm thinking, "Do they need this poor, broken-down middle-aged colored lady with three feet of intestines missing and a fused spine? There ain't nothing I can do that they can't do—they're white, they're young, they're Black, they're strong." And then finally, when it gets on my personal plate, then I've got to do something.

Carter: I want to give you this copy of my book, and this is what I wrote in it for you: "To my beautiful, tough-fighting sister Flo, welcome to the fight, old friend. And look out, you simpleminded political monsters, because now that my sister Flo is there we are going to win this sixteenth round in short order, because we are only seeking to find peace. But we are intelligent enough to know that peace can only come after the struggle, because freedom and justice have got to come first, and only then will there be peace."

Since I've been here I've had to put down being a prizefighter. Since I've been here behind these walls, I've seen that all the warriors—and I'm a warrior, I love to fight, and not only do I love to fight, I *can* fight, I'm a winner—but I've seen throughout these years that many of the he-males are acting and looking like females, and so there's not too many warriors left out there. So I saw that if I had to fight, I was fightin' by myself. So you had to stop bein' a warrior and start bein' a teacher. So I did have to study the law, and I became very proficient in the law. And if we start to impeach Byrne, that will give them an issue to give it back to the politicians—.

Flo: All right, let me tell you something, honey. Their ass just ain't that strong. We thought when we picketed the White House that they didn't pay any attention. We thought when we picketed the Waldorf and they came in on those demonstrations, they weren't taking notice. But honey, we discovered that Nixon was freaking out because *one man* was picketing. They are not cool. I will listen to any remedy that is superior to this one, but I want to tell you, honey, I've been around these kinds of people, and they really are weak. See, they're not like you, they can't stand any pressure. It's like the story I always tell, there's this Black lady at the dentist's, and she's not smart, she ain't got no mink, nothin', she ain't nothin' like we are—she ain't a smart-ass Black lady, she's just a very intelligent but very square lady. And the dentist, once he hit her tongue with his drill, then he hit the inside of her jaw, and just now he hit her gum. So all of a sudden he becomes aware that she has a fairly tight grip on his testicles, and he stops, not daring to move, and says, "What is this?" She looks up at him with a very pleasant expression, very benign, and she says, "Now, we're not going to hurt each other, are we, doctor?"

Now you are the patient, and you've had evidence that there was perjured testimony, you've had two versions, led by their Black designee, and so forth. And now we got the testicles. Honey, they can't afford to find out how much we can squeeze—giving it back to politicians is the last thing he wants to do, because there are a lot of politicians in this thing that want his ass. And they might just as soon turn us loose on him just to get rid of him. So I would be willing to take my chances on this.

See, this is a jockocracy, and you are a jock, and if they're making it this hard for you, then what's going to happen to a plain old nigger? An athlete is a de-niggerized nigger, so you're an aristocrat among Black people. When they take an aristocrat and *re*-niggerize him after they done *de*-niggerized him, then you know how tentative de-niggerization is, and how little we can any of us count on it. It doesn't matter if you're a lawyer, if you're a judge like Bruce Wright, you turn in your balls with your long black dress, and then you can be re-niggerized in one fell swoop, that is to let everybody know that when you get de-niggerized, re-niggerization is just around the corner. Because what they're saying to the world is, no matter how high you fly, when we want your ass we'll bring you right back down into the gutter.

With John Lindsay on *AM America*, ABC-TV, 1975

"Racism is coast to coast and border to border."

Interview with Robert Abrams, Borough President of the Bronx, on The Urban Challenge, *WNYC-TV, New York, January 25, 1976:*

Bob: Flo Kennedy has been described as one of the loudest, rudest, and most audacious people you can find anywhere. Yet while that may be true, I seem to find her one of the softest, kindest people I know. So I guess she is an absolutely irrepressible and incongruous person. People who may be meeting her for the first time will get to know what I am talking about. . . .

Flo, what do we have to do to bring about changes in this society?

Flo: The first thing we have to do is to stop shucking each other. I mean when we had the city crisis, for example, and we had the mayor and the governor and people running around pretending to solve it, never talking about the multibillion dollar armaments budget, it was perfectly obvious that all we had to do was to declare a moratorium on arms spending. Okay? The fact is that neither Carey nor Beame nor anybody else talked about leading the uniformed unemployed people, the uniformed service people who were threatening to strike. Can you believe we have gone back two or three decades by taking the pensions of workers who worked for the city government? Can you believe that we are continuing to pay those incredible, horrible debt services, as they call it, which is money to banks?

Even those of us who are not damaged by closeups and shutdowns and all are being shucked by the banks. We should march on the banks, obviously, in my opinion. Do you understand that I put a $2,200 deposit in the bank about twelve days ago and it needed fifteen days to cover it? In the first place, you have charter banks, about ten charter banks. So if you bank at Dime Savings Bank and probably the First Women's Bank you are actually adding four or five days of the bank's right to control your money. They have millions and millions, probably billions of dollars of savings of us good people (you know, like the good people in Germany who didn't know what was going on at Dachau ten miles away). They take our money and they hold it lo these many days, and I feel this is the kind of issue that politicians should be concerned about. I am going to talk to my friend who is an official of the New York State Savings Bank Association and see what he is going to do about it. But there's terrible discrimination in the banking community against the good people. I am not talking now about the women, or the Black people, or the gay people, all of whom I adore. Or the farm workers or ex-prison inmates or the ex-mental hospital patients. I am talking about the good secretaries and nurses and domestic workers and housewives. And these good people put their pittances in the banks, and these charter banks, by refusing to issue new charters, hold millions and millions of dollars and get the interest on it, and we in the meantime continue to have to pay, in addition to all that, these tremendous debt services—what is it, one and a half billion dollars?

Bob: Let me ask you this. We know you are critical of many in our city, state, and federal government. Are there any out there in the public arena whom you admire?

Flo: Oh, yes; I demand less of people the higher they go. Now a lot of anti-Establishmentarians don't believe in the electoral process, but I dig all the members of the Black caucus, and I dig most of the women in the women's caucus that I know. Now there are some right-wing women—I don't dig Louise Day Hicks, who is a pig—I call her a sow—and I don't dig Rosemary Gunning, for example. But most of the women in politics that are not utter sows and pigs, I dig. My own choices of presidential candidates are Fred Harris and Julian Bond, if he runs, and I dig Birch Bayh. My favorites are my favorites, but I usually have one favorite who can win and another favorite who can't win, but needs a small check and a little help. I think we should be active in everything we like. When you go to the dentist, you don't want the dentist telling you about your good teeth, you want the dentist telling you about what's wrong with you. I see myself concerned with the pathology of oppression and I find myself acting as a pathologist. I talk for the most part in public about what I find is wrong.

Bob: You are known as the friend of the underdog. Who are some of the underdogs with whom you are siding?

Flo: Well I'm still siding with Rap Brown, who is up in prison full of gunshot wounds. I am still siding with Joanne Chesimard, and with the future of Joann Little. I am very concerned about Inez Garcia, and about Yvonne Wanrow, a native American whose child was molested by an old man who also raped the babysitter's kid and gave her venereal disease, and then when he came in at five o'clock in the morning drunk and falling all over and lurching toward her three-year-old, and Yvonne had a broken leg, she shot and killed him. Now she is facing twenty years. I want to know what people like Scoop-the-Poop Jackson are going to do about that. He is concerned about Soviet Jewry, but he is not worried about the Indians in the State of Washington. In fact, if you say something to him about a reservation, he will think you are talking about a Holiday Inn.

Bob: You are not criticizing him for his concern for the treatment of Soviet Jewry! You want his concern to be broader than that?

Flo: I am, in the sense that I think he is a shuck. I think he is very concerned about maintaining the armaments level, but I think he uses the need to arm Israel as a way to keep Boeing happy. But I may be wrong about that. If Jews in the Soviet Union are oppressed, as they undoubtedly are, then he is entitled to be concerned about that. But if that concern is really a part of the fact that he wants armaments sold in what we call the Middle East—we don't like to say North Africa. We don't like the word Africa used any more than it has to be, so we say Middle East, but the fact is, it is Africa. Now that Angola is bursting open, there's a whole implication of arming so many people around Israel, Syria, Saudi Arabia, the whole area is beginning to have much more significance to the Black people. The connection between arming the North African area and the fate of the Angolas of this country is getting more important because much of the armaments are coming by way of that area, and it is a complicated matter. I think it is all right for Jackson to be concerned about Soviet Jewry; I think every Jewish person and non-Jewish person should be concerned about the oppression of Jews and Israelis or anyone else. What I am saying is that I suspect his motives, since this native American woman from Spokane, Washington, his own state, is getting such a terrible deal, and the native Americans up there in Yakima are having horrible times.

Bob: Our time is running out, and I would like to have your assessment of race relations in America today.

Flo: I went to "Wednesdays in Mississippi" about 1964 with a group of Black and white women. We went to Jackson and out into the hinterlands, and on the plane coming back I said to them, "You know, racism is not limited to Mississippi," and what I say now when I lecture in the South is that they have no corner on racism. Boston and Louisville, not to mention Canarsie and Forest Hills, and the recent Channel 13 special on Rosedale, show us that racism is coast to coast and border to border. I was in Canada and Australia this summer, and sexism is like a bad case of athlete's foot or a toothache. You don't want either one, but racism is the crux of the worst problem in the world, in my opinion.

Bob: Are we doing better or worse than white-dominated countries elsewhere in terms of our race relations?

Flo: In some ways we are much better than Australia. The first aboriginal graduated from college only in 1962, but we have a lot of Black people who are college graduates in this country.

Bob: Our time is up, the irrepresible Flo Kennedy. Thank you very much.

Flo Kennedy and Her 'Pro Rata Share'

Flo Kennedy is a walking, talking example of activism in the Seventies. To catch the flavor of her personality and her views, reporter Melinda Voss interviewed her and listened to her speak at a race relations conference recently at Drake University in Des Moines.

By Melinda Voss
(Register Staff Writer)

If Florynce Kennedy tells you she's "just a middle-aged colored lady," don't believe her.

She's much more than that. Her saucy tongue and sharp brain have taken her through Columbia University Law School and placed her at the forefront of various liberation struggles for the past 20 years.

"I'm for people coming together to challenge oppressors," she says.

At 58, Flo says her "hustle" is talking — when she's not writing books, attending conventions of welfare mothers, creating a new organization or relaxing (if that ever happens).

She has lectured at more than 200 colleges and universities in the past two years. Comparing what she's doing with practicing law, she says:

"It's a much better hustle, plus it's more political because you can say what you want, don't give a damn whether they like it or not and take the next plane out."

Flo is not known for being timid.

Gaining acceptance to Columbia Law School in late 1940s was no easy task for a black person, let alone a black woman.

"They told me they were keeping me out because I was a woman rather than because I was black," says Flo, who has home bases in both New York City and San Francisco. "I told them some of my more cynical friends thought I was being kept out because I was black.

"At that time, blacks were suing schools, so they managed to find a place for me, while a white woman friend of mine, who had better grades than I, got nowhere."

Since then, Flo has taken on

Florynce Kennedy, speaking in Des Moines   (Register Staff Photograph by Thomas Hooper)

the Catholic Church, challenging its tax-exempt status in a suit charging that the church illegally spends money to influence legislation, particularly on abortion.

Flo views politics as a "major sport."

"The fight for any liberation struggle is an interesting fight," she says. "And, frankly, I'm in the struggle against oppression because it's fun, in addition to everything else.

"I could never run for nothing because I'm always making enemies. But that's why I wouldn't run for anything — because I wouldn't be able to make enemies."

Nevertheless, she's self-confident. "I happen to be a very conceited person," she says, "and . . . I have found I can use white people faster than they can use me."

Flo Kennedy probably makes some listeners wince just because she doesn't bother masking her speeches in fancy language. Flo uses the vernacular of "little people."

But if she turns some folks off by her brashness and forthrightness, she also turns others on.

After each of her appearances on the Drake campus — her topics were titled "Black

Women in the Year 2000," "For Women Only" and "The Pathology of Oppression" — people flocked to her.

A founder of the Feminist Party, Ms. Kennedy also is the co-author of one of the first major books on abortion, "Abortion Rap," which she wrote with Diane Schulder. Her second book, "The Pathology of Oppression," is soon to be published by Viking.

Besides being an organizer, Flo goes for individuality.

"I love the idea of individuality," she says, 'That's one of the reasons I continue to wear nail polish, false eyelashes and an Afro."

But, she isn't out to change the whole world.

"I don't think it's my job to drink up the Atlantic Ocean. I just want to deal with my pro rata share," she says.

Her share, means taking a fair number of jabs against the government and other "oppressors."

"Racism is alive and well all over America, just as sexism is alive and well," she says, "And the more out-to-lunch an area is, the easier it is to control."

Her philosophy is perhaps best embodied in one of her frequent sayings:

"Take it easy, but as I always say, take it."

Flo Kennedy is immen[se]ly quotable. Here are a few e[xam]ples from the Drake co[nfer]ence:

● On "oppression" and "[liber]ation":

"Often a person is no[t in] favor of giving money [to a] hospital because they ain't [sick.] But if they suddenly [need] dialysis, they get all ex[cited] about how you're going to [give] access to the kidney mac[hine.] That is damn typical of [the] oppressed mentality."

"What you must underst[and] is oppression does not end [with] the niggers. It does not [end] with the poor people, it doe[sn't] end with the women, or [the] pregnant women. It goes [up] the line to the executive [who] has his bag searched in [the] airport."

"A liberation struggle is [like] a struggle against dirt. [No] matter what type of bath [you] take . . . in three weeks y[ou'll] smell like you've never see[n a] bathtub. What we don't un[der]stand about a libera[tion] struggle is you never win [it] any more than you "win" cl[ean] dishes. As soon as you eat [off] them, the dishes are d[irty] again."

● On the women's moveme[nt:]

"If it's a movement, I so[me]times think it needs a la[xa]tive."

"How can you even [talk] about a movement when you['ve] had 21 years of 'I Love Lu[cy'] and feminism hasn't change[d it?] You got a new series this ye[ar.] What'd you get: 'Dirty Sally.[']

"You don't have to be wh[is]tling Dixie when you're ly[ing] on the ground with a car [on] your ankle. If you're lying [on] the ground with a car on y[our] ankle, it's not your conscie[nce] that needs raising, it's the c[on]science of the person in the [car] that needs raising."

"As far as black women [are] concerned, I would certainly [be] most appalled if they all rush[ed] into the women's moveme[nt.] It's clear that most bla[ck] people should be involved wi[th] the problems of the black libe[r]ation struggle."

"If I were the Establishment and had the big guns, I'd much rather see one lion come through the door than 500 mice."

"Women and the Law," discussion and interview with Lisa Feiner on Outreach: Celebrate Women, *on WNET-TV, New York, produced by Miriam Bogert, Sunday, February 1, 1976*

Lisa Feiner: Flo, do you think the economic crunch is going to hurt women worse than men?

Flo: Well, of course—it always does. Don't forget that the law can be a justice system, but it can also be a niggerizing tool. And institutions treat people differently, in class terms—it's a favorite example where women are concerned to see how law is used to niggerize them. You have the good people protected by the laws, you have the bad people punished by the laws, and then you have what I call the "niggers," not just Black people; it includes the homosexual women, it includes the prostitutes and other focuses of cleanups, like the massage parlors, which don't cause nearly as much damage as cigarettes and liquor in the Times Square area—you have 52,000 people dying from lung cancer every year, and no one ever dies from the ministrations of a massage parlor.

So you find the criminal actually taking women hostage, putting them in prison, in order to make "good women" out of them, and the same things happens with a temporary niggerization, like when a pregnant woman wants to terminate her pregnancy—she too is niggerized by the law.

Lisa: Flo, do you say a person is niggerized when they don't have political power? Is that what you're saying?

Flo: Well, if they have the power, as Alice Sant'Andrea says, they simply do not use it, and what the feminist movement is about, over the protests of many anti-rebel women, is simply to say, "We will try to teach those of you who care how to use the power you have." If you have an electric light bulb and you never turn it on, then it will not give any light, and your iron won't iron unless it's plugged in. So we're trying to plug women into the nature of power, you see, and therefore we want to teach them how to deal with oppressive institutions.

Lisa: Is there any guarantee that women can unite?

Flo: I think unity is a mistake. Let the whores unite, let the lesbians go into the gay community, let each group stay segregated if they want to. It's a mistake to tell people who have been programmed to be horizontally hostile to unite. If I were the Establishment and had the big loaded guns of the various oppressive institutions—law and medicine and the academic community—I would much prefer to see one lion come through the door than 500 mice. So I think it a big mistake to urge people to unite, because then you can set up a Martin Luther King and a Malcolm X and kill off the entire group. . . . It's not that that would be the choice, but we don't have a choice. The housewife is worried about the feminists, the old woman is worried about the kids, the whore is worrying about the feminists, the feminist is deploring the prostitute's status, but everything that happens to a whore is happening to a housewife, and yet we're saying how degrading it is.

So it's important that women organize around the things they agree on, and to those that say, "I'm not for women's lib," my position is if you can't say the whole word after seven years, do us a favor and get out of the way.

. . . I think it's important that women understand the issues, even if they say they're not for the feminist movement, because I distinguish between a feminist and a woman. Recently four Black women gave a luncheon for LaDonna Harris and there was not one empty seat. Now many of those women were not feminists, but the feminist movement has raised the consciousness of every single woman, and I think women's activity in electoral politics is extremely important, but I also think it's important to understand there are at least two kinds of women who get to be politicians. Some of the segregationist women are as bad as the pigs—I call them "sows"—and then there are the other kind, who are just women who are trying to do something to improve society. But I do think that whenever you have a struggle situation, our Establishment makes some women into a kind of whore in the political sense, so that she would do what the john, who may be the racist community or just anti-women, wanted; so the anti-ERA community has the Ku Klux Klan support, the John Birch Society support. And therefore you have people like Phyllis Schlafly, who are anti-women, in my terms, although many women agree with her.

So I think we've got to understand that it's a little more complicated, but struggle always pays off, and whenever women get discouraged I remind them that the barefoot Vietnamese, with no Pentagon, won over a multibillion-dollar machine. So as long as women are prepared to struggle, we don't need everybody. We just need those who are prepared to struggle, and we will affect electoral politics, the banking community, the health community, the Equal Rights Amendment, and all the rest. The media are the reason the ERA does so poorly, because jockocracy is always covered and the ERA is usually whited out.

Lisa: Ann, you have doubts about ERA—maybe we could hash it out right here. What were your doubts?

Ann Giordano: I thought it wasn't as important as the laws we now have on the books, that aren't enforced. What's important is that we change men's attitudes, and the movement seems to me to be geared toward educating women, when it should be thinking about educating men.

Flo: But when Liz Holtzman retired Manny Cellar as head of the House Judiciary Committee, believe me, that educated a lot of politicians. The best education is to put the pressure on the most sensitive area, which I don't want to say on television, and make them understand that if they want to be comfortable, they've got to yield to some of our minimal, peripheral demands. And believe me, Ann Giordano would not have been confused on the ERA had we had an opportunity to spend as many hours talking about the Equal Rights Amendment as they spend on the jockocracy, with the sports and the golf games and the balls rolling around here and there. So what we do is permit the media to spend that time on sports and ignore us, and as long as we do that everyone will be confused. . . .

"If you want to know where the apathy is, you're probably sitting on it."

From a speech at Radford College, Virginia, February 9, 1976

Today is the ninth of February and this is Radford College and most of the people are sitting out there staring, so let's go on with "Striped Christmas." The brave ones are on stage.

I'm dreaming of a striped Christmas
Like Richard Nixon never knew,
Where a sheriff's badge glistens
And Nixon listens
To hear pigs' feet come and go,
I'm dreaming of a striped Christmas,
May courts continue to indict,
And may futures of poor Blacks be bright,
And more prisoners be wealthy and white.

Okay. Everybody that came up and sang is invited back to my room after everything is over tonight. We'll have some cookies and we'll talk about bravery. It's always nice to reward the people that get up off their ass.

We're going to talk about niggerization, but not just about niggerization of Black people. Although of course we are the original niggers, and as a matter of fact we're not exactly proud about being the original niggers but we're sometimes a little jealous when other people try to compete with us. So we're sometimes uncomfortable about feminism, and sometimes we take the position that the Environmental Protection activity is an attempt to take center stage, and of course my position is that any time you're on center stage and somebody else attempts to take it, just don't let him push you off. Just stay there and be glad they joined you, because in this society there are not too many people ready to take center stage, as you've just seen.

We really weren't going to do anything particularly dangerous or anything that would get you arrested or in trouble, we were just going to sing some slightly impudent songs, and look how scary it was for a lot of people. And those are some of the people who whine and complain the most. I normally find that people who complain about apathy are frequently people who themselves are apathetic and really need an excuse for their own apathy. They say, "This is an apathetic town," as if that somehow keeps them from doing their number, right? And I don't think that any of us is free from that tendency. I think it's normal in a pathological society. Regardless of how many of us try to be analysts or doctors, in connection with that pathology, we're all subject to it. A doctor who is dealing with an epidemic is not immune from the epidemic or from that disease which causes the epidemic. So just because some of us try to understand the nature of the pathology of our society, we're not saying that we are not ourselves subject to those symptoms.

Now what I try to do in explaining about the apathy of our society is to combine that explanation with a few remedies and a few techniques and a few strategies and a few tips as to how to deal with that particular pathology. I'm not here to change a lot of people's minds and I'm not here to ingratiate myself. I'm not really here to make friends, although I may incidentally influence some people. You see, I've long ago discovered that when we go to the dentist, he or she may hurt us, but the fact remains that we still go. So if I'm right about any number of things, and I'm sure I'm wrong about a lot of them, what I'm saying is my attempt to give you what I think you need to have in this short period of time that I'm going to be on this campus.

But I really don't care whether I'm loved, respected, whatever, so any of you who feel like leaving, or if you really have to leave legitimately or illegitimately or whatever, don't hesitate. Sometimes people say, "Gee, about twenty people walked out on you." Of course if twenty people walk out on me, I'll just talk to the red seats. But when they say that, I say, "You know, I get a little nervous if somebody doesn't walk out." Because you see, if you're really trying to change society, you scare people. And if you're talking to scared people, they're liable just to faint, in a body. So as far as I'm concerned, I'm not doing what the average people who come here are trying to do. I'm sixty years old day after tomorrow, so I'm not going to pass this way ever again, right?

Somebody's here who heard me on the Phil Donahue show. But you see when I go on these TV shows, I'm pretty obnoxious because I happen to think that this is a very obnoxious society, and I don't think that people who are suffering from an obnoxious society have to get on and call it our beloved country. And I understand that there are different techniques for survival, so even though I may not have the highest respect for Pearl Bailey or Sammy Davis, Jr., or any of the rest of the people that suck the pigs of our society, I'm not suggesting that they're wrong, because I also see what happens to the Eartha Kitts of our society. She spoke at a party given by the Johnson crowd and told Ladybird something about the war in Vietnam, and immediately the CIA or the FBI was on her ass and she managed to get a big dossier, and Black people didn't say shit. They applauded her for coming out against the power structure, but when they didn't hear her records or see her on these crappy talk shows, they just forgot about her.

And we have done the same thing in the general community about Supreme Court Justice William O. Douglas. All of us who relate to the civil rights or civil liberties area of our society know that William O. Douglas was one of the best Supreme Court Justices we had—and that isn't saying a hell of a lot, because you know if he'd been any better, he'd probably have been killed or wiped out. And even as it was, there were attempts to impeach him, one of which was led by Smilin' Whitey Jerry Fraud, whom y'all call President Ford. And you see how he was hounded off the Supreme Court bench by the pigocrats of this society with the cooperation of the media—you know how the media have a way of shit-covering the chocolate and chocolate-covering the shit, and one of their tricks is to make something good rotten and something rotten good. . . .

To get back to the show that one of the singers mentioned, this was the Phil Donahue Show, in Chicago. I went on that show and I was feeling very crazy. At my age you don't have to worry about who's going to dig you, so I wore my Super-Dike shirt which was given to me by some gay friends of mine in San Francisco. I'm nervous too about this issue of lesbianism, but my moxie overcame my nervousness and so I wore this shirt. And I'm thinking to myself, I got it all worked out in my head. What you have to do when you're scared about anything political is to work it out in your head, get your answers first, because by now, even if you're only eighteen or nineteen, you've got their criticism in your head. You know what they're going to say. But instead of saying, "Oh, no, I'm not going to do that," you're supposed to say, "Let me figure now, what is the political answer to that attitude?" I call it KMA, Kiss My Ass, but you're supposed to work out your own because you probably don't use that kind of language.

So I'm going to Chicago to do the Phil Donahue Show, and I'm going to wear this Super-Dike shirt. But I wanted the lesbian community to understand that I realize that to lesbians who are kind of hip, "dike" is like "nigger"; if any white person comes to my house with a shirt that says "nigger," they're going to have to do some quick explaining. So I explained at the outset that this had been given to me by a gay group, that it wasn't just a commercial thing, that I wasn't just trying to be cute. Then we do the show, and I sing this song, "My Country, 'Tis of Thee, Sweet Land of Bigotry," which offends everybody, which I had anticipated, obviously, and now I finally get a call. Phil comes running up and says, "Do you want to take a hostile call, Flo?" And I say, "Sure." I love a chance to be evil or crazy.

And this lady gets on, a cupcake, Susie Cream Cheese, and she says, "Who do you think you are? What do you think you are, why don't you stay in your place, why don't you help your own people?" meaning Black people. At the end of it, her voice rises in indignation and she says, "And besides, you're a lesbian!" Now that is supposed to be the ultimate put-down, but for some reason I did not get pissed. Sometimes I just don't feel like getting pissed. I get very easily pissed, I'm the most pissable person you ever saw in your life, but I was in a silly mood.

So I said, "Now, see there," in a very patient voice. "Just because I'm wearing my Super-Dike sweatshirt, you think I'm a lesbian." I said, "I guess if I were wearing a string of pearls, you'd think I was an oyster."

Politically what happens about this kind of thing is really important, because that thinking on her part, my part, your part, the whole community's part is a matter of niggerization. We've got to analyze that, because as good people, most of us are not niggers. Even most Black people are not niggers. The Black people that get ahead on the campus are very often what I call vanilla wafers, Oreos, and chocolate cupcakes—they're people who do not offend the Establishment beyond a very discreet level. So that when you have people in power, you must understand, whether it's Pearl Bailey or Sammy Davis or anybody else, you cannot count on them. You cannot count on the Secretary of Transportation Colemans of this world to put down the Establishment, because the only way that they can put the Establishment down is if we disrupt sufficiently to give them a higher sellout price. They are no more interested in losing their jobs as Secretary or Ambassador than you are in failing your course, being thrown off the faculty, being fired from the staff, or being flunked and not permitted to go to graduate school. We somehow have it worked out in our heads that they are supposed to take risks that none of us will take. And

With Leon Heath (in the glasses) and Tony Russo at the Gay Rights Conference, Columbia University, 1975 ▶

most of you would not even risk walking up on this stage and singing some silly songs, so you see how riskless we want to live.

In other words, we want to live a riskless life, we want security and we need it badly, and you have no right to expect anybody else to think less of security than you do. We have no right to criticize Pearl Bailey or Sammy Davis, Jr. You can say, as you probably do, that they've got money and they can hire a lawyer. But they don't want to hire a lawyer, they want to send their kids to school. And if you are so security-oriented that you can't walk up on this stage, then you have no legitimate basis for criticizing the William Colemans of this world who grant the SST Concorde permission to land in Dulles and JFK Airports. What I'm telling you is that the good people of this world have a responsibility as silent or minimally active collaborators with the pathology of this society. I'm not saying I want you to get suspended or arrested or lead a march of thousands in Radford, because you couldn't do it. I'm saying that you've got to do something, and until you do that something that involves a risk, you shouldn't, though of course you will, complain about anybody else's apathy. You are the apathetic one that you can control, and you have no legitimate basis for criticizing anybody else. . . .

"Women and Negroes have become the enthusiastic sponsors of the campaign for their own suppression."

From a paper written for a sociology class at Columbia University, January 1946

A COMPARATIVE STUDY—ACCENTUATING THE SIMILARITIES—OF THE SOCIETAL POSITION OF WOMEN AND NEGROES

. . . The similarities of the societal positions of women and Negroes are fundamental rather than superficial. The obvious differences are accentuated by the fact that women are supposed to occupy a privileged position. No such pretense is usually made where the Negro is concerned, but a dispassionate consideration of the economic, sociological, historical, psychological, political, and even physiological aspects reveals some rather startling parallels.

The majority of both groups are generally dependent economically upon the dominant group. Great lengths are attained to insure these dependencies. The necessity for an F.E.P.C. (Fair Employment Practices Committee) in a "Democracy," and support clauses in divorce codes, which according to Hobhouse existed in pre-Christian societies, and which Monica Hunter, Naomi M. Griffen, Ruth Benedict, and Cora Du Bois refer to in their accounts of various primitive societies, may be accepted as proof of the excessive abuses prevalent.

More than any other aspect of culture, the economic factor determines cultural development and direction. The political and social implications of this fact are infinite. It is therefore of primary importance to examine carefully the means by which women as a group and Negroes as a group are rendered *hors de combat* by being deprived of economic equality and independence. The far-reaching effects of their economic incompetencies leave not the minutest detail of their lives unaffected.

Women and Negroes are less apt to be hired and more apt to be fired than a similarly equipped member of the currently dominant group. Exceptions are made for extraordinary competence or during emergencies such as wartime or political revolutions. Both women and Negroes command lower wages, and are usually confined to lower-bracket positions.

In times of economic stress working women and Negroes arouse the resentment of those of the dominant group who are unemployed. Thus a returned serviceman may be especially upset to find his job occupied by a woman or Negro. Without entering into a which-came-first-the-chicken-or-the-egg argument, it seems sufficient to point out that rivalry for jobs provides a source of serious friction.

Industry frequently adds insult to injury by exploiting the subordinate group to lower wage scales or break strikes. A dual purpose is served, since this divide-and-rule technique further alienates society from those women or Negroes thus exploited. It goes without saying that the disdain is directed not at the employer but at the tool.

Both groups are barred from many specialized fields. Prestige of a position tends to decline upon their entrance. The withholding of training and education precludes development of potentialities. Exclusion from intimate situations where powerful combines are made places a definite barrier in their path. Even those women or Negroes who have attained some prominence in a preferential field are only tolerated in exclusive clubs, at banquets, or on golf courses with equally distinguished members of the dominant group. In the isolated instances where such chummy relationships prevail, the adoption of patronage and subtle condescension saves the day for the dominants.

The preeminence of those exceptionals among the weaker group is paradoxically viewed. Many conflicting theories and rationalizations are encountered: "Determination will win". . . "The majority (e.g. of women or Negroes) are inferior; these are the exceptions that prove the rule" . . . (bosh) . . . "This woman has a masculine mind" . . . or . . . "This Negro has 'white' blood" . . . what "Negro" hasn't? . . . "Women are getting all the best jobs" . . . "Negroes are 'taking over' the theatre" . . .

This magnifying of hard-won advancement makes it seem that a weak gnarled tree that pushes through the concrete in Brooklyn is a threat to miles of centuries-old forests which have flourished in fertile lands where the best of expert care has been lavished.

How are subordinate groups kept in subordination? Is their suppression a reflection of the will of all of the dominants? Do those who are submerged struggle to reach the level of their "betters"? If not, why not? How, if at all, are the submerged groups rewarded? How punished? Why do not the "superiors" crush them entirely? Women are much loved; Negroes are generally ignored, distrusted, pitied, or even disliked; do not these differences make any attempt to draw parallels seem a bit ridiculous? . . .

The psychological implications are vastly important in any consideration of personal-social relationships. The geographical, temperamental, financial, political, social, psychological, physiological, and historical are but a few of the most abstract factors which enter into every formula. For example: a customer is asking for a pound of butter . . . Alabama or New York? . . . Humbly or peremptorily? . . . Mink coat or Union Square special? . . . New Deal and O.P.A. or Republicans and "free enterprise"? . . . Does the butcher read *P.M.* or the *Daily News*? Is he young or old? . . . a Coughlin-Bilbo fan or Henry Wallace devotee? . . . All generalizations ignore these variables. . . .

Social sanctions take many forms. There are written laws governing franchise, property, political participation, and legal articulation. Social legislation reflects the comparative insignificance of women and Negroes. Educational budgets and medical care for Negroes or women have long been unequal. In housing, Negro districts are invariably slumlike. The kitchen where the average housewife spends the majority of her time is often the least spacious, attractive, comfortable, or even practical room of the house. Overwork is the lot of most of the members of the subordinate groups. When their health suffers due to this insanitary environment, their poor health immediately becomes the "reason" for their exclusion from desirable endeavor or choice programs. . . .

The unwritten laws are often more convenient and certainly more difficult to combat. Some are rational, most are nonrational or irrational. Many paradoxes and inconsistencies exist. There are great discrepancies between theory and practices.

Nonsupport cases belie the exaltation of motherhood so often heard. Societal penalties and punishments are more severe for sex "transgressions" by women or Negroes. Both are regarded as evil and dangerous. The Christian and other religious influences, and the white southerner, are but two sources from which such ideas have come. Overemphasis of the potency of women and Negroes in personal-societal relations serves to place an almost insurmountable barrier between these groups whenever it is advantageous. Sex taboos do not prevent miscegenation, but usually guarantee secrecy and therefore minimize the possibilities for legalized union and familial solidarity. There's no denying that sex drives are frequently far more democratic than contemporary societal pretence.

Paradoxically, criminal action by women or Negroes may be approached with extraordinary leniency; depending upon the offense, a paternal we-don't-expect-much-of-you attitude is frequently encountered. A Negro who cohabits with a white southern woman is almost certainly doomed to die; a Negro who kills another Negro in a brawl may be rescued by his white employer. In rare conformance with the theory that they are the weaker sex, women may receive preferential treatment in criminal courts.

Indeed, so numerous are the devices employed to delineate and emphasize the desired role that it is difficult to account for the many digressions that exist. Fiction and nonfiction, movies (with silly Billy Burke and groveling Ingrid Bergman, shuffling Stepin Fetchit, and Mammy Louise Beavers as "typical" women and Negroes), radio, drama, myths and legends, gossip and rumor, implication and innuendo leave little to the average imagination as to what is acceptable to "society."

A passive woman or Negro is presented with a ready-made role. Choice may be made from a wide range of conceptualizations which are considered ideal and/or average. Individual distinctions are minimized. Accomplishment outside circumscribed areas is discouraged.

Clothing is designed to accentuate the societal roles which have been chosen for the weaker group. Any concerted attempt to emulate or imitate the dominant group in dress is frowned upon—or laughed at. Women in slacks or a well-dressed Negro in a small southern town may be subjected to numerous embarrassments.

Religious participation is encouraged. Futile, blind alley endeavor is sponsored. Docility, forbearance, reticence, faithfulness, blind loyalty, silent suffering, acceptance of the *status quo*, and recognition of the divine right of the dominants are dramatized and applauded by society. Eager for status, the subordinate group accepts the role assigned by the powers-that-be. *Hence comes the irony.*

The subordinates become the enthusiastic sponsors of the campaign for their own suppression!

Endless complexity results from the fact that the majority of a subordinate group, though rejecting the ignominious position, will accept and popularize the devices through which the suppression is maintained. . . .

Thus, the longer the history of an inferior position, the greater the necessity for a break with tradition. Little effort is required by either group to further the submergence of those chosen, once religion and the prescribed pattern are accepted. The program becomes self-perpetuating. The desire to be identified with the dominant group results in the least significant of the societal underlings' becoming the unpaid guardians and champions of their exploiters' theories.

Rewards for conformance are spurious or superficial. Security and independence for the entire group are never expected or offered without a death struggle. The inevitability of the societal position is accepted by many of the most militant opposers to inequality.

Reforms are usually much too little and centuries too late. Reforms are at best not the result of intellectual conviction but of emotional effort. The recognitions of rights are considered concessions; sentimental reasons are offered to explain long-overdue justices. Progress results from struggle. Little fundamental change can be cited. Superficial progress has been merely a shifting of emphasis rather than an alteration of balance. Progress has seemed to some extent related to societal advancement.

Women and Negroes are but two of hundreds of groups within groups which occupy subordinate positions.

Foremost authorities to the contrary notwithstanding, I am convinced that the glorification—without qualification—of family life militates against the achievement of full equality for women. It would be interesting to see how many marriages would result without the church, *True Stories*, Myrna Loy, sex myths, and the *Ladies' Home Journal*. It would be more interesting to see how many monogamous marriages would endure if polygamy were legalized and popularized, and children's support were guaranteed by the states.

If women weren't coaxed and lured from industry and professions by societal cupids, those who are unsuited to marriage and breeding could direct their energies into other channels. Without pleading a case for a doctrine of individualism, it would seem that a recognition of the infinite variations among women and Negroes will lessen the occurrence of the every-girl-should-marry, women's-place-is-in-the-home philosophy as well as the more diabolical but no less effective keep-the-Negro-in-his-place attitude. Few societies at any cultural level provide for an acceptance of an independent life for large numbers of unmarried women. Emancipation for women and Negroes would seem to be contingent upon the emancipation of societal thought. This is, of course, question-begging at its worst, since there remains to be solved the problem of how to revolutionize the theories and thinking of "civilized" society.

If a study of this type has any value, it lies in the possible counteraction to the divide-and-rule technique which minority dominants invariably employ. Recognition of the similarity of their position can hasten the formation of alliances to combat the forces which advocate the suppression of many for the aggrandizement of the few.

The continuation of conscious or unconscious subordination of one group by another will hasten the coarsening of the moral fibre of society. Psychological maladjustments result from the difficulty of reconciling pretense with practice. Personal-social behavior is cramped when societal sanctions and taboos are at too great variance with logic and humanitarian proclivities.

Societal impoverishment inevitably results from policies of discrimination, segregation, and limitation. That such policies are absolutely necessary disproves the much-publicized contention that women and/or Negroes are "naturally" inferior. Bitterness and societal unrest arise out of attempts to exclude women and Negroes from full participation in societal endeavor.

No amount of segregation separates one unit of society from society as a whole. Thus, general societal health is ever contingent upon the health of its least significant member.

Exclusivistic tendencies deprive society of innumerable skills and contributions. The dissatisfied minorities within the subordinate groups provide an ever-present threat to societal peace. Need it again be necessary to call the attention of those who defend the *status quo* to the fact that it has never been a question of whether or not a subordinate group is capable of self-rule and equal right, but rather whether or not any group is worthy of the right to dominance and autocracy?

mfp

free press

20¢

Flo Kennedy's act

by Rachael Kamel

ANN ARBOR — Be prepared to find yourself on stage if you want to catch Flo Kennedy's act, because she starts off every appearance by hauling her audience up front to sing about women, power, and all the reasons we have to hate rich whitemen.

Kennedy — a Black feminist and self-described "anti-establishmentarian" — was in Ann Arbor this weekend (12-13) for 'Approaching 1984,' a symposium on the CIA, the FBI, and related corporate government operations (see story this page).

Kennedy's political theater is impossible to just consume: it challenges, mocks and finally provokes her audience into an active role. You can move with her — as an audience of women here did Saturday (12) afternoon — or against her — as many did during her talk on Rockefeller that night (see story page 3) — but you've got to move.

At her afternoon appearance, sponsored by the women's studies program, one woman announced that the corporate university will soon vote on whether to give the program department status. "I don't understand you people," Kennedy commented. "What are you letting them vote for? You ought to just demand that they do what you want."

She was even more emphatic that night. "Radicalism can become an excuse for paralysis," she said,

'the power of the people will not be held down because the power of women is gonna turn the world around'

"Nothing is quite so embarrassing and pitiful as the smallnesses of a great man. There was something childish and hysterical in Churchill's recurrent attempts to focus on Russia as the bogey man in the dark."

In March 1946 Winston Churchill delivered his "Iron Curtain" speech in Fulton, Missouri, which launched the Cold War. A week later I wrote this paper for a class at Columbia University. I'm still proud that 30 years ago I was saying the following:

MISSOURI MESSAGE

The significance of Winston Churchill's speech in Fulton, Missouri, on March 6, 1946, can scarcely be overestimated. It is far too soon to determine whether it marked the beginning or the ending of an era. (Inasmuch as his public appearances continue, the American audiences are applauding instead of booing, one may think the worst or the best according to one's position in relation to the fence.)

The speech was not a spontaneous expression. It was infinitely more than the irresponsible ravings of a tired, disillusioned, rejected, unhappy, old-fashioned, bitter old man. Newspaper accounts indicate that not only Prime Minister Attlee and Prime Minister Mackenzie King, but also President Truman, Secretary of State James Byrnes, and Bernard Baruch had *a prior* knowledge of the approach that Churchill would make to the complex problem of international relations. Thus Churchill's speech becomes a major move in a gigantic chess game, the outcome of which may mean world progress or world destruction.

Churchill made the issues very clear, notwithstanding continual recourse to vague concepts and name-calling. He became the Metternich of our era. The political and social superstructure of the era of Metternich crashed in the early nineteenth century, when the determination of men to eat and grow and progress conflicted with the hostility generated by the Machiavellian statesmanship of the guardians of tottering empires.

President Truman assumed the ignominious role of vice-president in charge of the maintenance of the *status quo*. His role became analogous to that of the weak, well-meaning Alexander I of Russia during and after the Congress of Vienna. His introduction of Winston Churchill cannot fail to be interpreted as tacit if tentative approval of the phoney focus on Russia, the plan for competition and war rather than cooperation and possible peace, the brush-off of the hunted, homeless Jewish peoples in Europe, and the hundreds of millions of Indians, Chinese, and other Asiatics who are finding the present state of affairs most uncomfortable if not intolerable.

The message in the city where stands a lunatic asylum was not just a message to Missourians. It was not merely a message to Americans, Canadians, and Englishmen. It was not only a warning to the Russians but also a warning to the inhabitants of Hong Kong, Ceylon, Athens, and

Palestine. A message from one of the inmates of the nearby institution may have been less euphonic and oratorical, but could easily have been less likely to upset the delicate balance between atom bomb war and sacrifice for peace.

Churchill's message must have aroused many emotions. It may have lent a spark of encouragement to a patient ex-Nazi who longs only for the confusion of disunity in Germany to make another stab at rule by "blood and iron" instead of "majority resolutions." It may have increased the hopelessness of some desperate underground worker who longed for the triumph of the "democratic principles." Franco must certainly have breathed easier.

Winston Churchill made many dire predictions, but he does not have a high batting average as a prophet. Once he lauded Mussolini and the Fascists, and said that if he were Italian he would join their movement. According to the round-faced ex-prime minister, there is no hope for the sickened world. Prognosis: negative. But even worse than shaking his head over the patient, the self-appointed spokesman for a number of reticent consultants advocates pounding the sick nations with bullets and bombs.

But what does Churchill want? Considering the great discrepancy between what he said he wanted and that which would result from the plans he suggests, we are forced to suspect that ambivalence and rationalizations veiled a multitude of dangerous and suicidal propositions. Nothing is quite so embarrassing and pitiful as the smallnesses of a great man. There was something childish and hysterical in his recurrent attempts to focus on Russia as the bogey man in the dark instead of stepping over, turning on the light, and facing the fact that there are lots worse things than imagined bogey men.

Let us suppose for the moment that there were no Russia. That Poland, Iran, Trieste, China, Manchuria, and India were not "menaced" by the great red horned monster of the East. Then what? Would a combined armed forces of English and American men and boys be an adequate substitute for food and homes of the dispossessed Jews of concentration camp fame? Would the intermingling of British and Americans and the interchanging of students and gagged, handcuffed scientists solve the problem of wealth and plenty for the clerical and royal "worthies," and famine and disease for the unfortunate "nobodies"?

What of bread, and schools, and Peron, and shoes, and Hong Kong, and Greece, and South Africa? Will silencing the Russians hypnotize a hungry man (English-speaking, Christian, or what-have-you) into thinking he has a full meal? Hardly.

But it isn't as easy as that. Russia is here to stay, it seems. It would also seem that Communism is something more than the "accidental beneficiary of a temporary discontent." Countries have a way of growing stronger when they have rid themselves of some of the shackles of their royal patrons. America is a case in point. Some statistician could amuse himself trying to compare the numbers of Indians killed so that America could share in the bounty of the rich "new" continent, with those of Russian aristocrats murdered during the revolutions. Of course the Indians weren't Christian, and they were in the way. But it only goes to prove that tenderness and the desire to get peoople out of the way at any cost are antithetical.

Even if Anglo-American solidarity became a reality instead of Master Churchill's dream, getting Russia out of the way would be no matter of tender (firm) treatment. Russia with a population of nearly two hundred million, India, China, South and Central America with other hundreds of millions, could make a serious unpleasantness between the English and Americans and the rest of the world rather awkward.

Unfortunately, however, the brotherhood of the English-speaking seems to exist only in the metaphysical figment of Mr. Churchill's imagination. After all, Mr. Churchill was recently rejected by the English-speaking people of his own country. Our English-speaking labor leaders, sharecroppers, and homeless veterans certainly must be a bit dubious about the fraternal regard of the (English-speaking) National Association of Manufacturers, the poll-taxers, and a majority of the congressmen. Lingual affinity isn't all. In the British West Indies as in our own Star-Spangled America, the ability to speak English is secondary to the skin pigment content in the establishment of brotherly relations.

It would be such a shame if we knocked ourselves out getting rid of Russia, then found that most of our Anglo-American problems were something quite apart from Communism. It's easy to imagine how Mr. Churchill's chin would tremble when he found that moving the Russian troops from Iran wouldn't get the British troops out of Greece. The ubiquitous "unrest," and "disorders," and "uprisings" did not result from Communism. Mr. Churchill in pursuing his will-o'-the-wisp has stumbled upon the common error of mistaking the result for the cause.

It is indeed difficult to determine what Churchill wants. It is well-nigh impossible to find, with any consistency, what he does not want. Now let's see. He doesn't want Russian expansionism. Good. That must mean he's opposed to imperialism. Well—er, not exactly. He wants free elections throughout the world. Fine. National self-determination. For India? Greece? Please! Such rude interruptions. He wants *peace*. Combined military, "nobody knows what Russia will do." He waxes sentimental over the worker in his little cottage and sponsors any program that denies a decent home life to South African workers. He wants to dangle an Anglo-American atom bomb over the world, but woe unto any attempt by "other" countries to buy uranium, conduct research on atomic power, or even suggest that a world organization take precedence over chauvinistic bullying and sovereign tyranny.

It's heartwarming to hear him say a kind (if deprecating) word for UNO. It would have been easy to think that the plans for a unified and expanded air force, army, navy, and atom bomb arsenal were leading to war. Arming a nation is an expensive undertaking, and sometimes so much money is spent that a country is forced to go to war just to protect the investment, and keep the bored soldiers occupied. The price of a gun can buy a lot of bread.

Rather simply, it is a question of feeding people who complain of hunger or shooting them. Lots of people, even Americans and Britishers, would just as soon share their sugar and flour with the hungry Asiatics and

Europeans as go over and keep a gun in their protruding ribs.

The UNO is too young and tender to handle the atom bomb problem, according to our eloquent guest, but is apparently old and strong enough to withstand a solid blow below the belt from two of the "big" three.

Much vagueness was misted over the Missouri double talk by frequent reference to "Christian civilization." The intent was doubtless to sweeten the poisoned custard. Since the term excludes the cultures from which Christianity borrowed most of its philosophy, legends, codes, and rationalizations, one is left rather in the dark, which may possibly be exactly what was desired. The possible inferences from such dangerous abstractions may warrant a demand for greater clarity if not explanation. Certain audiences should have the right to wonder exactly what "Christian" and "civilization" mean to Churchill.

Mr. Truman is quoted as having referred to his presentation of Churchill as "the greatest pleasure and privilege since I became President of the United States." Apparently he and many somnolent Americans regarded the speech as an isolated incident rather than as part of a process. Such assertion invariably begets counter-assertion. To point to the fact that Churchill spoke as a private citizen is gibberish. In the first place, few private citizens have local, syndicated, and foreign correspondents to record and disseminate their words of wisdom. Secondly, the hand-washing attitude of Attlee, for example, gives unlimited power without responsibility to the erstwhile leader of the British parliament.

After all, a "fire-bug," or a house-breaker, or a black marketeer is respected as a private citizen only to a certain point. It remains for history to determine whether this type of assertion can endanger the public welfare.

If the hero-worshipping American people aren't awakened from their lethargy by this history-making speech from a sleepy Missouri town, there may yet be the chance to learn that the atomic bomb—even at its best—is not a defense measure, even when one's head is in the sand.

"The question arises . . . whether all lawyers are the same. This is like asking whether everything that gets into a sewer is garbage."

"The Whorehouse Theory of Law,"* from Law Against the People: Essays to Demystify Law, Order and the Courts, *edited by Robert Lefcourt, Random House, 1971. This essay was based on a speech I delivered at the Columbia Law School Forum in March 1970.*

Ours is a prostitute society.[1] The system of justice, and most especially the legal profession, is a whorehouse serving those best able to afford the luxuries of justice offered to preferred customers. The lawyer, in these terms, is analogous to a prostitute. The difference between the two is simple. The prostitute is honest—the buck is her aim. The lawyer is dishonest—he claims that justice, service to mankind, is his primary

*Copyright © 1971 by Florynce Kennedy

purpose. The lawyer's deception of the people springs from his actual money-making role; he represents the client who puts the highest fee on the table.

Assuming that a concern for humanity is consistent with the person who avoids corruption, that is, the person who goes "straight," the lawyer is still a prostitute. As a law student, he is taught not only to park his humanity, but to think only in terms of money, power, and the "law." It follows that many lawyers wish to be in the pay of the business and government "houses." That is their highest aim—to be in a house where the richest johns come.

These are the clients who demand and get the best services the prostitute can offer. They are also the most racist, the most genocidal, and the worst polluters of the environment. The more delinquent the business or government client, the greater the employment opportunity for lawyers. Some of the two-bit-whore lawyers have spent lives of great disappointment because they have not been recruited and raised to "call girl" status in the major Wall Street firms or the MICE—Military-Industrial-Complex-Establishmentarians.

I think that where oppressed people are involved, it is customarily the guilt of the oppressor that is projected into a microcosmic corner, as it were, and made to apply only to the victims—the narcotics addict and the person immediately above him, the pusher, and other examples of society's projection of guilt and anger, while the Turkish farmer who grows the opium and the international racketeers who distribute the product are the greatest beneficiaries of the laws, protected by the whores in the Bureau of Narcotics, customs courts, and other government agencies. This contradicion is quite consistent at all levels of our society. The victim of society's attack is always the victimized!

Of course it is true that other professionals and most businessmen, and perhaps especially those in the medical profession, could fit the whorehouse characterization. Our history and literature are sprinkled liberally with "professionals" who have gone "straight" and revealed the numerous ways that they have sold themselves and their professional services for the almighty dollar. But the legal profession outdoes the other fields. For it is through the principles of law that men and women lose their liberties, and thus their lives.

The question arises, in discussing the generic sense of the whorehouse as representative of the whole legal system, whether all lawyers are the same. This is like asking whether everything that gets into a sewer is garbage. Because the shit is in the sewer means that it is garbage, of course, although distinctions can be made between better quality or lesser quality garbage.

The Wall Street lawyer, for example, services and represents, in my opinion anyway, the most delinquent johns in our society, whereas the average lawyer for hire just uses the law as a hustle. The typical lawyer represents either side: for example, the wife or husband in a matrimonial case. It is the *gelt* not the guilt that determines whether the client is acceptable in most cases. In that sense, the law is a hustle. Since this particular kind of lawyer does not represent the largest or most delinquent business people, a "hustle lawyer" is naturally less a menace because his hustle is to protect less powerful and less influential people. He is less infectious to the general community, less a shield for the carriers of the white plague of racism, war, poverty, and imperialism. And less often is there an Establishmentarian interest in his clientele. If a man and wife appear before a judge—the madam, if you wish—the dispute is not one which directly damages the whole society, except to the degree that the institution of marriage is institutionalized slavery.

People ask me whether, as a lawyer, I am not, in my own terms, a whore (especially since I'm a woman). The answer is, "of course." I have described my practice as a hustle ever since I discovered that the practice of law had much more to do with money-making than justice. I try to tell it like it is. But whether the hustler in a small, private practice tells it straight or not, this lawyer tends to be a less virulent prostitute than a major law firm that services the MICE.

The MICE are the clients that decimate the society and threaten the world. The MICE are the genocidal developers of biological and chemical warfare, the makers of the planes which siphon off the money from the hospitals and schools and divert it into the building of airplanes to be deposited in the rice paddies of Vietnam, Cambodia, and Laos.

The MICE, of course, also include people who do not actually contribute to the war arsenal. They are the makers of tomato paste, dog food, bird chow, and the shit-on-a-shingle that the GIs eat in the rice paddies, and which ghetto Blacks buy overpriced. The MICE are the national advertisers who conspire with the Madison Avenue fifteen percenters to repackage a box of crackers so the people can't get into it without a crowbar. The MICE observe with approval and/or subsidize the "soul" stations' radio format, whose white owners beam sugar-coated bullshit to the Black community on the theory that "that's what *they* want."

Since the MICE are in alliance with the most delinquent business people, they must have a confederacy with lawyers. The whole legal-government-business community is analogous to a National Association of Whorehouses (NAW). The legal whores in NAW include the legal departments of the television and telephone companies, whose committees are humping it with the state and federal regulatory agencies such as the F.C.C. (Federal Communications Commission), the state public utilities commissions, and members of Congress who are former customers or inmates of the NAW "house." The regulatory agents are also former inmates in, clients of, or presently housed in a NAW "Affiliate House" (AH!). They tend to be bought-off political hogs in retirement from various NAW installations throughout the country, such as members of the supine New York Public Services Commission, who in the late Sixties and early Seventies were entertaining pleas of "Don't whip us" from the public utilities community, such as the New York Telephone Company and Consolidated Edison, when those companies projected multimillion-dollar rate rises.

Whereas the wealthy legal whores of NAW and AH spread their disease to millions of people, screwing them on a daily basis, the prosecutors and district attorneys, bodyguards for the MICE, are poorly paid, highly

THE MEGAPHONE

SOUTHWESTERN UNIVERSITY *Georgetown, Texas*

Vol. 69, No. 2

October 9, 1975

FLO, SPEAK OUT!

by Marion Ross

"One reason people don't speak out against oppression is that we have all been programmed to have a sense of guilt — not enough to make us neurotic or crazy, but just enough to inhibit us from attacking the oppressors."

This conclusion was made by **Florynce Kennedy** concerning the pathology of oppression. Besides practicing law, lecturing, and writing books, Ms. Kennedy is the champion defender of oppressed people everywhere.

This dynamic lecturer will be at Southwestern Wednesday in a program sponsored by the Ideas and Issues Committee. She will give a speech in the Main Lounge of the SUB on the "Pathology of Oppression" and will respond to questions and comments from the audience.

After graduating from Columbia University law school, the best job Flo could find was as a $50-a-week law clerk. She later established a private law practice including mostly celebrities as clients. But most of her life has been spent in a constant battle against oppression.

Flo labels four types of oppression: personal, private, public, and political. Her fight for equality does not end with either the civil rights movement or the feminist movement, but it entails all aspects of our oppressive society. She organizes and executes demonstrations, a task wherein she has developed expertise. Flo has staged several effective demonstrations. Among them are a Harvard Yard pee-in to protest the lack of toilet facilities for women at the University, and a suit against the Catholic Church to deprive it of tax-free status on the grounds that it engaged in political activity by lobbying against more liberal abortion laws. Stephanie Caruana says of her, "When Flo decides to picket some deserving governmental agency or movie studio, she doesn't wait to find out who, if anyone, is going with her. She would, if need be, picket all alone, calling a sidewalk press conference at the same time. She herself is a one-woman demonstration, and the rest of us, if we happen to be there, are incidental."

During Flo's years of combat experience she has formulated an understanding and philosophy of oppression probably unmatched by any other demonstrative individual or institution. She perceives oppression as a fault of the people: "Clearly, the role of the good people in the politics of oppression is extremely important. One thing that happens is that good people are a little too ruth and couth in a ruthless and uncouth society. Good people are so busy trying to be good that they don't want to hurt anybody. They don't kill flies, they don't eat meat, they don't wear fur coats. The point is, always see if you can end the corruption; but if you can't end it, honey, get your share, because you may not live long enough to end it. I'm not saying everyone should get in on the machinery of oppression, but people should be aware that just by living in this society, you're in on it automatically. "Between fear and guilt, few people are prepared to act against the establish-

ment. It's as though you've got a car sitting on your ankle but the good people are afraid to take it off because they might scratch the paint. Anybody who wants to scratch the paint is considered a militant. People who call militants are merely victims who dare to complain in an appropriate way. The real militants are the good people who think they should do something to protect the oppression.

"Part of the politics of oppression is that the oppressor takes the money that should be used to run the country or provide services and then begs you to contribute for the things that you should be getting for your tax money. You pay taxes and you get the Trident (a US missile costing $13 billion) — and you don't even get a ride in the Trident and HEW gets only a small fraction of what is spent on the Trident, which is why we need a telethon for cerebral palsy research. I suggest we take the position that we will do absolutely nothing in terms of volunteering for anything until our human needs have equal parity with the Trident. I think we should switch the Pentagon budget with the HEW budget and have a telethon for the Trident."

Florynce Kennedy is an impressive figure who asserts her beliefs with positive, explosive action. Her attitudes may seem formidable, but it certainly gets to the heart of the matter. "I think we must be prepared to treat our enemies like enemies," Flo reasons. "Humanism that extends to Nixon is like people picnicking on the beach while others are drowning in the ocean. We don't need to change the world, but we ought not to lead an oatmeal existence."

Ms. Kennedy is a revolutionary personality in our society. If you are interested in provocative, vibrant, and truly contemporary people, be sure to attend this Ideas and Issues program.

infectious two-bit whores. They prosecute people who are usually the victims of the pathological system of oppression. Their sadistic role is to cage and isolate their victims for cruel and inhuman punishment. Although not members of NAW, they are still held in high esteem, mostly for their screwing ability and high batting averages. They usually have a good chance to become criminal court judges or madams.

Every whorehouse has its madam. In a law firm the madam might be the senior partner. In state government, the attorney general usually plays that role. In a corporation, the chief "house counsel" assumes the position, obviously. But the superintendent of the entire national red light district, the superlawyer of them all, hence the superwhore, clearly has to be the United States Attorney General. Why? Because he is the apologist for the MICE *in toto*. He is the protagonist for the death-dealing Pentagon. He is chief counsel for the slickest of all the dicks, and the thumb-sucking FBI. He is supermadam, supersuperintendent of the National Association of Government houses (NAG).

It is he who decides that certain select "outside agitators" who want to close down the whorehouse will get hassled, rolled, bounced, or smashed. He assigns the lesser madams to NAG houses of "justice" where the rolled victims, the war protestors, draft resisters, hippies, Blacks, or Yippies try to fight back as best they can against overwhelming odds. This particular supermadam infects the country like an epidemic within the judicial whorehouse.

A whorehouse is where one finds it: the smell of injustice is unmistakable. Injustice floats in the air like incense in a bawdy house, or like Chanel No. 5 in a "respectable" house. When a lawyer and tenant-client visit a cheap whorehouse like the local landlord-tenant courthouse where the practice of high-paying landlord favoritism and corrupt tenant sellouts is the daily routine, the heavy odor of cheap incense is pervasive. Easily recognizable in the unaesthetic criminal courts is the strong odor of law and order and the cheap smell of racism and repression. The illusion of efficiency is ritualized and formalized in these courts by the judge or madam in his or her granny gown, surrounded by the uniformed attendants who are paid to keep the victims in line.

The greater the injustice, the greater the attempt to make the atmosphere acceptable. Accordingly, the greater the injustice, the more genteel the surroundings. In the higher courts, such as the state or federal "houses," it is always said that the "practice is cleaner" because it is here that one would expect that justice would be most seriously considered. But the whorehouses that are well-decorated, that smell wonderful, that make the litigants feel comfortable and welcome, are the dangerous death-dealing houses. Not only are the millions of workers ignored and their impotency legalized, but the Ku Klux Klan has been legally protected, without serious challenge, for a hundred years. These "respectable" houses of the higher courts present a humanitarian front, but their real aim is to keep a good business from failing.

Lawyers, being practical people, may be forgiven for following the practice of getting in on whatever corruption they cannot stop. Likewise, it seems safe to assume that every person has a humanitarian impulse with an inclination to follow it if a viable, decent choice were available. Many lawyers, in fact, have begun to reject the *quid pro quo*—money—with scorn. The pervasive corruption throughout society has given rise to a new kind of lawyer, especially in the last few years.

The so-called poverty lawyer represents clients in poor neighborhoods, frequently in civil matters. Civil representation includes landlord evictions, family court cases, and consumer fraud situations. There is also the old-style poverty lawyer, sometimes called the legal aid lawyer or public defender, who defends poor people in criminal courts. The service in either case is sporadic, mechanical, and of very poor quality. Nevertheless, these lawyers are trying to go straight in a whorehouse society.

Predictably, poverty lawyers usually practice out of ugly, small offices. In a half-assed attempt to "service the community," the federal government sets up offices in storefronts, which resident indigents occasionally burglarize to the perplexed horror of the supersincere staff. These law offices are actually Vaseline dispensers. The staffers comfort the rapees, but they cannot stop the screwing. They cannot stop the system that fucks people over. They have to operate by what I call the "ass-by-ass" technique. They get one ass out of the wringer at a time.

The whole legal system is devoted to the ass-by-ass approach to injustice through which the law forces people to back into a wringer. The poverty lawyer is then permitted to "get them out," thereby achieving a victory. Then the wringer starts up again or continues. The ongoing pressures of racism, materialism, war, greed, and poverty then force innumerable others back into thievery, drugs, unfair rental arrangements, larceny by banks and merchants. Poverty lawyers actually earn their living by allowing society to operate as a screwed-up washing machine from which the results are never clean. This failure of the societal washing machine constitutes a system of oppression. Oppression is a by-product of the malfunction.

Since the role of almost every lawyer is to perpetuate oppression in a corrupt, unjust Society of Whorehouses (SOW), it seems to leave very little alternative to the law students or young practitioners. They don't want to be whores, and they can't survive as virgins. What are the alternatives when practically every house worth entering has a NAW or AH member, a two-bit whore or corner hustler? It's very hard to find a shelter which is not a part of the prostitute system, and this is why the young people talk about bringing down the town and all the houses in it.

Yet the lawyer or law student may go "straight" without ever becoming a whore, in my opinion, by literally battling the system. It is simply not enough to walk away and permit the society of whorehouses to continue to wallow in filth. There are obviously fewer whorehouses than whores. Long lines of law school applicants are waiting for an opportunity to get in on the corruption. Walking away simply leaves a place for someone else, who will probably do a better job. Whorehouse madams breathe a sigh of relief when they see ill-suited virgins or ex-whores quietly walk away. They really don't want a bunch of nervous Nellies in the house, because they will just upset everything.

Steinem-Kennedy speak on humanism

By LYNN MARTIN, Kernel Staff Writer

"We are not leaders, as always billed by the press, we are individual women. The movement belongs to every woman in this room. And in the end it belongs to everyone. This is humanism," began Gloria Steinem in last night's forum on Women's Liberation.

Gloria Steinem, contributing editor of "New York" magazine, and Florynce Kennedy, author "Abortion Rap," spoke to a standing-room-only crowd in the Student Center Grand Ballroom last night.

The crowd was composed of students, faculty, staff and local citizens. As one student put it, "This was the largest crowd I've seen in the ballroom, and I've been here five years." Both women were periodically interrupted by shouts of agreement and loud applause.

Steinem and Kennedy's appearance was the first in a series of lectures sponsored by the Student Center Board.

Going back into history Steinem said the world has been ruled by a gynecocracy for 5000 years. During ancient times women usually regarded as being superior and often worshipped. Since this period women have allowed themselves to be taught to feel inferior said Steinem.

Second class citizens

Steinem pointed out some ideas that have originated down through the ages: ownership of children, marriage ("lock up women to be sure who the father was") and women as objects. Once the situation was locked up women became second-class citizens.

Women have always had the most undesirable tasks. "Definition of woman's task," said Steinem, "something no man wants to do."

Steinem said as long as the oppressed groups are united by the fact they look different, they are consigned to the role of second-class citizens and these groups must unite and fight to change this role.

At first woman inferiority was supported by science and mythology. Myths began about physical, mental and emotional inferiority. Steinem revealed a health study conducted on women from all parts of the world found no difference in intelligence and little physical difference.

Science has proven the female hormone to be a calming additive. On the other hand, the male hormone has been proven to be an irritable and aggressive one.

Steinem's statement, "The church is the myth-maker of all times," was followed by shouts of agreement and applause. She went on to say that in every great religion, there has been sexual oppression to gain control.

She posed the question of why nuns could not be priests, typists could not be bosses, nurses could not be doctors, etc. She answered her question by saying, "Perhaps a whole generation of us (women) should refuse to learn to type."

The idea that women can not get along with each other has proven to be a myth. Women are forming political caucuses all across the nation.

It is important that women are allowed at last to come together as women across the boundaries of race, class and economic standing. These boundaries, said Steinem, were set up by white male supremists to keep the oppressed groups out.

The sex angle is over emphasized. Steinem's definition of sexual liberation is the ability to say no as well as the ability to say yes.

Most men believe if the liberation is a success there will be less sex. According to Steinem, Dorothy Pittman Hughes, usually Steinem's lecture partner, said, "On the contrary, there will be more of it." Steinem added, "Many older men are so accustomed to submission, they don't know what co-operation is like."

She went on to say, "The penis envy is a male chauvinistic notion. It only exists as a condition of society because second-class society envies the first-class distinction—the penis."

According to Steinem, women's liberation is the beginning of love—not the end of it. Love cannot survive in an unequal situation. She said women have to respect themselves before love can work.

In a question from the floor, a young married woman asked how more money could be appropriated for the wives of students to go to school. Steinem told her that in cases of wives sending husbands to school, she would suggest that a working arrangement be made to allow the wife to attend. If that were not possible, she suggested the couple take turns attending college.

Mass media has left the impression that the movement is not for all women. But according to Steinem, middle age housewives make the most radical liberationists.

A political movement

The movement is political and politics effect all women. It is not something to let the men handle alone. Consumer reports show women constitute 80% of consumer sales. Industry controls money, money makes men and men run the government. Therefore, since women are the largest consumers, they should be the majority influence in politics.

The movement will make all men and women equals if it is a success. Bobby Seale, according to Steinem, said, "A real man does not depend on the subjugation of anybody."

"If we leave here and nobody makes trouble," ended Steinem, "we won't have succeeded."

"At 55 I have no illusions about being a sex object," responded Florynce Kennedy to a question posed in the all woman reception held Wednesday afternoon.

During the reception Kennedy stated that Kentucky women needed to campaign against legislative candidates who are on record opposing abortion repeal

She said, "Make every single candidate who loses feel he didn't get elected because he opposed the repeal."

The main argument was blockage of menial jobs performed by educated women. These jobs could be filled with welfare recepients and women who are currently working in domestic fields.

'Jockcratic value'

Kennedy introduced a new term 'jockcratic value', and applied it to such issues as the UK athletic program.

During the forum, discussion became divided on the funding of the athletic program. An unidentified student posed the question of how to go about finding out where the money comes from for such things as new cars for some athletes.

Kennedy said to take the matter to the Health Education and Welfare Board. She also advocated doing anything possible to expose the situation.

Kennedy said, "I think that all government offices should be composed of 30% black women, 30% black men, 30% white women, and 10% in proportion to the rest of the population."

'At age 55, I have no illusions of being a sex object.'

FLORYNCE KENNEDY
(Staff photo by Jim Wight)

Black woman choice for president

She added, "My first choice in the race now is Shirley Chislom. My second choice is McGovern."

Steinem said she would support McGovern.

Kennedy repeatedly urged the audience to pressure advertising and industry in Kentucky and make them submit to women's demands.

Advocates change at UK

Some needed changes at UK listed by both women were:
▶ Remedial history.
▶ Women's studies.
▶ More black studies.
▶ Change racist and sexist textbooks.

▶ Professor changes—There are two in the law school who are self-declared racists.

▶ Black recruitment on campus. One percent of UK population is black, with 10% black population in the state.

▶ Equal hiring, promotion and pay for women and non-white men.

▶ Set up a UK sponsored and paid childcare center for students, faculty and staff.

▶ Acquire equal money for women's groups and athletic program.

▶ Abolish the nepotism rule that the wife of a professor cannot be hired in the same department.

▶ Change the local newspaper's rule that classifies ads under sex.

GLORIA STEINEM
(Staff photo by Dave Robertson)

The way to begin upsetting the daily routine of the whorehouse is by accepting, for the most part, those clients and those cases that are clearly anti-SOW, anti-NAW, and anti-MICE. One way to survive while battling the system is practicing as a lawyer-hustler. A part of the whorehouse mystique is that a person must be abnormal, and cannot possibly earn a living, if he or she remains outside the whorehouse. Yet a lawyer-hustler whose primary purpose is to effect justice by disrupting or exposing an unjust system is not a contradiction.

For example, if a client opposed the war machine through some direct action, and especially if the case is not an "ass-by-ass" rescue but one which could theoretically expose a part of the war machine, then the lawyer who takes that case is a "straight" or "right on" attorney. In no sense is that lawyer a whore in my terms, even if paid. One of the differences between rape and a honeymoon night is consent. The abandonment of appropriate concern for oppressed humanity is what makes a lawyer a whore. The "straight" lawyers who best confront the Establishment, who best threaten the whorehouse system, are those who protest the conditions of the most oppressed in society as they reject the system.

Obviously, it would be desirable for those who have been oppressed to become "straight" lawyers, say Black lawyers for Black people who resist, women lawyers for women activists. Alas, this cannot happen so easily, because a well-institutionalized oppressive society aims to make prostitutes out of "upward mobiles" from the oppressed groups. It by no means follows that because one has been oppressed, one will fight oppression. Widespread notions to that effect notwithstanding, one has only to note that mostly white lawyers represent the Black Panther Party prisoners, to note that lawyers for an oppressed group are not always of that group. Activist women would prefer women lawyers. But they often find that although women lawyers are not wholehearted participants in the *quid pro quo* of corruption, which is money, they are too often completely dedicated to getting a chance to be agents for the oppressors, to join a MAW, SOW, or AH.

Lawyers who are analyzing their roles in anti-Establishment terms are saying that their disinclination to affiliate with SOW, NAW, or one of the other houses is not personal, but social and political. In the generic sense, they know that as whores, they must be well-housed, well-dressed, and walking evidence of conspicuous consumption, but they would not be happy. One of the reasons the government, at the insistence of the MICE, has become even more repressive than before is because it is unable to make others happy; it is, therefore, very easy for the leaders to punish people without too much discomfort. It's part of their way of life—to divorce themselves from an honest concern for humanity. It is not so unusual, therefore, for most lawyers who regard themselves as "relevant straights" or anti-Establishmentarians to see themselves using the law as a weapon against Establishment repression and against the system itself.

Of course, my attempts to accomplish that end have made me feel like I was trying to level the Pentagon with a wet noodle. I feel that the courts and the legal system are so thoroughly a part of the whole system of prosecution, persecution, and prostitution that an anti-Establishmentarian hustler like myself might be as well off simply using the law as a source of income, and disrupting the Establishment whenever my laziness and timidity permit. It's more fun that way. What's the revolution going to be for, if it's not going to bring more fun, anyway?

[1]*Two important aspects of my experience have been the practice of law and participation in the Women's Liberation Movement. Sometimes an amalgamation of the two constitutes important insights. "Prostitution" might seem peculiar to feminism. One of my major political attempts has been to demonstrate the political nature of group variants. Thus, I use here the concept of prostitution in this extended, this political sense.*

All oppressed people who do not die quickly collaborate in some way with their oppressor. Wives, for example, stand behind the husbands, are the powers behind the thrones. Prostitutes, on the contrary, are defined by those who stand in front of: A prostitute is an out-front collaborator. I see lawyers similarly: as out-front collaborators, they shield the oppressor.

I leave aside for the moment whether in a just society a legal profession would be necessary. This profession has always been of an essentially apologetic nature: an apology and concealment for injustices perpetrated by those in power. However, prostitutes, because they are exposed to society as oil that greases the wheel–the alternative to rape–have a special choice forced upon them.

"Just by nobody doing nothing the old bullshit mountain grows and grows. Chocolate-covered, of course. We must take our little teaspoons and get to work. We can't wait for shovels."

"Institutionalized Oppression vs. the Female," from Sisterhood Is Powerful, Robin Morgan, ed., Random House, 1970.

People who have trouble accepting the thesis that women are an oppressed group might be somewhat placated by my theory of the *circularity of oppression*. It should be noted, from the jump, that there can be no really pervasive system of oppression, such as that in the United States, without the consent of the oppressed. People who have not withdrawn consent usually deny that they are oppressed. It follows. However, although the concept of circularity fails to suggest that some groups are far more restricted, segregated, boycotted, ostracized, and insulted than others, it does succeed in suggesting one reason for the uncomfortably solid basis for the male backlash.

Men are outraged, turned off, and wigged out, by threats that women might withdraw consent to oppression, because they—men— subconsciously (and often consciously) know that they—men—are oppressed. Women, as they loudly proclaim their rejection of further oppression, will arouse men to turn upon the established order. First, women will ignore or take care of the male backlash by any means necessary. In acknowledging their oppression, women will do well to reject their own roles in the hierarchy of institutionalized oppression.

At least one answer to the failure of any number of people, especially women, to accept as a fact the contention that women are oppressed, might lie in their experience of having been the victim of an oppressive woman, i.e., women being utilized as agents for oppressors.

Women are frequently oppressive in one-to-one situations. In those cases the oppressees tend to be their children, other family members, especially husbands, superintendents, or other domestic or nonpolitical public servants, e.g., waiters.

I see our society, however defined, as an excellent example of institutionalized oppression. *Where a system of oppression has become institutionalized it is unnecessary for individuals to be oppressive.* So it is that where Blacks are concerned (there we go again analogizing women and Black people; it's too perfect to ignore) whites can say, "But I never feel the slightest prejudice!" So, also, a man may say, "I'd hire a woman art director in a minute!"

Even if thousands of white male personnel directors made such declarations, such is the System that the overwhelming majority of art directors in major advertising agencies would be white and male. Just by nobody doing nothing the old bullshit mountain just grows and grows. Chocolate-covered, of course. We must take our little teaspoons and get to work. We can't wait for shovels.

It may be the church, the husband, the TV series, or a sister-in-law who persuades the pregnant woman that she should run for cover the second she dons a maternity dress. Surely the personnel director does not decree that she hover over the crib, the creeper, the crawler, and the cuddly until puberty. Women in their brainwashed consentual condition frequently act out their role of hovering mother without any noticeable pressure from anyone. Note "noticeable."

Dictates, from so many sources that you couldn't even count them, wind like soft cotton-candy fiberglass to bind the woman to the BPBP status—Barefoot-Pregnant-and-Behind-the-Plow. Although the BPBP status of peasant days now translates into various updated versions, there is little doubt that sex and the female ability to bear children is a frequent rationalization for ever so many of the (at least) fifty-seven varieties of rationale for oppressing women. What difference does it make whether the rationalizations arise from suspicion, tradition, or competition? It's women's job to put their power to work to slow it down or break it up.

Very usually consent to oppression is obtained by the issuance of a license to oppress. Since not all women seek a license to oppress, and since children are frequently the objects for women's oppression and not all women have access to children, consent is sometimes obtained through the ennoblement of suffering and sacrifice. Quite often, women consent to the system of oppression in exchange for a Vaseline-dispensing franchise. The franchise for dispensation of Vaseline is not wholly distinguishable from the honor of sacrifice and suffering, but has the added dimension of giving the female a superior status. She ministers to the suffering natives in her role as missionary, nun, or nurse, in exchange for which she suffers a second-class treatment from male missionaries, priests, or doctors. But she is so superior to the natives, novitiates, sinners, and bedridden that she glides serenely through the bullshit as if it were a field of daisies.

Coalitions of welfare spies, euphemistically dubbed social investigators, with welfare victims, called clients, are a good example of salutary coalition of the oppressed.

The concepts of *horizontal hostility* and *dumping* are an integral part of the circularity of oppression in an institutionalized system. Horizontal hostility may be expressed in sibling rivalry or in competitive dueling which wrecks not only office tranquality or suburban domesticity but also some radical political groups and, it must be sadly said, some women's liberation groups. Considerable headway toward a refocusing of hostility *upward* can be seen in the New York State area where broad coalitions of women's liberation groups joined with such victimized pioneers as Bill Baird and Dr. Nathan Rappaport to demand, not reform, but repeal of abortion laws. Yet upon sober consideration, horizontal hostility is most understandable. Oppressed people are frequently very oppressive when first liberated. And why wouldn't they be? They know best two positions. Somebody's foot on their neck or their foot on somebody's neck. Rednecks and poor white trash have traditionally dominated the Ku Klux Klan in the South, even as racist social workers and schoolteachers have infiltrated the ranks of those assigned to babysit the Black communities in the North. To avoid these destructive effects of horizontal disruptiveness, women need some minimal political and/or social awareness of the pathology of the oppressed when confronted by divide-and-conquer experts. How else would it be so easy for Jews—who have never been placed in concentration camps by Black people, or kept out of country clubs by Black people, or pushed out of upstate resorts by Black people—to fall for the line that Black anti-Semitism was a greater threat to them than the Establishment's divide-and-conquer techniques?

Similarly, even as they huddle together in the cold, damp atmosphere of their new-found liberation, and until they don the cozy raiment of "How beautiful we!" women who have rejected the Establishmentarian goodies (pink mops, wigs, women's magazine romances, a door-held-open, and miniskirts) often clash with each other before they learn to share and enjoy their newfound freedom. Some direct their hostility understandably to male counterparts rather than vertically toward the institutions that program us all, e.g., the media and the church.

A lack of a sense of considerable worth is another reason for horizontal hostility, consent to oppression, and the circularity of oppression. Values are learned at the parents' knee, at the laundromat, at church, at club meetings, and on TV networks. One Establishmentarian device, usually resorted to in newspapers and TV or other mass media, is to show women sacrificing and suffering. She quits her job so that she can follow *him* to South America or some such place.

Women are dirt searchers; their greatest worth is eradicating rings on collars and tables. Never mind real estate boards' corruption and racism, here's your soapsuds. Everything she is doing is peripheral, expendable, crucial, and nonnegotiable. Cleanliness is next to godliness.

She quits her job to have a baby. Magazine articles ponder the question of whether a wife can be a mother *and* a career woman. Never any problem being a *wife, hostess, chauffeur, gardener, cook, home typist, nurse, seamstress, social secretary, purchasing agent,* and/or *baby-manufacturing machine*. A woman may be discouraged from studying law. "The books are *so* heavy." But do they weigh more than a six-month-old baby? TV commercials reduce the female worth by depicting the young wife crying over sink spots and water marks on goblets. What will his mother say? Make a good pudding so's

Ms. Kennedy Speaks ...

By combining a high-style street rap and political insight, Flo has become one of the few feminists who make humor work *for* change, not against it.

—*Gloria Steinem*

FLORYNCE KENNEDY

♀ **LECTURER**

♀ **ATTORNEY**

♀ **CATALYST**

Second in the "Awareness '74 - The Total Man" Series

TUESDAY, FEB. 25

10:00 AM

Norton Aud.   FREE

"THE PATHOLOGY OF OPPRESSION"

OPPRESSION

"If you've been hit a lot, you tend to stay sore for a while. Trying to help an oppressed person is like trying to put your arm around somebody with a sunburn."

REVOLUTION

"You can't dump one cup of sugar into the ocean and expect to get syrup. If everybody sweetened her own cup of water, then things would begin to change."

TACTICS

"Unity in a Movement situation can be overrated. If you were the Establishment, which would you rather see coming in the door: one lion or five hundred mice?"

"Don't agonize. Organize."

POWER

"Women have at least three kinds of power: Dollar Power, to boycott with; Vote Power, to take over structures with, and maybe even get somebody elected; and Body Power, to get out and support our friends and make a damned nuisance of ourselves with everybody else."

MOTHERHOOD

"Being a mother is a noble status, right? Right. So why does it change when you put 'unwed' or 'welfare' in front of it?"

MARRIAGE

"Going in and out of a closet, your mind is on what you really want in there. But the minute the door locks, all you want is out."

WOMEN WHO LIKE THINGS THE WAY THEY ARE

"Women who say they're contented just having a nice husband and two beautiful children—fine; I'm glad. Of course, I always wonder what happens if one of the children *isn't* beautiful . . . and if housework is so rewarding, why don't men do it, too? But this Movement isn't about getting some woman to leave her husband. It's about social justice."

"Just because you're not feeling sick doesn't mean you should close the hospitals."

ON HERSELF

"My parents gave us a fantastic sense of security and worth. By the time the bigots got around to telling us we were nobody, we already *knew* we were somebody."

"I know we're termites. But if all the termites got together, the house would fall down."

There will be an informal discussion with Florynce Kennedy on Mon., Feb. 25 in the ABC room of the SUB, sponsored by the Young Academics.

you'll be loved. Get a strong deodorant! Women get so excited, they smell! Poor dears.

Men are scarcely less peripheral and irrelevant in their day-to-day or weekend activities than women. They should be prepared to join with women to force society to liberate everybody from irrelevant, peripheral, societal bullshit. But for the foreseeable future some women will act as if getting in on the corruption is more desirable than ending it.

Freud was at his most fraudulent (forgive, I couldn't help it) when he talked about women's frustrations and hostility in terms of "penis envy." One would have thought that even the most pompous and fatuous of asses would have gathered that women were less interested in standing at urinals than in standing on an equal basis before the bar of justice! As with most, if not all, systems of injustice and institutionalized oppression, the law had a leading role in oppressing women. It still has.

Some considerable time ago, anachronistic laws depriving women of most, if not all, civil and property laws were rewritten or repealed. But try to rent an apartment without a husband's (or some man's) signature. I can't begin to tell how many times a woman, separated from her husband, had to get him to sign a lease or help her get a charge account. Brothers or fathers often have to co-sign or countersign auto loans or chattel mortgages. This comes as a superirony, when, as is occasionally the case, the woman in question earns more, or has a longer and/or more impressive work record.

As a rule, of course, the men, especially if they're white, do have the better jobs and the more impressive work record. That's because of sex bigotry, the buddy system, and various other below-the-belt Establishmentarian characteristics.

Women with really good jobs and connections are often kowtowed to, like the "Negro" who has "made it." Women who know what's good for them lapse into old role styles when they really need or desperately want something, like an apartment, or a part in a play, or a really cool job.

The kind of female who doesn't pull punches even to get an important Precious becomes known as strident, strong, a ball-breaker, or crazy. If they survive the ridicule, scarcasm, hostility, demotions, and demerits, such women frequently fare better than the pliables. But the casualty rate is high.

Survivors of the gamut often are among those most impatient with feminism or female liberation. They scrambled their way up and why can't anybody else? Such women are gleefully quoted by the Establishment, even as the "Uncles" Roy Wilkins and Bayard Rustin are widely quoted when they take Black activists to task or defend pig Establishmentarians.

I predict that the Harriet Van Hornes who sniff at such beautiful zaps as the 1968 women's liberation demonstration against the Miss America Pageant, or the hollow, bewigged, superchic Pamela Masons who seem so bright and brittle until they have to deal with the matter of women's liberation, will meet with less tolerance than the Uncle Toms and the white maggots who feed off the few edibles in the garbage dump that the civil rights "fight" turned out to be.

Just as the students bypassed some of the turn-the-other-cheek, beat-me-daddy-eight-to-the-bar bullshit that Black people grooved on, so, I predict, women will begin almost where the students left off, and *they* are starting more fires than get into the papers.

Some of the same reasons might account for the speed with which the women's movement will take off, once it taxies the field for a season or two. Students and women, unlike Black people, didn't see themselves as oppressed; therefore when they were niggerized they didn't respond with a shuffle and a "S'cuse me, boss." Of course, Black students are in the vanguard of the student movement. This, if my theory is right, is because they knew they were scheduled for oppression and withdrew their consent: "Hell, no, we won't go," "No Vietnamese ever called me Nigger," etc. So Black students were indeed not representative of the Black community, or the shit would have hit the fan a long time ago.

But women are doers, and dreamers, and activists by the nature of their permissible roles. They do most of the buying, most of the lying ("Honey, call them and say I have to see an out-of-town client on the weekend"; "Dear, say I have a virus"—Hangover Hal; "Say we'll send the rent in on Friday"; "Change the appointment 'til next week") and a major portion of the hassling: with the landlord, merchants, family, etc. Women are more ready than most for the liberation struggle. We have only to direct our hostility from the vertical *down* (the kids, the merchants, the family, co-workers, and other women), and from the horizontal—to the vertical *up*. According to my *modus operandi* this means systems and institutions less than people.

Kicking ass should be only where an ass is protecting the System. Ass-kicking should be undertaken regardless of the sex, the ethnicity, or the charm of the oppressor's agent. As the struggles intensify, the oppressor tends to select more attractive agents, frequently from among the oppressed.

It is for this reason that I have considerable difficulty with the sisterhood mystique: "We are all sisters," "Don't criticize a 'sister' publicly," etc. When a female judge asks my client where the bruises are when she complains about being assaulted by her husband (as did Family Court Judge Sylvia Jaffin Liese), and makes smart remarks about her being overweight, and when another female judge is so hostile that she disqualifies herself but refuses to order a combative husband out of the house (even though he owns property elsewhere with suitable living quarters)—these judges are not my sisters. And if the same pair of female Family Court judges concur in decisions to return a three-year-old child to her mother and stepfather only a few months before the child's body is recovered from the river and her stepfather accused of her death? (Foster parents had pleaded to keep the child and had pointed to the evidences of physical abuse, to no avail.) No, these judges are not my sisters. Such females, in my opinion, are agents of an oppressive System, which the Family represents without a doubt.

Every form of bigotry can be found in ample supply in the legal system of our country. It would seem that Justice (usually depicted as a woman) is indeed blind to racism, sexism, war, and poverty.

Dean Willis Reese, a lanky man who talks with a lisp in a shrill voice and walks with a switch, hastened to assure me that I was being refused admission to Columbia Law School in 1948 not because I was Black, but because I was a woman. I leaned on the ethnic angle, saying that some of my more cynical friends thought I was being discriminated against because I was a Negro (we weren't saying "Black" in those days), and in any case it felt the same. Law school admissions opened the door just wide enough for *me*, but not for my friend Pat Jones, who was a Barnard graduate, with a slightly higher law aptitude level and slightly lower undergraduate average, but white.

Many senior partners, or hiring partners in Establishment law firms still have the nerve to say they don't normally hire women. Some, perhaps most, firms will accept a woman if she is in the upper percentile of her law school class. (So, also, they'll accept supersmart Jews.)

Of course, the law schools assist by screening out the women and the Blacks "from the gitgo." Nowadays the tokens have become a trickle. Much of the clash of Black students on campus and the predictable upcoming clashes involving women is due to the "expectancy gap" which prevails when a bigot decides to go straight. The crabgrass liberal-bigot anticipates a good sport, a dazzled recipient with damp hands and misty eyes near to overflowing with gratitude—but is confronted by a cool, if not coldly suspicious, potential foe—a creditor sullenly receiving a minuscule payment of an unconscionably late I.O.U. Black students now—and female students in seasons to come—will break up the bank.

"There is a chill, almost icy reserve towards Women's Liberation among Black women, which carries into the struggle for abortion law repeal."

"Black Genocide," from Abortion Rap, *by Diane Schulder and Florynce Kennedy, McGraw-Hill, 1971*

Black people know that part of our revolutionary strength lies in the fact that we outnumber the pigs—and the pigs realize this too. This is why they are trying to eliminate as many people as possible, before they reach their inevitable DOOM. ALL POWER TO THE PEOPLE!

—Brenda Hyson, in *The Black Panther*, Saturday, July 4, 1970

The overwhelmingly white Women's Liberation contingent was rather nonplussed by the failure of the Black community and the Third World people to join in on the struggle to repeal the New York State abortion laws. Outside the white community there was scarcely an audible rustle for or against reform, or repeal of laws or practices relating to abortion. In short, the Black community seemed preoccupied with other problems or totally uninvolved. To the extent that the views of the Black community were publicly expressed, they were almost always diametrically opposed to the ideas encountered in the eye of the storm for abortion repeal. On several radio programs Black men and women (and, in at least one case, people from the Muslim community) denounced abortion as racist genocide, directed at Black people.

Moreover, there was an immediate and emphatic response by the Black Panther party a few days after the new abortion law became effective. This response was reminiscent of the position taken at the Black Power Conference in 1967, in Newark, New Jersey, where there was a consensus that birth control and abortion were both forms of Black genocide. At that time there was a workshop on "Black women and the Home" from which a rather generally worded statement was issued:

". . . Black women commit themselves to: a self-preservation and continuity through educating and exposing to our people the genocidal practices by racist societies."[1]

This resolution was predicated on considerable discussion in which it was very clear that the consensus was against contraception.

Some revolutionaries in the Black community take the position that Black revolutionary forces will be decimated by birth control and abortion. Dire predictions about "population explosions" or sudden offers of long-denied birth control information only serve to confirm well-founded suspicions of racist motives.

Many of the arguments emanating from the Black community have been set forth by Brenda Hyson in the July 4, 1970, issue of *The Black Panther*. This article is a well-articulated exposition of views held by many varied Black groups. Her article was directed at the abortion law passed by the New York State Legislature, effective July 1, 1970.

The *Panther* article took a dim view of the idea that the new law was a victory:

". . . Perhaps it is a victory for the white middle-class mother who wants to have a smaller family, thereby enabling her to have more material goods or more time to participate in whatever fancies her at the moment. But most of all it is a victory for the oppressive ruling class who will use this law to kill off Black and other oppressed people before they are born."

This *Panther* view was similar to that stated in the Manifesto from the 1967 National Conference on Black Power:

"Black people who live under imperialist governments in America, Asia, Africa and Latin America stand at the cross-roads of either an expanding revolution or ruthless extermination. It is incumbent for us to get our own house in order to fully utilize the potentialities of the revolution or to resist our own execution."[2]

The *Panther* article also expressed an emotional and sentimental view of the Black family. Brenda Hyson labeled the true problem as capitalist greed:

"Black women love large families, and the only reason that they would want to eliminate them is to rid them of the pain and the agony of trying to survive. Why in a country where farmers like Eastland are given large sums of public funds to not grow food, where food is actually burned, must Black mothers kill their unborn children? So they won't go hungry? Absurd! Eliminating ourselves is not the solution to the hunger problem in America nor any other problem that could exist from a so-called unwanted pregnancy in the context of this capitalistic society. The solution lies in overthrowing this system and returning the means of production back to the people—REVOLUTION."

The specter of enforced abortions is almost upon us. Pregnant women in New York, prior to the new law, had sometimes been told that they could get an abortion only if they agreed to be sterilized. Women on welfare are sometimes threatened with being removed from the rolls if they have had a relationship with a man, let alone have another child. Cynicism about the new abortion law is related to cynicism about the law generally. As the Panther writer so well put it:

"The abortion law hides behind the guise of helping women, when in reality it will attempt to destroy our people. How long do you think it will take for voluntary abortion to turn into involuntary abortion, into compulsory sterilization? Black people are aware that laws made supposedly to ensure our well-being are often put into practice in such a way that they ensure our deaths. The current welfare laws are one of the classic examples."

Finally, the article strongly decried the poor health services available at hospitals and other treatment facilities, about which there can be no dispute.

Notable exceptions to those who equate abortion with Black genocide include Black women such as Florence Rice of the Harlem Consumer Education Council, Shirley Chisholm, first Black congresswoman, and the many Black women who contacted us for abortion information during the course of the case. Among them were several youngsters under sixteen. The *amicus* brief filed by Emily Goodman had as one of its signators Percy E. Sutton, Borough President of Manhattan and a former New York State assemblyman, who was one of the first sponsors of abortion law reform in the New York State Assembly.

At least three small groups of Black and Puerto Rican Women's Liberation groups participated in plans for the spring 1970 demonstration against abortion oppression. Speaking for groups, and as individuals, several Black women related horrendous experiences they had had in near-fatal attempts to terminate unwelcome pregnancies. One young Black woman told of becoming pregnant while working for the New York Telephone Company. Unable to obtain an abortion, she worked as long as she could, then was forced to seek welfare. The baby was born prematurely and was kept in the hospital. She encountered endless difficulties getting her welfare checks. She had no place to live, could not bring the baby home from the hospital, and her life was in total chaos.

Several Harlem Hospital physicians verified the rumors that a number of Black women died each month as a result of incomplete abortions or infections caused by self-induced or illegal abortions.

That a discrepancy exists between the Black genocide position and the plight of many women and children in the Black and Puerto Rican community is very clear. This seeming contradiction might be accounted for in a number of ways:

1. Other day-to-day problems in the Black community, less dramatic, but chronic and ongoing, are felt to have priority. This would account for the impatience, amounting almost to annoyance, evinced by Black people

and community groups invited to participate in the struggle for repeal of abortion laws. Abortion is a relatively rare crisis as contrasted to such problems as unemployment, racism, poverty, bad housing, police rioting, and war.

2. Distrust of the white women's movement, a natural consequence of the D and C (divide and conquer) techniques of the oppressive Establishment. Even young Black women, on and off campus, disdain the women's movement and declare that Black liberation has priority. They describe Women's Liberation as a media-promoted fad and charge that it is sometimes used to divert attention from racism. Black women apparently feel patronized by white women. Some few may see them as rivals for the affection and attention of Black men. Others suspect white women of attempting to play the role of the missionary's wife, dispensing Vaseline to the raped native.

However much white women evince concern for male chauvinism in the Black community, however eloquently they declaim their solicitous regard for the hundreds of Black women who die annually in Harlem Hospital and other institutions that service predominantly Black communities, there is a chill, almost icy reserve toward Women's Liberation among Black women—if it is taken into account at all—and this carries into the struggle for abortion law repeal.

However, this is gradually changing due to the cumulative effect of the Free-Our-Sisters/Free-Ourselves demonstration in support of the New Haven Panther women; also the successful Free Joan Bird campaign which resulted in her release on July 6, 1970, after fourteen months in the Women's House of Detention, and the supportive action for telephone workers on strike by the Gay Liberation Front, women's groups, and at the May 28, 1970, Conference for Women.

3. A residual, subsurface religious bias not dredged up and dealt with, and probably not even acknowledged as such. Many Black people, who are not themselves religious, have been reared in circumstances where their parents and community are heavily influenced by religious concepts.

4. The habit of accepting oppression, without any relevant reaction, except horizontally or self-directed guilt.

5. A distrust of systems, especially courts, as well as a feeling of aloofness to wooing "movements" which historically (e. g. the labor movement) tend to use Black people as troops, then return to the white "buddy system" as soon as the time comes to allocate the conquered territory.

6. Some of the people active in population control, family planning, and so on, have a bad stench of racism. In the spring of 1970 a radio panel of Third World women on WBAI-FM discussed their antipathy toward contraception and abortion. They cited the testing of birth control pills in South America and Puerto Rico. This clearly impressed them more than the concern of the white women's movement with *machismo* in the Puerto Rican community.

Early concern for population control was most often focused upon nonwhite areas. For example, in India, where transistor radios are given to young men who consent to having vasectomies which render them infertile, white racism seems symbolically to be making a transistor radio the *quid pro quo* for a man's manhood.[3] Recently, Planned Parenthood send out a fund-raising pamphlet entitled "Overpopulation." They asked for contributions to help build Planned Parenthood clinics "in Asia, Africa, or Latin America."

In our opinion the Black genocide argument is subject to certain objections. Of girls who drop out of high school, a large proportion are from the Black or nonwhite communities and a major reason for leaving school is pregnancy, which competes with economics and boredom to motivate the dropout.

Black majorities in places like South Africa and Mississippi are not noticeably revolutionary. No evidence has come to our attention that mothers of large broods led the rebellions in Watts, Detroit, or Newark, although Mothers for Adequate Welfare in Roxbury precipitated the Boston rebellion with their sit-in.

Women hampered by children tend not to be in the vanguard, and male revolutionaries frequently abandon their children when the going gets rough. Perhaps the thought is that the parents will continue to consent to oppression, but will reproduce large numbers of children who will snatch them from the claws of the oppressors in their old age. This concept of breeding revolutionaries, rather then revolutions, is appropriate in a society where the old people do the voting and the youngsters do the fighting and dying. Breeding revolutions can be fatal, whereas breeding revolutionaries is not too far removed from a cultural past where Black women were encouraged to be breeding machines for their slave masters.

It might shock Black radicals to entertain the possibility that religious programming combined with certain of the slaver's social values, plus a soupçon of male chauvinism, account for the volume of the contention that a legalization of a women's right to terminate an unwanted pregnancy is Black genocide. In any case, Friends of the Fetus in the Black Community have permitted a number of potential revolutionaries to languish in orphanages and foster homes, despite widely broadcast pleas for rescue (for revolutionary or whatever purpose).

If abortion or other forms of birth control are used by oppressors against a certain class of people, there might easily come a time when all women will have to fight against the imposition of abortions. Like any other problem, abortion must be approached openly and dialectically and not in a mechanistic manner. Enforced sterilization is not merely a nightmare of the future, since it has often been ordered in the case of welfare mothers, and has been used as well as a precondition for an abortion.

We favor the right of women, Black and white, to have the choice of deciding whether they wish to have babies. To the degree that Black people equate the repeal of abortion laws with compulsory sterilization, they obviously must oppose it. However, among the silent majority there would appear to be bleeding women in the emergency rooms of hospitals who could use the help of those who have been espousing the Black genocide theory.

A further irony in the Black genocide position is that here it is the opponents of governmental control of Black communities who urge the continuation of state interference in the personal lives of Black people. It would seem more understandable for these anti-Establishmentarians to seek community control of such matters. This control might better result if abortion laws were repealed and free choice prevailed.

Nevertheless, the white women's movement must be careful not to use the Black women's plight to make their case for them. White women must let the Black movement formulate its own ideas and strategies in its own time and way.

That Black women are beginning to publicly oppose the Black genocide position is further evidenced by a recent article in *Black America:*

"Don't call me sister if you can't call me wife. Dig it! This is not a catch phrase, or one of the ten top Black sayings of the week. This is a sentiment taking a strong hold on many sisters who are no longer willing to be the punch line of some brother's joke. The sisters say it and they mean business. No more fatherless Black babies, no more weeping Black unwed mothers. Sisters are firm in this stand, and they warn, 'Don't cry Black Genocide!' "[4]

[1]*Resolution from the National Conference on Black Power. These resolutions represented the distillation of the first major national dialogue by 1,300 Black Americans on the creative possibilities inherent in the concept of Black Power. There were a great number of resolutions from the seventeen workshops–at which there were delegates from 39 states, Bermuda, and 190 organizations.*

[2]*Presented together with the Resolutions, Newark, New Jersey, 1967.*

[3]*"In Bogota, Colombia, there is a new billboard advertising a service formerly only whispered about–family planning.*

"Radical young priests, along with their lay supporters, are taking the line that family planning is being fostered by 'imperialist United States agencies' in place of social and economic aid. Many of the radicals believe that only a change in basic social and economic institutions can solve Colombia's problems.

" 'Washington is trying to give us the pill because they think it is a simple solution to our problems,' one priest is quoted as having said. 'Oh, God, how Washington loves neat and simple solutions in Latin America! First it was the Alliance for Progress, which they are quietly burying. Now it is the pill.' " (From an article "Colombians Get Aid on Family Planning," by H. J. Maidenberg, New York Times, July 15, 1970.)

[4]*Carolyn Jones, "Abortion and Black Women," Black America, Vol. 1, No. 5, September 1970.*

148   With Liz Reid, Australian delegate to the International Women's Year Conference, Mexico City, 1975

This complaint was served on the Internal Revenue Service in 1972. However, Planned Parenthood, the feminist community, and the abortionists and gynecologists could not, among them, raise funds to take the suit to federal court. Irene Davall and I had already spent the equivalent of $40,000 in legal research, and I decided it was approaching nigger nobility to pursue it. It is here included since the abortion backlash, the anti-gay movement within the church, and Ellen McCormack's illegal campaign funding make it more relevant than ever.

COMPLAINT RE:

Archdiocese of New York

Terence Cardinal Cooke

Birthright

Knights of Columbus

This is a request to have the tax-exempt/tax-deductibility status of the above-named groups and individuality status of the above-named groups and individuals revoked based on their political lobbying activities to preserve archaic abortion laws which threaten the lives and safety of women in this country. A combination of the Archidocese of New York, Terence Cardinal Cooke, Birthright, and the Knights of Columbus have been actively engaged in conduct in violation of the tax-exempt status of the Church.

The Internal Revenue Code, in defining organizations that are exempt from taxation, states:

"Corporations . . . organized and operated exclusively for religious, charitable . . . or educational purposes . . . no substantial part of the activities of which is *carrying on propaganda* or *otherwise attempting to influence legislation, and* which does *not participate in,* or intervene in (including the publishing or distributing of statements) *any political campaign* in behalf of any candidate for public office."[1]

Internal Revenue Code sec. 501 (c)(3). (Emphasis supplied.)

A. PARTICIPATION IN CAMPAIGNS

The above-named groups and individuals have participated in and intervened in (including the publishing and distributing of statements) political campaigns both in behalf of and against candidates for public office. Under the Internal Revenue Code, there is a total bar against this kind of activity.

Tax-exempt organizations must be operated exclusively for exempt purposes. Federal Regulations set forth two main tests to determine whether an organization is organized exclusively for exempt purposes or whether it fails to qualify for exemption and is an "action" group. The groups named have become "action" groups as defined in both tests expressed in the regulations. The test relating to political campaigns is as follows:

"An organization is an 'action' organization if it participates or intervenes, directly or indirectly, in any political campaign on behalf of or in opposition to any candidate for public office. The term "candidate for public office" means an individual who offers himself, or is proposed by others, as a contestant for an elective office, whether such office be national, state, or local. Activities which constitute participation or intervention in a political campaign on behalf of or in opposition to a candidate include but are not limited to, the publication or distribution of written or printed statements or the making of oral statements on behalf of or in opposition to such a candidate."

Treas. Reg. sec. 1. 501(c)(3)-1.(c)(iii).

Recently, the Archdiocese has spent much money, time, effort, and energy on abortion legislation. There have been direct and indirect threats of organized pressures for or against legislators depending on whether their stand was in accordance with the Church position.

In April 1971 a plea from Cardinal Cooke requesting Roman Catholics in the New York Archdiocese to make their views against abortion known to the state's elected officials was read in the 407 parishes of the Archdiocese. "There are bills in Albany right now that would stop this slaughter of the innocent unborn," the Cardinal said in his message. "I suggest that you write, phone, telegraph, and speak to the state's lawmakers and make your support of life known to them in a clear manner. (*New York Times*, April 25, 1971; Exhibit 1)

Many people have wondered how and why the liberalized New York abortion law, passed by the legislature in 1970, was repealed by it and rolled back to its archaic form in the Spring of 1972 (although reasserted by veto of the Governor).

The *Long Island Catholic* (a paper which is ordered through one's local priest and for which he is then billed), tells a lot of the story. Beginning in early 1972, busloads of people streamed to Albany to pressure legislators to work for passage of the Donovan-Crawford bills (restrictive). As the *Long Island Catholic* put it: "The organizers would like to see a busload of people from every two parishes in the diocese." (*Long Island Catholic*, December 16, 1971; Exhibit 2) Upon information and belief, these activities were funded or sponsored by the diocese.

In early April 1972 a pastoral letter on abortion, prepared by all the New York bishops, was read at all masses. (Exhibit 3) At this time, political activity became intensified. The *Long Island Catholic* carried a statement on "The Hell of an Abortion," a tearout ad entitled "Tell Your Legislator," and a form letter urging passage of the Donovan-Crawford bill, followed by a list of the names of the legislators. (*Long Island Catholic*, April 13, 1972; Exhibit 4) There followed a period of pressure upon individual legislators that is unprecedented in New York.

In the Spring of 1972, the political activism of the named groups was clearly tied to political campaigns of candidates. As the *Long Island Catholic* headlined it: "Pro-life Rally Planned for Nassau; *Tying to Primary Voting*." (*Long Island Catholic*, April 20, 1972; Exhibit 5) On April 16, 1972, 10,000 persons demonstrated against the liberalized abortion law under the sponsorship of the Knights of Columbus. Cardinal Cooke designated the day as "Right to Life" Sunday. On April 17, 600 demonstrators rallied on the steps to the New York State Capitol. (*New York Times,* April 18, 1972; Exhibit 6)

The enormous tax-exempt funds of these groups (the Archdiocese has assets of over $640,000,000 in New York City alone), coupled with the tremendous moral pressure brought to bear following the reading of the Bishops' letter, finally culminating in an exchange of letters between President Richard Milhous Nixon and Terence Cardinal Cooke a day or two before the vote—helped to force a vote in the New York legislature overturning the liberalized law, that women's groups (non-tax-exempt, of course) had fought so hard to obtain.

Governor Rockefeller, in vetoing the Donovan-Crawford bill, stated: "At no time have I seen a session of the legislature so characterized by inordinate pressures as in the 1972 session in the area of abortion. . . ." (*New York Times,* May 16, 1972; Exhibit 7) Cardinal Cooke, after its passage in the legislature, personally and specifically asked Governor Rockefeller not to veto the Donovan-Crawford bill. (*Long Island Catholic,* May 18, 1972; Exhibit 8)

So, the hundreds of thousands of women who depend upon New York State for a relatively safe and hygienic operation were saved by a hair's breadth. But, we cannot allow this flagrant violation of the law to continue. There is clear evidence that these tax-exempt groups plan to continue and intensify their political activity in the coming year.

On May 18, 1972, just two days after the *New York Times'* report of Governor Rockefeller's statement concerning "inordinate pressures in the legislature," Paul Driscoll, a coordinator for the diocese, spoke most strongly in favor of restoring New York's old (restrictive) abortion law. There followed a list of names of Long Island assemblymen and senators and how they had voted on the state's abortion law. For the restrictive law: 10 Republican and 1 Democratic assemblymen; 6 Republican senators. For the liberalized law: 2 Republican and 4 Democratic assemblymen; 1 Republican senator. (*Long Island Catholic,* May 18, 1972; Exhibit 8) It is clear that these church-financed groups have participated in the past, and pla to participate in the future, in the political campaigns, both for and against the legislators listed.

In November 1970, Assemblyman Balletta had been defeated by Catholic groups because of his vote on abortion. "ABORT BALLETTA" had been their slogan, spread on bumper stickers. (*Village Voice,* March 25, 1971; Exhibit 9)

A questionnaire on the New York abortion law, specifically requesting answers to four questions on the Donovan-Crawford bill, was prepared by the Human Life Committee of St. Mary's Parish in Roslyn and sent to all senators and assemblymen in the area as well as to candidates who declared for these offices. The answers, or lack of reply, were listed next to the legislator's or candidate's name in the *Long Island Catholic*. (April 27, 1972; Exhibit 10)

Earlier Monsignor Thomas McGovern, spokesman for the Archdiocese of New York, is quoted as having said that Right to Life groups have their headquarters in the building of the Archdiocese, which provides them with free office space, free phones, and a priest to answer their calls. (*Village Voice,* March 25, 1971; Exhibit 9)

Groups funded by the named tax-exempt organizations are going even farther. Yelling "Stop abortion!" members of "right to life" groups were carried out of the Assembly after staging a brief sit-down near the Speaker's rostrum. (*Long Island Catholic,* April 27, 1972; Exhibit 10)

The high level of organization is available to these tax-exempt groups largely because of their funding and because their pressure is so much the more difficult to resist because of their coming on as the "Church" with closer connection to God and "His" will. The Church is organized as a strict hierarchy, with the Pope at the top. The Pope has been unbending in his stand on both contraception and abortion. (*New York Times,* November 17, 1970; Exhibit 11) And individual legislators have been subjected to pressures in their individual parishes. All this, of course, is in blatant and flagrant violation of the First Amendment's proscription against the "establishment of religion." In recent times, separation of church and state has never been more clearly breached in this country.

This campaign of pressure (terror, in some cases) by a minority group is being waged on a national scale. Just one instance will suffice (although this can be documented state by state). It is reported that when the letter on abortion by Nevada's bishop was read in all Catholic churches one Sunday, several state senators said they were contacted in their homes following the reading of the letter. One assemblyman said he received 50 phone calls and another said he received a call every fifteen minutes during the day. (*Las Vegas Review Journal,* March 5, 1971; Exhibit 12)

B. INFLUENCING LEGISLATION

In addition to intervening in elections (against which there is a total prohibition), these tax-exempt groups have also organized a substantial part of their activities, recently, to carry on propaganda and otherwise attempt to influence legislation concerning abortion.

This activity is, also, in violation of the federal income tax regulations and would, again, classify these groups as "action" organizations:

"An organization is an 'action' organization if a substantial part of its activities is attempting to influence legislation by propaganda or otherwise. For this purpose, an organization will be regarded as attempting to influence legislation if the organization:

"(a) Contacts, or urges the public to contact, members of a legislative body for the purpose of proposing, supporting, or opposing legislation, or

"(b) Advocates the adoption or rejection of legislation.

"The term 'legislation,' as used in this subdivision, includes action by the Congress, by any State legislature, by any local council or similar governing body, or by the public in a referendum, initiative, constitutional amendment, or similar procedure. An organization will not fail to meet the operational test merely because it advocates, as an insubstantial part of its activities, the adoption or rejection of legislation." *Treas. Reg. 1.501(c)(3)-1.(c)(ii).*

I. Influencing legislation by carrying on propaganda

The propaganda has taken various forms. A common form has been the pastoral letter. But this has not been a mere innocent statement of policy that happened to be mentioned from the pulpit. The letter by Terence Cardinal Cooke to the Catholic bishops was denounced by Reverend Howard Moody:

"The seeds that Cardinal Cooke planted are bearing fruit of an ugly sort, with his followers in Right to Life groups, in Friends of the Fetus, or advocates of fetus power. With less restraint and more hostility and hatred in their heart they threaten legislators and label as 'subhuman criminals' all those who would support the present repeal law on the book." (Village Voice, *May 13, 1971; Exhibit 13*)

These pastoral letters, again, are being coordinated all over the country. One, by Patrick Cardinal O'Boyle, archbishop of Washington, D.C., was inserted into the Congressional Record (March 8, 1971; Exhibit 14). Similarly, in Massachusetts, at the time hearings were being held in the legislature, the Catholic bishops of Massachusetts urged the defeat of any move to liberalize Massachusetts abortion laws, in a letter read at Catholic masses throughout the state. (*Boston Globe,* February 28, 1972; Exhibit 15) And in Massachusetts, after a bitter name-calling fight led by Archbishop Humberto Medeiros, Massachusetts women may find themselves with a more restrictive abortion law than ever, based on rights of fetuses as superior to those of women. Other propaganda has been, and will be, organized nationwide. A Florida newspaper, for example, headlines: "Abortion Bills Face Organized Catholic Opposition." (Fort Lauderdale, *News and Sun-Sentinel,* March 5, 1970; Exhibit 16) And one article in the Catholic paper mentions fights over abortion legislation in New Jersey, Ohio, Mississippi, and Massachusetts. (*Long Island Catholic,* April 13, 1972; Exhibit 17)

In New York alone, the Archdiocese has expended considerable funds for full-page ads for Birthright. (e.g., *New York Times,* April 13, 1971; Exhibit 18)

Despite all their activities, at Catholic forums on abortion, bishops have been accused of "timidity" in upholding the orthodox Catholic faith! At one Roman Catholic forum, attended by people from 34 states and 6 foreign countries, a speaker drew applause when he said that Catholic bishops of New York had failed to oppose with sufficient vigor that state's abortion law because they wanted tax money for their schools. It would have been better to sacrifice the schools and to uphold moral principles involved in abortion, urged John J. Mulloy, a Philadelphia teacher and writer. (*New York Times,* June 21, 1971; Exhibit 19) The women of New York State do not want their constitutional rights dictated by a sectarian forum. And they are, of course, particularly enraged that the tax-exempt money and tax-deductible contributions are being used to fight against women.

The "timidity" referred to above, if it ever existed, is certainly not apparent now. Propaganda efforts have become intensified. And the United States bishops have already organized a so-called "Week of Prayer" amid other activities for October 1972. This, as part of a proposal in which the bishops reaffirmed the Church's teaching against abortion. (*Long Island Catholic,* April 20, 1972; Exhibit 20)

II. Otherwise influencing legislation

The named tax-exempt groups have attempted to influence legislation in other ways as well. In New York State, actions included, but were not limited to:

(a) A massive lobby in the New York State capitol. (*Long Island Catholic,* December 16, 1971; Exhibit 21)

(b) Pledges supporting a New York bill for restrictive laws to be passed out in churches, collected at the end of mass, and sent to Albany to be presented to the state legislature. (See telegram; Exhibit 22)

(c) The New York State Right to Life Committee urged individuals to write letters, make telephone calls, send telegrams, and make personal visits and group visits to Earl Brydges, majority leader, and Perry Duryea, speaker of the Assembly. (*Long Island Catholic,* April 13, 1972; Exhibit 23)

(d) Bishop Francis A. Mugavero of the Brooklyn diocese, himself, made an "urgent" appeal to the state legislature asking that the Donovan-Crawford bill be brought out of the codes committee of both the Assembly and the Senate. (*Long Island Catholic,* May 4, 1972; Exhibit 24)

(e) Two priests were arrested in Albany, at a rally at the capitol, for blocking a revolving door to protest New York's liberal abortion law. (*Long Island Catholic,* May 4, 1972; Exhibit 24)

(f) A church lobbyist was retained in Albany.

(g) President Nixon and Cardinal Cooke engaged in prejudicial correspondence only days before the vote on the New York law. (*Long Island Catholic,* May 11, 1972; Exhibit 25)

Again, these kinds of activities can be observed nationwide. In Washington, D.C., a Nixon commission on abortion, which came up with a moderate view, was labeled as a "valley of death" by Monsignor James McHugh, one of the directors of the United States Catholic Conference. (*Long Island Catholic,* March 23, 1972; Exhibit 26)

Catholic groups and individuals, heeding the call of the Church, have flaunted court decisions which have come down in various states declaring abortion laws unconstitutional.

In Connecticut, after a large group of women (*Women* v. *Conn.*) finally succeeded in having that state's abortion law declared unconstitutional, they were forced to bring a contempt of court action against Catholic Governor Meskill for his unprecedented action in pushing through a new and restrictive law similar to the one declared invalid by the court. The *New York Times* declared: "Tough abortion law in Connecticut is attributed to Meskill and Catholics." And, congressmen were convinced "that the impetus for the bill . . . came directly from the Archdiocese." Their high degree of organization and fanaticism combined with tax-exempt funding allowed them to do the following:

"Clergymen and lobbyists supporting the church position walked the colonnaded halls of the Capitol building to button-hole fence-sitting legislators throughout the special session. During the final hours before the bill's passage, members of the Connecticut Citizens Right to Life Committee and the Connecticut Catholic Conference continued to press Senators who had voted in favor of a mild amendment to permit abortions in cases of rape and incest." (*The New York Times,* May 25, 1972; Exhibit 27)

And, in New York State, a self-styled friend of all the unborn fetuses, bachelor Robert Byrn, associated with Fordham Law School, head of the Metropolitan Right to Life Committee, and author of the minority report on abortion prepared for the New York State legislature, will not allow women to rest secure with their rights. First, he brought an action to enjoin all abortions under the liberalized law, as champion and "guardian" of all fetuses. (*Daily News,* December 4, 1971; Exhibit 28) This suit, originally sustained by Judge Francis X. Smith, was later overturned. A second suit, after Governor Rockefeller's veto of the Donovan-Crawford bill, was allegedly brought to reinstate the Donovan-Crawford position.

In an excellent analysis, "The Politics of Abortion" (*Nation,* June 5, 1972; Exhibit 29), we see how the participation in abortion politics of these tax-exempt groups (properly labeled "mercenaries") may lead to one of the very kinds of involvements that the tax-deductible guidelines were designed to protect against: power politics and tax-deductible funds. The author outlines a power struggle between the right wing and liberal wing of the Republican party—a struggle between Nixon and Rockefeller. Funds of Church groups are obviously not supposed to be used in this way.

The evidence attached hereto shows that the activities by the named groups and individuals to influence legislation are not insubstantial. The abortion issue is headlined on the front pages of the Church paper. It receives more publicity than any of their other activities. And they are not presenting their material in a calm, dispassionate, objective, or nonpartisan manner.

C. FINANCIAL REPORT

The Archdiocese of New York has issued a report setting its net worth at $643,000,000. (*New York Times,* April 5, 1972; Exhibit 30)

Upon information and belief, a substantial amount of these assets are used not purely for charitable or religious purposes, but are organized as business ventures. The assets so organized should henceforward be taxed.

D. CONSTITUTIONAL ISSUES

In addition to the fact that the Church is violating the requirements of a federal statute, important constitutional issues are also involved:

I. The Church is violating the basic principles set forth in the First Amendment, of separation of Church and State. (See *Abortion Rap,* McGraw-Hill, by Schulder and Kennedy).

II. The State is fostering the establishment of a particular religious viewpoint.

III. The Church is lobbying for a statute that has already been declared unconstitutional in various states. Women's basic constitutional rights are being lobbied against, at the taxpayer's expense.

IV. A basic unfairness and denial of equal protection is being perpetuated by the Internal Revenue Service in that groups who do less lobbying, propagandizing, and influencing of campaigns than the Roman Catholic Church are denied tax-exempt status. A few examples: (a) The Sierra Club; (b) Americans United for Separation of Church and State, which lost its tax-exempt status, lobbying for separation of church and state; (c) The Civil Liberties Legal Defense Fund, denied tax-exempt status, although organized purely for the support of indigents in civil liberties cases, which carries on no lobbying or political activity of any kind and which denies such activities to its grantees in special written contracts.

V. First Amendment rights of speech and petition of other groups are chilled and violated because they are denied equal treatment.

E. CONCLUSION

Since the above-named groups and individuals have:

(1) tried to influence legislation in a substantial manner,
(2) participated in political campaigns of candidates for public office, they no longer qualify for either tax-exempt status or for tax deductibility of contributions to them.[2]

Unless we hear from you within ten days, we shall ask for relief from the federal court: (a) ordering you to remove tax-exempt status and/or tax deductibility from the named organizations; and/or (b) enjoining said organizations and individuals from continuing activities prohibited by statute and federal regulations. Five hundred palintiffs have indicated a desire to bring a court action.

Your failure to act in light of such flagrant, public violations of the tax laws may have already caused irreparable harm to countless women.

Your inaction in this matter is in sharp contrast with your reported activity against many smaller groups, such as *Akwesasne Notes,* the nation's largest circulation Indian newspaper. (*The Nishnawbe News,* May 1972; Exhibit 31)

We are particularly irritated in light of the clear denominational nature of the abortion struggle by the Church and its affiliates and the hypocrisy of those who use rationalizations concerning the "sanctity of life," while supporting mass destruction of life in Vietnam. Cardinal Cooke is still "military vicar."

If this has been an oversight on your part, we hope this complaint will spur you to action.

Finally, would you please furnish us with the following:
1. The status of the tax-exempt status of the named organizations;
2. The specific section of the Internal Revenue Code under which they are covered;
3. Whether donor's contributions are tax-deductible;

4. Whether any of their assets are currently being taxed.
Sincerely,

The Feminist Party

by

FLORYNCE R. KENNEDY
Media Workshop Chapter
Feminist Party

IRENE DAVALL
National Coordinator
Feminist Party

"I have carried out my contracts, I refused to be pitiful, I have successfully fought against tears, but I seriously consider abandoning this work, as I never before have. United Airlines personnel showed malice."

MEMORANDUM OF: FLORYNCE R. KENNEDY, COMPLAINANT— AGE 59, BLACK, FEMALE, ATTORNEY, LECTURER, 8 EAST 48th STREET, NEW YORK 10017, PL 93223
NATURE OF COMPLAINANT'S CHARGES: OVERBOOKED FLIGHT, MISREPRESENTATION OF COMPUTER READOUT, RACISM AND SEXISM IN SEAT ASSIGNMENT, BREACH OF CONTRACT, ASSAULT AND BATTERY, PERSONAL INJURY
DEFENDANTS: UNITED AIRLINES
ASSAILANTS: J.J. MOHRMANN, SUPERVISOR
        MS. GRAY
DATE OF COMPLAINED CONDUCT: SUNDAY, 2 MARCH, 1975, c. 12:30-c. 1:45 P.M.
PLACE OF ASSAULT: SATELLITE TICKETING AND RESERVATION AREA, UNITED AIRLINES, NEWARK AIRPORT

I arrived at Newark Airport at about 12:30 P.M. Sunday, 2 March, 1975, where I was met by Jesse Banks and my sister, Joy Kennedy. I had reconfirmed my corrected reservation for a nonstop United Airlines flight to Cedar Rapids. After several minutes at the computer, the U.A. agent told me that my reservation did not appear on the computer, but that I could get a seat assignment at the gate area. I advised him and all subsequent personnel that I had a contract for an Iowa City, Iowa, speaking engagement, that I had personally confirmed my 1:40 U.A. flight and that I was being met in Cedar Rapids by University of Iowa people. I noted that about 20% of my gross income is paid to airlines.

My sister was not allowed to accompany me past security since they were not ticketed, but promised to wait for ten minutes in case I had further problems and had to change terminals.

Shortly after I reached the gate area, I noted the time: 12:40 P.M. I spoke to a Ms. Nozer. She indicated that there was no reservation either for 3 March as my ticket indicated, or for my reconfirmed 2 March reservation. After several trips to the rear office, she held my ticket and told me to have a seat in the boarding area, *where I would receive a seat assignment.* It is important to note that her instruction did not indicate any doubt in contingency.

I sat in the boarding area; then I noted a male, white passenger who had also been told he did not appear on the computer was given a boarding pass. *I charge that this was a discriminatory seating assignment. I further charge that U.A.'s instruction after holding my ticket was part of a policy of preventing a change to a competitive carrier.* I joined the queue of unassigned passengers as the uniformed white male announced that someone would bring over a seating chart "in 30 seconds." I was about third in line. Numerous white male passengers had received boarding passes long after the 15-minutes-before-flight-time after which I'd been advised that my reservation would be forfeited. With a $1,000-plus-expenses contract involved, which had to be carried out within 36 hours, I was not casual about reservations. Had there been any doubt of seat availabilities, I could have taken a 4 P.M. flight from more convenient La Guardia. My agent could have advised the university and I could have avoided the mad rush for the 1:40 flight.

By the time U.A. personnel Gray and Supervisor J. J. Mohrmann arrived with the seating chart there were eight or ten persons on the line. The male attendant phoned someone to say to send no more passengers. This indicates an awareness of overbooking practice.

Having boarded many planes with eight or ten empty seats while five or six standbys were rejected, I kept asking for security to be called to check whether there were empty seats or to be allowed to go on board the carrier myself *to count the empty seats.* Instead Mohrmann went on board. Meanwhile someone told the attendants there was one more seat. I begged for that seat; it was given to a white male without the formality of a boarding pass.

I asked again to be allowed to see how many empty seats there were and walked over to pick up my luggage, which was beside the door. I picked up my briefcase and totebag; then *I was grabbed by Ms. Gray and*

Picketing National Airlines, San Francisco, 1973

punched in the face by Mohrmann. He later said he thought I would try to force my way onto the plane. I saw stars, but pointed out that the job of preventing such a thing was security's and I again demanded that security be called so that a report could be made and witnesses queried. I was dazed, I felt my lip swelling, and I was fighting tears.

Even after that, a young white male who had come only a minute or so before flight time was slipped through the door to board the plane. I am well-known as a sarcastic, acerbic person, but I was trying to be my best self, while yet protesting, since I couldn't believe I wouldn't finally make the plane.

I charge racism and sexism in seat assignments, as well as fraud, overbooking, and misrepresentations as to confirmed reservations. They closed the flight and ticketed me to an American Airlines Chicago flight with a change to a United Flight. I reached Chicago and rushed to Ozark, where I rebooked myself to Cedar Rapids, where I waited two hours for my Iowa parties.

Mohrmann and Gray had punched and pushed me so violently that I could have fallen to the floor except that Gray had pinned my arms and clamped my torso. I was hanging onto my luggage so that my elbow was awkwardly twisted. Yet they refused to call security so that I could make a report. Moreover, they refused to let me use a United Airlines phone to call security so that I could make a report. Ms. Gray went to Mohrmann's office after I questioned her refusal, returned and directed me to a pay phone. As I started to phone, the porter came to carry my bags to American Airlines. I indicated that I expected U.A. to pay him and received a blank stare. The porter was kind and solicitous and explained about the bus to American Airlines and waited until I boarded the bus. I gave him $1.50 for fear he mightn't otherwise get paid.

As I sat on the Chicago flight holding ice to my swelling lips and face I asked myself where did I go wrong. The airlines industry collects between $6,000 and $10,000 per annum from me, and I had endured innumerable degrading searches, and now this.

I charge United Airlines with the practice of denying computer listings where overbooking occurs and there are too few "no shows." The computer can't be seen by the passengers, like old butcher scales, which also can't be seen by the customer.

I have carried out my contracts, I refused to be pitiful, I have successfully fought against tears, but I seriously consider abandoning this work, as I never before have. United Airlines personnel showed malice.

CC: RALPH NADER, 5 PUBLIC CITIZEN, INC., P.O. BOX 19404, WASHINGTON D.C. 20036

Ken Neilson, CARS' liaison to the Committee to Defeat S.I, asked me to speak at an anti-S.I rally. I was going to be on the road, and suggested this petition instead.

**Coalition
Against
Racism &
Sexism**

8 East 48th St.
New York, N.Y.
10017
PL 9-3223
(212)

"Move on over or we'll move on over you."

FLORYNCE R. KENNEDY SPEAKS OUT FOR DEFEAT OF S.1

S.1 is the common name for the Criminal Justice Reform Act of 1975, designated S.1 and H.R. 3907 in the Senate and House respectively. S.1 is also another step in the Nazification of America. Boston was a big step forward in that movement. The forces of the right wing are always busy and we must energize ourselves to meet the challenge. But since it's going to be a long war, we're not going to take the joy out of our lives. We must take every opportunity to declare our short-range, as well as, long-range determination to defeat this Fascist-inspired legislation.

The cerebral response of those of us who oppose S.1 has failed to capture the attention of the public and has given the print and press an excuse to continue their Munich approach to the issue.

The big cities are suffering from Pentagonorrhoea. For instance, New York taxpayers have been paying $20.00 for every dollar that goes to Washington, D.C. The Munich Syndrome is becoming more and more apparent in the pathology of our oppressive society. The oppressed and the oppressors are moving closer and ever closer to the pattern of conduct reminiscent of the Storm Troopers, the gauleiters, and the "good" Germans of the Nazi society under Hitler.

The "good" Germans of Munich professed ignorance and innocence, as well as, impotence to know about or change the situation at the Dachau Concentration Camp ten miles away. So, also, New England and Eastern liberals, students, Blacks, and relevant whites, ignore the Boston bid for the unenviable title of Racist-Sexist Capital of the Western World. The cradle of liberty is likely to kill the baby of freedom in the Bicentennial Year of 1976.

The S.1 Bill gives an easier opportunity for the Munich Syndrome and the wise monkey syndrome, in that 8,500 people marching to menace Black people is a fact harder to ignore than a Federal statute which is in the process of being enacted.

FLORYNCE RAE KENNEDY
Lawyer, Founder of the Feminist Party, Lecturer,
Manhattan Coordinator of CARS (Coalition Against Racism and Sexism)

P E T I T I O N

I SUPPORT THE ABOVE STATEMENT.

N A M E   A D D R E S S

OTHER COLORS

Flo is the greatest Black woman that ever happened to my country, Australia.

Lana Cantrell, singer

Flo Kennedy is the greatest dynamo of our time and my number one muse. If it were not for her being Flo, I would not be Sandra.

Sandra Hochman, poet, novelist, film maker

"Flo Kennedy? Isn't she that far-out Black woman with the hat—and buttons like 'Nixon Eats Lettuce' and 'Defeat the Fetus Fetishists'?

"Isn't she the lawyer who calls herself a middle-aged colored lady? And she's always dressed in leather pants and turbans and has bracelets and rings all over?"

Yes, Florynce (her mother believed if you couldn't afford anything else, you could at least have a "y" in your name)

Kennedy *is* all these things. And many, many more.

Most important, and often unrealized, is that Flo Kennedy is really what sisterhood is all about. Or is supposed to be about.

It's true that there is no one funnier, wittier, more caustic than Flo Kennedy. Who else would support the decriminalization of prostitution by saying, "No one ever died of a blow job"? But there is also no one more supportive, giving, loving, helpful, protective to her friends. Nor does there seem to be much her friends would not do for her—if only she would let them!

I think of the clever, wonderful, unique, extraordinary, hilarious, potent, effective Flo Kennedy confrontations I've witnessed or, even better, participated in. Like the time our Fire Island house was cited for an improperly placed garbage can, and Flo told the cops, "Arrest me, you'll just make me rich and famous." Or the time 200 of us, organized by Florynce, stormed a segregated beachside community (no Blacks, Jews, Catholics, or in fact anybody but neo-Nazis and other

With Irene Davall, Lana Cantrell, and Robin Tyler, presenting International Women's Year award to Lana, Australian Consulate, New York, 1975

assorted Fascists); like the time during the Columbia campus "riots" when she referred to David Susskind as "that ivy-covered salami," or when we sang "Richard the Red-Necked Reindeer" while devouring the Watergate hearings on TV.

At the same time, I do not forget that when I hurt my neck (picking up a baby!) it was Flo who helped me wash my hair (well, actually she got the project started, then had Joy, her biological sister, take over, so she could go on to other things —as promised); who accompanied me for false-alarm breast X-rays, followed by "the-least-you-deserve-after-that-is-lunch-at-the-Plaza-and-the-sale-at-Saks." Or when my *Tenant Survival* book came out, and the publisher, not taking care of business, got a call from Flo promising to "get their ass"; or during inevitable disasters with a co-author, Flo's late-night assurances that she would stand by me unless she dies! Then there was the time I was asked stupid and humiliating questions on a TV interview program; it was Flo Kennedy who made all the frustration go away with, "Honey, why don't we give them the Toilet Paper Award for their Arrogance?"

As I write this, Flo, I am remembering that you will be sixty in a couple of weeks. I know you walked out on the acupuncturist who said he could add years to your life. But Flo, keep on trucking! You are needed. You are loved.

Emily Jane Goodman, attorney, co-author of **Women, Money and Power**

Flo Kennedy is that point on the graph of human experience where the curves of intellect, sensitivity, and brass balls intersect at their respective maxima. In short, she is a shining black ball.

Burton I. Monasch, attorney

If your thing is swinging on a star, that's A-OK with Flo, but just don't expect her to stand around watching you.

Flo is a great teacher, and I soon learned that while I had always written personal letters praising or condemning media programs, I could harness my personal energy to organizational protest and thus speak with the voice of ten organizations. Flo harnesses the hate energy motivating people's actions or desires for action. She gives direction, incentive, opportunity, and encouragement as well as support to such action. I am hooked on Flo, and have nowhere to go but up.

Ken Neilson, Coalition Against Racism and Sexism

Bangles, bracelets, rings, outrageous outfits. African jewel in the middle of her forehead.

Speaking the truth as she sees it, in her living room, on TV, on college campuses, at demonstrations and rallies, regardless: "Honey, if they pay me $1,000 to speak, they must want to hear what's on my mind. And if they pay me nothing, they are certainly going to hear exactly what is on my mind."

In her personal relationships —generous, a catalyst to bring out the best in people, to start their minds turning; tolerant of everything but laziness, stupidity, meanness; unapologetic; wanting to kick up as much dust as she can while she's on this earth; encouraging; supportive; able to see the potential in each individual; brilliant, creative mind, always wanting to be in control, unafraid.

Diane Schulder, attorney, co-author of **Abortion Rap**

Flo Kennedy was a fantastic lecturer and the students have never been so enthusiastic about a guest lecturer.

Patricia Taylor, Director of Activities, California State College, Stanislaus

---

I wish to express our appreciation . . . for enabling us to experience Florynce Kennedy. I say "experience" because Ms. Kennedy's stay with us was a mental and physical exercise. She was a dynamic personality that swept across the campus and challenged people's ideas and actions. She was a unique part of our Community Forum series and will be remembered as a highlight of the 1974-75 season.

Pamela S. Wilson, Community Forum Coordination, Hood College, Frederick, Maryland

---

Regarding Ms. Kennedy—she was fantastic!! I can't say enough. A beautiful person who gave us a marvelous program.

Patricia A. Larson, Program Director, Saint Cloud State College, St. Cloud, Minnesota

---

She was superb; enormously energetic and generous with her time, and inspiring to an audience of 300 who sat totally involved for two and a half hours.

Judith Barnet, Cape Cod Community College

Thank you very much for arranging for Florynce Kennedy to be our convocation speaker. From the time she met the press, through the informal luncheon following the lecture, she was great. As you well know, she has very definite ideas and projects them in a most forceful manner, whether to a member of the press, a Black male student or a white female administrator. She was most refreshing!

Allen J. Matherne, Dean, Community Services, Genesee Community College, Flint, Michigan

---

Good heavens! Flo did it again. She blew this place over like a tornado in a haystack. Dynamite!—and you know, in spite of all the hot air, she reminded me of my mother.

William J. Slack, Coordinator, Campus Activities, Director, Gage Memorial Union, Coe College, Cedar Rapids, Iowa

---

Right on with Florynce. Appreciated her ideas and enthusiasm and willingness to share the same with the Belknap community. Ripple on with peace and contentment.

Roy K. Bunce, Dean of Students, Belknap College, Center Harbor, New Hampshire

---

Her dynamic personality and positive approach toward the subject of concern was quite refreshing. Anyone involved, whether sympathetic or otherwise, could not help but be impressed by her devotion and fiery assault on "The Pathology of Oppression," as she puts it. Her stamina is phenomenal as she radiated energy throughout the day from 2:30 drop-in session until her final reception at the girls' dorm.

William A. Plasschaert, John F. Kennedy Memorial Union, University of Dayton, Dayton, Ohio

I want to thank you . . . for sharing your precious time with us, making our conference "Race Relations in the Seventies: Toward the Year 2000" a fantastic success! Young women, especially Blacks, need so many positive images on which to pattern their lives and to reinforce their confidence in their abilities and renew their wills to struggle against so much oppression and racism in the world. But one can't be serious all the time, can one? And that's where I think you play the most important role: when we can smile and laugh at ourselves and with ourselves, we are at peace with ourselves. This also gives us the right to laugh and smile at others' follies and stupidity.

Linda C. McKeever, President, Black American Law Students Association, Drake University, Des Moines, Iowa

Just a heartfelt thank you for the two hours you gave to the class on "Human Sexual Behavior." Not only was it important that you be the one to discuss abortion laws, but also that you be the "altogether woman" for women students to admire (and they did). Your entire visit was an inspiration . . . and left a real spark behind. With women like you around, we are bound to win.

Ellen B. Kimmel, Ph.D., Director, University of South Florida, Tampa

It has been a long time indeed since I have had the opportunity and pleasure to work with someone as interesting and delightful as Florynce Kennedy. She is a beautiful person! After hearing her speak, one isn't left with any doubt about where she stands on issues. She is honest; she is open—there are no façades—she is real and genuine.

Mary Yates, Program Advisor, North Texas State University, Denton

May I thank you for helping to make possible the visit of Miss Kennedy. She gave most generously of her time and immediately identified herself with the concerns of our students and the greater Charleston community. Our Black students particularly identified with her, as one remarked to me after the program, "She's real cool."

Edwin D. Hoffman, Dean of Instruction, West Virginia State College, Institute

I would like to thank you for the role you played in "kicking off" the University of Colorado Medical Center Women's Association Spring Series of Events. We feel your appearance on our Campus accomplished the goals we had developed for the series. Number one, your speech "shook out" some cobwebs of the mind and presented a new philosophy for us to ponder. Number two, your presence increased our visibility immensely.

Laura Sowell, UCMC Women's Association, University of Colorado Medical Center, Denver

SHE IS EVERYWHERE

Rugged simplicity of style
Disdainful of high-fashion splash
Clothed in banners flying bright
As bombs burst in the air
Mind and tongue aflash
On a safari of truth and light.
She is everywhere.

Ten red talons glare
Adding a regal dimension
Atop fingers bold handsome aware
Ensuring your rapt attention.
Large eyes forever listening
Open serenely on a tawny face.
She is everywhere.

The tinkle of a pendant
Pinned up body messages
Forewarn the greedy and arrogant
Self-inflicted cruelty beware
Endure her unrelenting scorn
Masked by fragile flesh overspent.
She is everywhere.

Her magic carpet is not driftless
It alights to dazzle
On potato salad and chicken feast
The fearful, spirited and shiftless
Their tears and anger to unravel
A moment to achieve and defend at least.
She is everywhere.

Supersister of four
She has mothered and fathered
A community of uncountable score.
A woman who never says good-bye
Herself a spritely child unbothered
No man can match her lullaby.
She is everywhere.

Her sorcery enchants and dispels
Cobwebs, bats and pale angels of hell.
Gracefully coiled on a low couch
Disciples surround the tales she tells.
Marching boots, back bent, shoulders slouch
Yet elegant as a tall long hood of a Cord car.
She is everywhere.

A pulp science-fiction writer
A genius aborted
The marriage was undone
But she is never unescorted.
Jewels taken once and set adrift
By a poet lawyer Southern son.
She is everywhere.

Gives and takes curses and names
Caresses and kisses
Brooks no time for phony games.
The mystery of the nature of us
Unfolds in her graying hair
Stop moaning, get on with it, what's the fuss.
She is everywhere.

Leonard Cohen, Civil Court Judge

BALLAD OF HARRIET TUBMAN

Dedicated to Flo Kennedy

I'm Harriet Tubman, people,
I am Harriet, the slave.
I am Harriet, the Free Woman,
Free within my grave.

How far is the road to Canada?
How far do I have to go?
How far is the road to Maryland
And the hatred that I know?
How far is the road to Maryland
And the hatred that I know?

Tell my brothers yonder
That Harriet is free.
Please tell my brothers yonder
No more auction block for me.
Please tell my brothers yonder
No more auction block for me.

I stabbed that overseer.
I took his rusty knife.
For I killed that overseer.
I took his lowdown dirty life.
For three long years I waited.

Three years I kept my hate.
Three years before I killed,
Three years I had to wait.

I'm Harriet Tubman, people,
I am Harriet the slave.
I am Harriet the Free Woman,
Free within my grave.
Done shook the dust of Maryland,
Clean off my weary feet
I am on my way to Canada
And Freedom's Golden Street.

I came through swamps and mountains,
I waded many a creek
Now tell my brothers yonder
That Harriet is free.
I conducted the Underground Railroad
To set my people free
I never lost a passenger and
Never charged a fee.

I came through swamps and mountains
And waded many a creek.
Please tell my brother yonder
That Harriet is free.
Yes, Please
Yes, tell my brothers yonder
No more auction block for me.

The Reverend Frederick Douglass
Kirkpatrick